Assessment
and
Intervention
With Children and Adolescents:

Developmental and Multicultural Approaches

Second Edition

Ann Vernon
Roberto Clemente

American Counseling Association
5999 Stevenson Avenue
Alexandria, VA 22304
www.counseling.org

Assessment
and
Intervention
With Children and Adolescents:
Developmental and Multicultural Approaches
✳
Second Edition

10   9   8   7   6   5   4   3   2   1

American Counseling Association
5999 Stevenson Avenue
Alexandria, VA 22304

Director of Publications
Carolyn C. Baker

Production Manager
Bonny E. Gaston

Copy Editor
Elaine Dunn

Cover Design
Martha Woolsey

Library of Congress Cataloging-in-Publication Data
Vernon, Ann.
Assessment and intervention with children and adolescents:
developmental and multicultural approaches / Ann Vernon,
Roberto Clemente.—2nd ed.
    p.   cm.
Includes bibliographical references and index.
ISBN 1-55620-239-3 (alk. paper)
1. Children—Counseling of.   2. Youth—Counseling of.
3. Developmental psychology.   I. Clemente, Roberto.   II. Title.

BF637.C6V466 2004
158′.3′083—dc22

2004004231

✳

*To my father, Maurice Suhumskie, for teaching me
self-discipline and perseverance.*

—Ann Vernon

A mi familia en el tiempo de las mariposas. Cu dragoste.

—Roberto Clemente

✳

Contents

Preface   vii
Acknowledgments   ix
About the Authors   xi
Introduction   xiii

✳

Part I

Concepts of Developmental Theory, Multicultural Considerations, Assessment, and Intervention

Chapter 1
The Child Assessment Process   3

Chapter 2
Methods of Developmental Assessment   33

Chapter 3
Methods of Multicultural Assessment   57

Chapter 4
Designing Developmentally and Culturally
Responsive Interventions   73

✳

Part II

Application of Developmental and Multicultural Theories: Typical Problems, Assessment, and Intervention

Chapter 5
Early Childhood: Assessment and Intervention   107

Chapter 6
Middle Childhood: Assessment and Intervention   135

Chapter 7
Early Adolescence: Assessment and Intervention 159

Chapter 8
Mid-Adolescence: Assessment and Intervention   193

Conclusion   223
References   225
Index   247

Preface

✳

Over the past 30 years, we gradually have recognized that counseling children and adolescents is much different than counseling adults. With the realization that adult models of assessment and intervention cannot be extrapolated to young clients, numerous books, games, and articles have focused on what works with the child and adolescent population. A proliferation of information is available on how to help children of divorce; children of alcoholic parents; children who have been sexually, physically, or emotionally abused; or children who live in stepfamilies. Heavy emphasis has been placed on how to work with suicidal, depressed, or chemically dependent youth.

✳

In addition to these trends, helping professionals are becoming more aware of the need to be culturally competent in this pluralistic society and are incorporating this knowledge into the counseling process with a younger clientele. Similarly, there is greater recognition of the need to apply knowledge of child and adolescent development to assessment and intervention with children and adolescents. However, much of the emphasis on applying developmental theory to counseling children has been through comprehensive counseling programs that emphasize prevention through classroom and small-group work, rather than intervention in individual counseling.

This book, *Assessment and Intervention With Children and Adolescents: Developmental and Multicultural Approaches*, was written to fill a void in the professional literature. Specifically, it addresses the individual counseling process with children and adolescents who exhibit more normal developmental problems or typical problems in their age group, rather than serious problems such as addictive behaviors, eating disorders, self-mutilation, or severe depression, which have been the focus of numerous publications. It also summarizes information on developmental theory and combines it with a practical approach to both assessment and intervention with school-age clients. In addition, this book provides helping professionals with strategies for increasing their own cultural competence and applying this in their work with youngsters. The cultural emphasis distinguishes this book from the original book, *Developmental Assessment and Intervention With Children and Adolescents* that I (Ann Vernon) wrote 10 years ago, and I am pleased that my colleague Dr. Roberto Clemente was able to contribute his expertise in this particular area to this work.

The first two chapters of this text discuss the special considerations and characteristics of developmental assessment, including specific age-appropriate informal assessment procedures. The third chapter addresses cultural assessment, and the fourth chapter describes how to design counseling interventions and gives over 40 examples of creative developmentally and culturally appropriate interventions. The remaining four chapters outline characteristics of normal development for four different age groups: early and middle childhood, and early and mid-adolescence. In each of these chapters, six case studies are presented, for the most part representing normal developmental problems, as well as cases that illustrate specific challenges for young multiethnic clients. Examples of assessments and interventions are described for each case study.

Assessment and Intervention With Children and Adolescents: Developmental and Multicultural Approaches is intended for school and mental health counselors, social workers, and school psychologists who counsel children and adolescents and who want a very practical resource to help them determine what the problem is, how it fits with the normal developmental sequence, how culture affects the experiences of young multiethnic clients, and how to address these issues. It is also a book that helps graduate students learn to combine theory with practice.

By reading this book, practitioners can learn how to help school-age clients and significant others deal more effectively with the challenges of growing up. It is our hope that this book can provide readers with practical information and user-friendly techniques to enhance their skills and give them new ideas in working with children and adolescents.

Acknowledgments

＊

We would like to thank the American Counseling Association Media Committee for accepting this publication and, in particular, Carolyn Baker for her support and assistance. Thanks also goes to the University of Northern Iowa graduate assistants Kathy Hedican, Lori Dobbin, and Randy Schultz for their numerous trips to the library and help with various aspects of this project.

All authors know that it takes many hours of dedication and hard work to write a book. Our appreciation goes to our families for their patience and understanding when we had to stay focused on our goal and had to forgo other activities. Finally, thanks to all the young clients who continually affirm the importance of the helping profession as we see them grow through the counseling process.

＊

About the Authors

Ann Vernon, PhD, LMHC, NCC, is professor and coordinator of the counselor education program at the University of Northern Iowa in Cedar Falls, Iowa. Prior to her position as counselor educator, Dr. Vernon was an elementary and secondary counselor. Dr. Vernon currently maintains a part-time private practice where she specializes in working with children, adolescents, and their parents.

In addition to teaching and counseling, Dr. Vernon is a frequent speaker at professional conferences and conducts workshops throughout the United States and abroad on a variety of topics pertaining to children and adolescents. She is the author of numerous books, chapters, and articles, including *Thinking, Feeling, Behaving; The Passport Programs; Developmental Assessment and Intervention With Children and Adolescents; Counseling Children and Adolescents;* and *What Works When With Children and Adolescents.*

Dr. Vernon is vice president of the Albert Ellis Board of Trustees and director of the Midwest Center for Rational-Emotive Behavior Therapy. She has been active in state, regional, and national professional counseling association activities.

Roberto Clemente, PhD, is an associate professor in the counselor education program at the University of Northern Iowa. He received his master's degree in school counseling from the University of Puerto Rico and his doctorate from Oregon State University in counselor education. Dr. Clemente was a school counselor in Puerto Rico. He is the author of several professional articles in state and national journals on multicultural counseling. He conducts workshops on diversity, multiculturalism, and artistic interventions throughout the United States. Also, Dr. Clemente serves as a consultant to Herzen Pedagogical University in St. Petersburg, Russia.

Introduction

※

*"I'm so concerned about my 6-year-old," explained a young parent
to the school counselor. "She's been such a well-adjusted child, but
suddenly she's convinced that there are monsters in her bedroom. She's
terrified of the dark, and bedtime has become a catastrophe. I just don't
understand why she's having these problems. As far as I can tell,
everything else is fine at home and at school. I need to know what I can
do to help her. Do you have any suggestions?"*

※

"Our fourth grader's teacher suggested that we confer with you,"
expressed Jason's parents to a mental health counselor. "Jason isn't doing
very well in school this year, and it's not because he doesn't have the ability. According to his teacher, Jason seems to think that he'll fail, no matter
what. When he was younger he was very confident about his abilities, but
during this past year, his performance has deteriorated and he just gives
up before he really tries to figure things out. We don't know whether this is
typical for this age, or whether we should have him evaluated? We know
that we have to do something before the problem gets worse."

A concerned mother stated to a school counselor during open house,
"It's like we're living with a stranger! We've always been such a close
Latino family, but now our 14-year-old son is very reluctant to speak
Spanish with us and seems embarrassed to bring friends home. When he's
not with his peers, he shuts himself off in his room. We realize that things
are different in this country, but we want him to appreciate his cultural
heritage. We don't know what to do."

How does one know what is typical or normal? How does a young
person's culture affect his or her life experiences? How does one determine
the exact nature of the problem and what to do about it? The answers to
these questions have significant implications for school counselors and
other human development professionals who routinely counsel children
and adolescents and consult with parents and teachers to facilitate healthy
development in a school-age clientele. With increasing frequency, these
professionals rely on developmental theories and cultural perspectives for
direction in assessing and treating problems pertinent to childhood and
adolescence. During the last 30 years, there has been heightened interest in
developmental concepts, primarily owing to three factors: (a) the increasing number of individuals who seek assistance for problems, many of

which are developmentally related; (b) the realization that it is more cost-effective to help people deal with problems before they reach a crisis state; and (c) the concept of prevention, which emphasizes early education to prevent crisis. Likewise, there has been increased emphasis on developing cultural competence as a result of the rapidly changing complexion of our society and the realization that culture cannot be ignored as an instrumental variable in the counseling experience.

According to Ivey (2000), development is the goal of counseling, and a developmental focus is the distinguishing characteristic of comprehensive school counseling programs (Gysbers & Henderson, 2000; Myrick, 1997). Borders and Drury (1992) noted, "Effective counseling programs are clearly based in human development theories" (p. 488). Interventions, curriculum, and student outcomes all should reflect developmental theories. Drum and Lawler (1988) described development as "a gradual, life-long process of mental and emotional growth resulting from and necessary to the resolution of certain critical tasks, issues, or conflicts that characterize specific periods of the life span" (p. 5). Although development occurs by degrees, these authors contended that conscious attention and specific intervention are important to prevent or overcome problems that may block progression through the hierarchical stages of development. This intervention may be in the form of prevention, which is the primary focus of developmentally based school counseling programs. Although there is no major existing problem at the prevention level, programs are designed to educate students about the normal developmental process, help them anticipate probable conflicts and issues, and teach them coping strategies. The most common method of introducing prevention programs is through classroom guidance (Borders & Drury, 1992; Tollerud & Nejedlo, 2004).

Intervention also occurs at the individual or small-group level to help children overcome problems that are just beginning to emerge, or where there is an unmet need that is blocking the healthy developmental process. The focus here is on appropriate assessment to determine the specific issue, the severity and intensity of the problem, and effective interventions. Although education and prevention are also important, assessing the problem and selecting appropriate developmental interventions are the critical tasks at this level.

In the case of recurring problems or more dysfunctional behavior, further assessment and directed intervention are imperative. Generally, problems of this nature are more serious than typical developmental problems, which can be ameliorated with less intense intervention.

A primary purpose of this book is to increase knowledge about child and adolescent development and the assessment of problems specific to this population. An additional focus is on how to address the developmental issues and problems experienced by ethnically diverse youth. Intended as a guidebook for the practitioner, this material should help parents, teachers, human development professionals, and clients understand the nature of a problem from a developmental perspective as well as a cultural perspective; learn practical ways to assess the problem; and identify specific, developmentally and culturally appropriate interventions to assist with problem resolution. Following an overview of the assessment and intervention process, the chapters outline typical child and adolescent problems; developmental and cultural assessment procedures; and assessments and interventions for early childhood (ages 4–5), middle childhood (ages 6–10), early adolescence (ages 11–14), and mid-adolescence (ages 15–18). The primary focus is the application of developmental and cultural considerations in assessment and intervention in individual counseling.

Part I

Concepts of Developmental Theory, Multicultural Considerations, Assessment, and Intervention

＊

There is a common saying that goes something like this: "If you don't know where you're going, you'll end up somewhere else." Although most counselors would agree that this makes sense, they do not automatically apply this wisdom within the context of the helping profession, particularly in terms of children and adolescents. In other words, although most professionals consider assessment and problem diagnosis as a prerequisite for determining intervention, this step is sometimes short-circuited with the child/adolescent population, because assessment may be defined too narrowly, it may be too time consuming, the instruments are not age appropriate, the results do not readily translate to interventions, or the helping professional is unable to adequately engage the young client in the assessment process. As a result, this integral part of the counseling process may be overlooked, which, in turn, has a negative effect on the outcome. A compounding problem occurs with young ethnically diverse clients, because many of the assessment measures are based on procedures and measures designed for European Americans and assumed to be appropriate for all children, regardless of their cultural background.

＊

The purpose of this book's first two chapters is to discuss the concept of developmental assessment as an effective assessment procedure with children and adolescents and to underscore the importance of developmental theory in relation to assessment and intervention with young clients. More specifically, these chapters identify characteristics of effective child assessment, with particular emphasis on how to develop a variety of creative, practical assessment techniques to use with children and adolescents. Examples of existing developmental assessment instruments also are described. The third chapter describes important multicultural considerations and assessment procedures.

In addition to the information on assessment, the fourth chapter describes the intervention process, including a four-stage intervention design process, guidelines for selecting and creating developmentally and culturally appropriate interventions for younger clients, and specific examples of interventions that have proved to be effective with children and adolescents. A case study illustrates application of the design process.

As stated in the Preface, we cannot merely extrapolate adult assessment procedures and intervention strategies to children and adolescents. Therefore, the intent of the following chapters is to bridge the gap between theory and practice by providing effective, practical methods of developmental and cultural assessment and intervention.

Chapter 1

The Child Assessment Process

✳

The importance of obtaining information directly from children and adolescents, rather than relying exclusively on behavioral observations or reports from parents, teachers, or other significant persons, is becoming more widely recognized by counselors and others in the helping profession (Garbarino & Stott, 1992; Stone & Lemanek, 1990; Wagner, 2003; Yule, 1993). This is due, in part, to an increased knowledge of the developmental process, which has resulted in a better understanding of the nature of childhood and the awareness that children are capable of providing data about their problems. According to Vernon (1999), it is "critical for counselors to consider developmental factors in problem conceptualization, in designing or selecting age-appropriate assessment instruments, and in developing interventions that take into account the developmental capabilities of the child" (p. 3). Flanery (1990) noted that because of children's uniquenesses, appropriate assessment that reflects the developmental capacities of children and provides insight into how the cognitive, emotional, and behavioral developmental processes affect the assessment process is very important. Furthermore, given the fact that children are not miniature adults, both Vernon (2002) and Prout (1999) cautioned that scaled-down versions of adult assessment techniques or adult models of normal/abnormal behavior cannot be extrapolated to young clients.

✳

Whereas adults are relatively stable in their development, the rate of growth in children is rapid, and Wagner (2003) and Yule (1993) stressed that practitioners who work with children must be more aware of developmental differences than those who work exclusively with adults. In fact, given the rapid changes that characterize early years, knowing what is developmentally appropriate is a prerequisite for identifying many childhood problems (Erk, 2004; LaGreca, 1990; Vernon, 2004). For instance, 2-year-olds who express emotion by throwing temper tantrums are behaving rather normally, whereas 10-year-olds should be able to express emotions in more appropriate ways. Similarly, it is normal for a 3- or 4-year-old to be somewhat anxious about separating from parents, but this behavior would be abnormal for a 15-year-old. "The same behavior may be developmentally appropriate at one age but indicative of pathology at another," noted Kamphaus and Frick (1996, p. 49). Yule emphasized that it is not only important to determine if the behavior is deviant but also critical to ascertain if it is interfering with the child's development or causing difficulties for the family or society.

Understanding age-appropriate behavior and developmental differences is critical in deciding whether a child's behavior is normal or abnormal and in gaining perspective about problems characterizing childhood and adolescence, "since certain behaviors are expected at certain stages" (Semrud-Clikeman, 1995, p. 10). Ginter and Glauser (2004) contended that accurate assessment must consider both developmental and cultural factors, noting that the range of developmentally based behaviors can vary dramatically from one culture to another.

The purpose of this chapter is to describe critical aspects of the assessment process, with emphasis on developmental assessment and specific considerations in the assessment process with children and adolescents. Critical cognitive, cultural, and developmental issues that affect the assessment process are discussed, as well as an overview of developmental theories, ethical considerations, and applications of the *Diagnostic and Statistical Manual of Mental Disorders—Fourth Edition—Text Revision (DSM–IV–TR;* American Psychiatric Association, 2000) with youths.

The Nature of Assessment

Whiston (2000) described assessment as "the broad term that implies the evaluation of individuals through a process that may involve test results and other sources of information" (p. 5). According to Whiston, assessment procedures are used to obtain information about clients that practitioners use to make clinical decisions as well as to provide information to clients. Assessment can facilitate problem solving by helping clients identify limitations as well as strengths that may affect the change process, and it can help clients make decisions. Additionally, assessment instruments measure developmental levels and can pinpoint developmental changes throughout the counseling process as well as at the end of counseling (Whiston, 2000). Hood and Johnson (2002) noted that the assessment process itself can be therapeutic because it helps clients clarify goals and develop a sense of perspective. The importance of good assessment cannot be underestimated. According to Whiston, if it is inaccurate or incomplete, the entire counseling process can be negatively affected because appropriate treatment cannot be selected without accurate assessment.

Assessment is an integral part of the counseling process, providing information not only in the problem assessment stage but also in subsequent stages (Hood & Johnson, 2002; Whiston, 2000). Hood and Johnson stressed how important it is for the client to recognize and accept the problem, noting that assessment procedures can increase sensitivity to the problem. Once the problem has been recognized, which is the first step of a typical problem-solving model, the counselor and client can move to the second step, which is identifying the problem in detail (Hood & Johnson, 2002) or conceptualizing and defining the client problem (Whiston, 2000). Assessment procedures can help clarify the nature of the problem and increase the likelihood that the counselor is accurately conceptualizing and defining the problem. Problem identification involves a diagnosis or classification, such as distinguishing between developmental and pathological problems. The third step in the process is generating alternatives to help resolve the problem, and assessment procedures help the counselor and the client identify various solutions (Hood & Johnson, 2002). Assessment can also help clients in the fourth step, decision making, by helping clients assess the advantages of alternatives. The final stage, verification, is when counselors evaluate whether the problem has been resolved or reduced. Assessment is an integral part of this step and includes such measures as self-monitoring techniques, satisfaction surveys, and goal attainment scaling (Hood & Johnson, 2002).

The purpose of assessment with children is to identify needs and priorities that lead to recommendations that will enhance their lives and assist with the decision-making process. Furthermore, it may promote self-awareness and enable children to cope with developmental issues before they become major problems (Hood & Johnson, 2002). Assessment procedures can be a shortcut to learning about a child, but because different procedures produce different types of information, it is important to consider what type of information is needed before selecting a particular assessment instrument or procedure. In addition, it is essential to understand the importance of developmental processes and deviations from normal development, as well as how the child experiences the assessment process.

Developmental Assessment

Developmental assessment emphasizes the assessment of individuals throughout the maturation process (Bradley, 1988). Instead of focusing solely on an individual at a particular age, developmental assessment is a broader concept that looks at specific characteristics within the context of the developmental sequence. As Bradley (1988) noted, "The approach is termed developmental assessment because it sees the aims of assessment, through various screening measures and instruments, as looking at how the individual moves through stages of development" (p. 136). The goal is to determine where the child or adolescent is in his or her development.

Developmental assessment focuses on the following characteristics (Drummond, 2004, p. 284):

1. The normality of client functioning in areas such as communication skills (verbal and nonverbal, listening and comprehension, receptive and expressive); cognitive skills (reasoning, thinking, memory, basic achievement, problem solving); physical development (gross and fine motor skills, sensory development, general development); emotional development (temperament, adjustment, self-concept, attitudes,

emotional expression); social development (interpersonal relationships with peers and family); self-care skills (ability to meet basic needs such as eating, drinking, dressing, toiletry); independent living skills (money management, functioning independently in home and community settings); work habits and adjustment (appropriate work habits and attitudes, job-seeking and job-keeping abilities, ability to work independently and get along with others); and adjustment problems (aggression, hyperactivity, acting out, depression, stress, withdrawal).

2. The historical factors that positively or negatively affect functioning of the child.
3. How the current status of family and school issues contributes positively or negatively to overall functioning.
4. The physical, psychological, and emotional health of the client at present.
5. The educational, social, physical, and psychological needs.
6. The expectations of the client and significant others.

Another characteristic of developmental assessment is the emphasis on qualitative versus quantitative methods. Qualitative assessment usually is not a standardized test, and there generally are not quantitative scores or tables that convert raw scores into percentile ranks or standard scores (Goldman, 1990). In a sense, qualitative methods are more "nontraditional," according to Goldman (1990, p. 205). Qualitative assessment emphasizes self-understanding within a developmental framework as well as a holistic approach, which avoids the specific measurement of the narrowly defined aspects of behavior, ability, or personality. Of particular importance is the fact that qualitative methods are not as precise as standardized tests, and the types of assessment procedures are more varied. Because of this, it is easier to adapt the method or the content to various ethnic, cultural, and sexual identity groups; to clients with disabilities; and to people from different socioeconomic levels.

A qualitative approach allows more active client involvement: "the client is not simply a 'passive responder' who is being measured, predicted, placed, or diagnosed" (Goldman, 1990, p. 205). This assures more client investment in the entire assessment and intervention process, which, in turn, results in more positive long-term effects. This type of assessment is also more dynamic rather than static, meaning that assessment is an ongoing process and there is less distinction between assessment and intervention (Drummond, 2000). Thus, although some initial assumptions are made on the basis of an assessment procedure administered early in the counseling process, this impression is tentative and may shift as new information is revealed in the course of counseling. Because developmental assessment is more ongoing, it diminishes some of the negative stigma about being "diagnosed and treated," and it is also tied more closely to interventions.

With this approach, the process of the counseling relationship does not have to be interrupted to give a standardized test.

In contrast to a structural, standardized assessment, which looks at how much or how little of a trait an individual possesses, the developmental approach looks for patterns and how these patterns relate to the total developmental process. In other words, rather than looking for a precise score, the developmental approach examines how the responses relate to the characteristics for a particular stage of development. For example, in the assessment of self-esteem, the School Form of the Coopersmith Self-Esteem Inventory yields six scores (Hood & Johnson, 2002). Instead of using an instrument such as this to indicate how much or how little self-esteem a child has, the developmental approach might make use of a self-portrait to determine how the child's view of him- or herself relates to stages of self-development. Looking at developmental patterns across different domains is also essential for a comprehensive assessment. For example, a gifted child may be average in his or her physical development, advanced in cognitive development, and below average in social and emotional development. The effective practitioner must assess all areas of development and not assume that the client is equally mature in all areas (Wagner, 2003).

Fadely and Hosler (1980) and Epanchin and Paul (1987) emphasized that developmental assessment should be comprehensive, including positive as well as deficit aspects of a child's functioning, so that the problem is assessed accurately from a total perspective. According to these authors, tests are given too often to determine what is wrong with a child, which results in a diagnosis of a disability but may not provide an overall view of the nature of the child. "Merely giving tests is not enough. There has to be a more comprehensive means of establishing the competencies of the child" (Fadely & Hosler, 1980, p. 4). Furthermore, focusing only on the deficits limits opportunities to facilitate optimal development in children (Wagner, 2003).

Kamphaus and Frick (1996) advocated viewing test results within the context of the child's environment, noting that an abused child's social anxiety may be much higher than his or her peers, but the child's behavior is more understandable when viewed within the context of mistrust associated with the abusive family environment. These authors also stressed that professionals should not assume that a child's behavior at one point in time is indicative of his or her personality, and that because children's behavior varies from one setting to another, it is critical to observe the child in different settings and take the context into consideration when making interpretations. Drummond (2000) concurred, emphasizing that multiple measures of assessment allow the professional to combine information from a variety of sources. He also suggested that, in addition to direct testing, naturalistic observation of the client in his or her environment and interviews with significant others are also valuable assessment measures.

Differentiation of assessment levels is also important so that extensive, time-consuming assessment is given only when absolutely necessary, according to Fadely and Hosler (1980). In their opinion, assessment should not be complex, because this prevents problem resolution at a more basic level. They contended that it is more practical to use a "first-level" informal assessment procedure that does not authenticate a diagnosis, as so many assessment instruments do, but instead provides relevant information that can be used to structure an intervention program. This first-level assessment often includes teachers and/or parents. Through involvement in the actual assessment, they tend to see the process as more valuable, and therefore invest more in the intervention process.

Developmental assessment is based on developmental psychology, which describes development as a process in which an individual gradually moves from the simple to the complex in interpersonal, emotional, moral, cognitive, and ego development (Berger, 2003; Berk, 2003; Charlesworth, 2003; McDevitt & Ormrod, 2002; Siegler, DeLoache, & Eisenberg, 2003). Although developmental theory generally has been characterized by an ordered sequence of stages, Drum and Lawler (1988) differentiated between those who describe the developmental process as involving internal change in the structure of the mind and those who believe that it consists of a discrete number of phases. Those who adhere to the latter view refer to stages as tasks or challenges at particular periods during the life span. How these challenges are handled influences happiness and well-being, as well as success in negotiating future stages. For example, if a child does not learn to express feelings effectively, intimacy likely will become an issue in adulthood until this earlier task has been resolved successfully. Erik Erikson was one of the leading theorists of this point of view.

Piaget was the renowned theorist who emphasized changes in the structure of the mind while also ascribing to the concept of sequential stages. The changes that occur at each stage affect how one thinks, which in turn influences how an individual views the external world. Essentially, the focus is on how the mind changes in complexity and how this affects the integration and processing of information.

Although development usually is presented as a hierarchical concept, Ivey (2000) expanded this linear model by introducing the concept of recycling of stages, noting that development can be linear, cyclical, and spiraling. Ivey stressed that although individuals develop in orderly progressions, they also repeat patterns. Thus, an individual may progress to a higher level but simultaneously may rework issues from a previous stage, which leads to new understanding. Ivey's model incorporates the traditional stage sequence notion and adds a new dimension that expands the theoretical concepts and seemingly reflects aspects of human growth and development more realistically.

Several developmental theorists' work has had a major impact on the nature of assessment across the life span. A brief overview is provided in the following section, with more in-depth coverage in subsequent chapters that specifically describes developmental stages and competencies corresponding to early and middle childhood and early and mid-adolescence.

Developmental Theories

"Developmental theory is a systematic statement of principles and generalizations that provides a coherent framework for studying and explaining development" (Berger, 2003, p. 35). Although this implies a universal pattern of development and that children who deviate from the norm are abnormal, Berger and Thompson (1991) emphasized the importance of relying on these principles as a general guideline but also recognizing uniquenesses, including gender and culture.

Cognitive Development

Jean Piaget clearly had a significant impact on the field of developmental psychology (Santrock, 2000). Piaget developed the conceptual framework that outlines key issues in cognitive development and emphasizes the development of rational thinking and stages of thought. Although environmental experiences are important, Piaget maintained that thoughts are the primary influence on children's actions (Berger, 2003; Santrock, 2000). According to Berk (2003), Piaget believed that children discover, or construct, their knowledge about the world through their own activity, which is why this theory is also referred to as a constructivist approach to cognitive development. As Berk noted, Piaget's theory assumes that all aspects of cognition develop in an integrated manner, that the stages always follow the same order and cannot be skipped, and that they are universal—they apply to all children everywhere. This is one of the criticisms of Piaget's theory, according to Kaplan (2000), who noted that there is evidence for and against the notion that children's cognitive development progresses through stages. Furthermore, some critics posited that Piaget underestimated how learning can affect intellectual development. Nevertheless, Piaget's stage theory continues to be relevant. According to his theory, children move through the following hierarchical stages of thought (Berger, 2003; Berk, 2003; Cobb, 2001):

1. *Sensorimotor.* This stage corresponds with infancy, lasting from birth until about age 2, and is divided into the following six substages because the differences between the newborn and the 2-year-old are so significant:

   - reflexive schemes (birth–1 month)
   - primary circular reactions (1–4 months)
   - secondary circular reactions (4–8 months)
   - coordination of secondary circular reactions (8–12 months)
   - tertiary circular reactions (12–18 months)
   - mental representation (18 months–2 years)

Organizing and coordinating sensations with physical movements and developing object permanence occur in this stage.

2. *Preoperational thought.* During this period, ranging from approximately age 2 to age 7, mental representation, primarily in the form of language and thought, emerges. More recent research (Ruffman, 1999) contradicts Piaget's original hypothesis that children at this age do not think logically. According to Ruffman, illogical reasoning occurs when children are dealing with unfamiliar topics, but that if tasks are simplified and relevant to their everyday lives, they are not as illogical as Piaget maintained.
3. *Concrete operational thought.* This stage is a major turning point in cognitive development. When children reach this stage, at about age 7, they can reason more logically and understand logical principles if they are applied to concrete examples. Their thinking is more flexible and organized than during the preschool years. Not only are they able to think more objectively, but also they are able to understand concepts such as identity, reversibility, reciprocity, and classification. This stage ends at approximately age 11.
4. *Formal operations.* Between the ages of 11 and 15, formal operational thought, characterized by abstract thinking, develops. Formal operational thinkers are able to develop hypotheses and make conclusions about effective ways to solve problems. The two phases of formal operational thought, assimilation and accommodation, correspond with early and later stages of adolescence. Piaget concluded that formal operational thought is often achieved completely in later adolescence, ages 15–20 (Kaplan, 2000; Santrock, 2000); however, some never complete this stage at all (Siegler et al., 2003).

Psychosocial Development

Erik Erikson (1963), a developmental psychologist, formulated a comprehensive theory of development that emphasized the importance of social relationships as well as feelings in a person's development (Meece, 2002). Erikson believed that all people have similar basic needs and that societal and cultural expectations, as well as personal relationships, influence the way people respond to those needs. According to Erikson's theory, although all children in every culture go through the same stages, each culture addresses the tasks associated with each stage differently. In other words, all children need to develop independence, but cultural norms will determine how this is done and to what degree.

This theory provides a general framework for understanding changes that occur throughout development and implies that unhealthy resolution of an issue may affect later development. There are eight stages in Erikson's model; the five that describe infancy, childhood, and adolescence are as follows (Kaplan, 2000; Meece, 2002):

- *Stage 1: Trust versus mistrust (0–12 months).* The primary task at this level is to develop trust that basic needs will be satisfied. If children are cared for in a warm, supportive manner, they develop trust, whereas if they are raised by caretakers who are angry and incapable of meeting the children's needs, they will learn to mistrust.
- *Stage 2: Autonomy versus shame and doubt (1–3 years).* Developing a feeling of control over behavior and learning to be self-sufficient are critical tasks at this stage. If children are not allowed to do some things on their own, they may develop doubt in their own abilities, which in turn affects their ability to develop self-confidence.
- *Stage 3: Initiative versus guilt (3–5 years).* Children need to develop a sense of self, be encouraged to initiate activities, and assume a sense of responsibility for their actions. If they are punished for expressing their own desires, they feel guilty, which leads to fear and nonassertiveness.
- *Stage 4: Industry versus inferiority (6–10 years).* Developing a sense of self-worth and competence through interaction with peers and academic experiences is central to this stage. Children who are constantly compared with others may feel inferior, whereas children with a sense of industry approach new tasks with persistence and enjoyment.
- *Stage 5: Identity versus role confusion (10–20 years).* Establishing a strong sense of identity and exploring alternatives concerning their career and future plans are the principal developmental tasks at this level. Adolescents develop role confusion if they are not able to develop a strong sense of identity.

One criticism of Erikson's theory is that it was based on studies of men, and as Gilligan (1982) noted, development may occur later or take on a different form for women. It is also important to note that while one of Erikson's major tasks is to develop independence, some cultures such as Asians, Latinos, and African Americans are more likely to value interdependence (Phinney, Ong, & Madden, 2000).

Ego Development

Loevinger (1976) was credited with the majority of the work done on ego development. She described a nine-stage model arranged in hierarchical order from the simple to the complex. Tasks at one stage must be accomplished before those at the next level can be initiated. The stages are as follows:

1. *Presocial stage.* The child sees no differentiation of self from environment.
2. *Impulsive stage.* Preoccupation with impulses (particularly sexual and aggressive) and a present orientation best describe this level of ego development.

3. *Self-protective stage.* During this stage, the child blames circumstances or others for problems and understands rules but uses them for personal gain. He or she learns to anticipate short-term reward and punishment.
4. *Conformist stage.* The child fears disapproval, perceives behavior as external, and is concerned about social acceptance, appearance, and reputation.
5. *Self-aware level.* At this level, there is an expanded consciousness of self and increasing appreciation of multiple possibilities in situations.
6. *Conscientious stage.* Characteristics of this stage include self-evaluation of goals, sense of responsibility and concern for others, and long-term perspectives.
7. *Individualistic stage.* A greater sense of individuality, need for emotional independence, and awareness of the conflict between personal needs and needs of others predominate this stage.
8. *Autonomous stage.* Individuals at this stage of development are able to recognize and handle conflict, allow others to be autonomous, and focus on self-fulfillment rather than on achievement.
9. *Integrated stage.* Although few people reach this stage, it could be described as an understanding of life's complexities.

Moral Development

According to Kaplan (2000), moral development is a cultural and social process, as well as a cognitive process. Moral decisions are based on logic and thought, but influenced by family and society. Determining how one should behave in various moral circumstances, how one thinks about rules, and how one feels about moral issues are all part of the moral development process.

Kohlberg (1980, 1984) and Gilligan (1982) have done extensive work on moral development. Kohlberg maintained that as children develop, their thoughts become more internally, rather than externally, controlled. Consistent with developmental theory, Kohlberg believed that moral development consists of three levels, each characterized by two stages that are described as follows:

- *Level 1: Preconventional moral reasoning.* The child has no internalization of moral values. This is a self-centered level, in which emphasis is placed on getting rewards and avoiding punishment (Berger, 2003).
  Stage 1: Punishment and obedience: Children obey because they are told to; rewards and punishments govern moral reasoning.
  Stage 2: Instrumental and relativist: Each person takes care of his or her own needs. Moral reasoning is based on self-interest; children obey when they want to or when they see it is in their best interests to do so.
- *Level 2: Conventional moral reasoning.* Children obey others' standards and rules.

Stage 3: "Good girl"–"Nice boy": Children want to be seen as "good kids." Good behavior pleases others. Social approval is more important than a reward (Berger, 2003).

Stage 4: "Law and order": Children make moral judgments based on their understanding of the law; they obey rules and respect authority (Meece, 2002).

- *Level 3: Postconventional moral reasoning.* At this stage, morality is not based on others' standards but is internalized. Emphasis is on moral principles.

    Stage 5: Social contract: The individual knows that laws are important and exist to protect human rights.

    Stage 6: Universal ethical principles: Universal principles of justice, equality, and fairness determine what is right or wrong. When they interfere with moral principles, unjust laws may be broken (Meece, 2002).

Although Kohlberg's model illustrated how children's moral judgment systematically changes with age, his work has been criticized because children in non-Western cultures do not advance as far in their moral judgment, despite the fact that they start out reasoning in a similar manner (Kaplan, 2000). Another concern is that Kohlberg asserted that people move from one stage to the next and once they reach the next stage, they do not exhibit characteristics from the previous level. It may be that as children and adolescents increasingly use higher stages of moral reasoning, they may also use lower stages.

Another prominent moral development theorist, Gilligan (1982), argued that Kohlberg's model is biased against females because it does not adequately recognize differences in the way males and females reason morally, nor does it reflect a relationship perspective that females value. According to Gilligan, males and females are socialized differently; males value justice and rights, whereas females value caring and responsibility for others. Gilligan developed the care perspective, which views people in relation to their connectedness with others. The focus is on relationships with others, interpersonal communication, and care and concern for others. Gilligan based her theory on a three-stage model: preconventional morality (concern for self and survival), conventional morality (concern for caring for others and being responsible), and postconventional morality (concern for self and concern for others are independent). Kaplan (2000) noted that Gilligan's work has broadened the focus on moral reasoning and has demonstrated that there are some male–female differences when confronting moral issues.

Interpersonal Development

Selman (1980, 1981) is a prominent researcher in the development of interpersonal understanding. According to Selman (1980) and Selman and Schultz (1998), the development of interpersonal understanding is reflected in the concept of social perspective taking, which is a process that enables a person to take on the perspective of another and relate it to his or her own. On the basis of extensive investigation, Selman (1980) and Selman and Schultz (1998) identified the following five-stage sequence of social perspective taking:

- *Level 0: Egocentric perspective taking (up to age 6).* The child can differentiate self and others, but not their points of view. There is no ability to relate perspectives, as "Stage 0 children believe that other people's thoughts and feelings are nearly identical to their own" (Bjorklund, 2000, p. 346).
- *Level 1: Subjective perspective taking (ages 6–8).* Although the child realizes that people feel differently because they have different experiences or information, he or she has overly simplistic perceptions of others' perspectives and tends to equate outward expressions with internal feelings.
- *Level 2: Second-person reciprocal perspective taking (ages 8–10).* At this stage, the child is able to see that people can have different viewpoints and possibly contradictory feelings about a situation. The child realizes that no one perspective is absolutely right.
- *Level 3: Third-person mutual perspective taking (ages 10–12).* The child in this stage talks about different points of view and can put him- or herself in another's place to see it from that perspective. He or she understands the advantages of trust, compromise, and cooperation.
- *Level 4: Social, symbolic perspective taking (ages 12–15+).* The adolescent is able to use principles of the social system to analyze and evaluate his or her own perspective and those of others. The adolescent recognizes that past events and present circumstances contribute to personality and behavior and that people are not always aware of why they act the way they do.

Social perspective taking helps children and adolescents understand and get along with others by looking at the world from other viewpoints. According to McDevitt and Ormrod (2002), social perspective taking "helps children make sense of actions that might otherwise be puzzling and choose responses that are most likely to achieve desired results and maintain positive interpersonal relationships" (p. 365).

The Assessment Process With Children

Understanding how developmental levels affect the assessment process results in more effective assessment. According to Stone and Lemanek (1990), the developmental literature is now providing a better understanding of children, and, as a result, more emphasis has been placed on designing assessment procedures that are more appropriate for children and adolescents. Children are limited in their ability to comprehend or respond appropriately to some assessment instruments, and their lack of life experiences also restricts their understanding of various concepts. The following considerations are important:

1. Instruments must be constructed in language suitable to the child's reading and comprehension level.
2. Instruments and other assessment methods should reflect the attention span capability of the child.
3. The format of the assessment instrument or procedure should be appropriate. Stone and Lemanek (1990) reported that forced-choice formats are not very effective, because children are likely to select the last alternative. Likewise, a yes/no format usually is responded to with a "yes" by preschoolers.
4. To maintain a younger child's interest, one needs to consider pictures, cartoons, and other creative techniques.
5. Questions that are relevant to the race, culture, or gender of the client facilitate attention to task and reflect sensitivity to people from various groups. Questions must be appropriate for the child's developmental level (Garbarino & Stott, 1992).
6. The examples used in the assessment instrument must be appropriate to the life experiences of the child.
7. Use props to stimulate memory, facilitate communication, or supplement language (Garbarino & Stott, 1992).

There are also some critical cognitive–developmental issues that have a major impact on the assessment process with children. Stone and Lemanek identified the following.

Emotional Understanding

Regardless of the type of problem, assessing emotions generally is an important aspect of the evaluation procedure. Assessors often assume mistakenly that children can readily identify and express how they feel. However, the development of emotional understanding is progressive, and young children cannot report their emotions accurately (Stone & Lemanek, 1990). In soliciting information about feelings, the child's developmental level of emotional understanding is a crucial factor. The following information should serve as a helpful guideline.

Young children can identify basic feelings accurately by observing facial expressions, although they sometimes confuse anger and sadness. They are better able to talk about their feelings and express them in appropriate ways. Although they do not realize that feelings may be disguised or that they may be experienced simultaneously, children do understand the idea of experiencing different emotions at different times (Berk, 1999).

As children get older, they understand that a person can have two conflicting emotions at the same time and rely more on their inner experiences or mental cues about what they or others are feeling (McDevitt & Ormrod, 2002). According to Berk (1999), children understand that they can change their feelings as well as hide them. The 7- to 11-year-olds also recognize negative emotions. Although younger children see themselves as the major cause of their parents' emotions, school-age children realize that they are not the cause of another person's emotional discomfort (Kaplan, 2000).

During adolescence, the understanding of emotions becomes more refined. Once children are past the emotional volatility of early adolescence, they become better able to understand the discrepancy between inner feelings and how these feelings are expressed (Vernon, 2004). They are also able to make causal assumptions about the feelings of others.

Concept of Self

When children are asked to complete an assessment of some aspect of their functioning, it is assumed that they have enough of a sense of "self" to make the assessment meaningful. This may not be the case, however, and it is important for the assessor to understand the development of self-concept.

Between the ages of 4 and 6, children tend to view the self as part of the body. There is an "all-or-none" conceptualization of personal traits and concrete descriptions of self based on behavior, activity, and physical appearance (Harter, 1999). From ages 8 to 11, children are able to incorporate psychological characteristics and social comparisons into self-descriptions (Siegler et al., 2003), are aware of different components of self, and can differentiate between mental and physical aspects of self. The 12- to 16-year-olds are able to use abstract self-descriptions that are based on dispositions, values, and beliefs. Adolescents have a more integrated and consistent self-identity (Siegler et al., 2003) and are capable of self-reflection and self-monitoring.

Because self-understanding progresses from the concrete and situation specific to the abstract and psychological dimension of self, assessment instruments and procedures must use more concrete, action-oriented questions for young children and then supplement this information with data from parents and teachers. At approximately 8 years of age, children have developed a more global sense of self, and the assessment becomes more meaningful (Harter, 2001).

Person Perception

The understanding of self and others appears to be interrelated. As with the development of the self-concept, there is a developmental progression in relation to how others are perceived that needs to be considered when designing or using assessment instruments. In short, "Person perception concerns how we size up the attributes of people with whom we are familiar" (Berk, 2003, p. 463).

Stone and Lemanek (1990) depicted 4- to 6-year-olds as capable of describing another person's behavior but not of explaining the behavior. At this age, descriptions of others tend to be concrete, such as "Maria has a puppy" or

"Antonio called me a name." There is confusion in the children's under-standing of what actions are intentional as opposed to accidental.

Next, 7- to 11-year-olds can describe others in relation to personal and psychological characteristics, but they still are not aware that others can have both positive and negative qualities. They are able to see that factors such as ability might be related to outcome, and they compare their feel-ings and thoughts with those of others (Selman & Schultz, 1998).

Adolescents are able to make psychological comparisons; can relate interests, abilities, and beliefs; and can explain and predict another person's behavior on the basis of a mutual perspective and societal con-cepts (Selman & Schultz, 1998). The adolescents' description of others is more complex.

This gradual shift from the concrete to the abstract in describing how others are perceived has implications for the assessment process. If asked to describe relationships with others, the preschooler will give a concrete response about physical appearance or a behavior, whereas the adolescent will explain dispositional causes of behavior and more complex relation-ship factors (Berk, 2003).

Language Skills

The quality of information obtained from a child obviously is influenced by the ability to communicate. Like other areas of development, language acquisition proceeds in a sequential order. By age 5, the basic dimensions are well developed (Bee & Henslin, 2003). However, it is important to remember that children have more limited comprehension, which affects the assessment process. Likewise, their experiences are not as expansive, and they may not have the necessary vocabulary to describe situations. The assessment instrument must reflect the appropriate reading level and the child's culture.

Assessing Childhood Problems: Using the DSM–IV–TR

How many times have you been puzzled by symptoms some young clients display that seem strange or disturbing? You ask yourself, "Do most children this age level behave this way?" "Is this what we should expect at this stage of development?" These questions are based on the challenging principle of normalcy. So is it normal, for example, that 8-year-old Carlos, who is always concerned about keeping his work area extremely clean and orderly and having his work done perfectly, vomits every morning before leaving for school? Most practitioners would say this is rather extreme behavior that goes beyond a child's normal desire to perform well in school.

Although the emphasis of this book is on effective developmental and culturally appropriate assessment and intervention with school-age clients, counselors must have at least a minimal understanding of age-related disorders that are disruptive and prevalent enough to appear in the

DSM–IV–TR (American Psychiatric Association, 2000) because some clients will display symptoms that are not culturally or developmentally normal. Ginter and Glauser (2004) used the term *developmental vectors* to refer to "those areas in human development that have been identified as areas expected to change during the life span" (p. 3). How the child progresses in the physical, cognitive, emotional, behavioral, and social vectors can reflect healthy, normal development. Likewise, failure to achieve these developmental changes could result in a *DSM–IV–TR* diagnosis. Although there are many disorders in children and adolescents, Erk (2004) listed the following most common disorders:

- adjustment disorders
- attention-deficit hyperactivity disorder
- disruptive behavior disorders (conduct and oppositional disorders)
- anxiety disorders (separation anxiety, specific phobia, social phobia, obsessive-compulsive disorder, posttraumatic stress disorder)
- mood and depressive disorders (major depressive disorder, dysthymic disorder, bipolar disorder)

In addition to this list, substance-related disorders, pervasive developmental disorders (Ginter & Glauser, 2004), and eating disorders (Scarano-Osika & Maloney, 2004) should be included.

Within the spectrum of childhood and adolescence, how does one determine what is normal or abnormal? Ginter and Glauser (2001) stressed that what might be considered abnormal for an adult may be normal for a child because the symptom falls within the expected range of a developmental vector. These authors also pointed out that teachers, parents, or counselors might see this behavior as abnormal because they lack understanding about what is normal for the child's age or situation. For example, how do you determine if the excessive energy and impulsiveness of a 7-year-old boy is an age-appropriate behavior or a disruptive behavior? Certainly, there are many factors involved in rendering a tentative diagnosis. However, Ginter and Glauser noted that it is normal for the boy's behavior to fluctuate throughout the day when he goes through periods of being tired or rested. And although the inclination might be to label this child with attention-deficit hyperactivity disorder (ADHD), the *DSM–IV–TR* states that "In early childhood, it may be difficult to distinguish symptoms of Attention-Deficit/Hyperactivity Disorder from age-appropriate behaviors in active children (e.g., running around or being noisy)" (American Psychiatric Association, 2000, p. 91). This statement is a clear indication not only of the difficulty in rendering a diagnosis but also of the importance of considering the symptoms within the context of normal development.

The *DSM* is a manual based on the medical model that classifies disorders, not people. The intent is not to identify what constitutes normal development, but according to Ginter and Glauser (2004), the diagnostic criteria listed in the *DSM* provides a way to logically infer what is developmentally expected. A simple way to understand this classification system without losing focus of normal and cultural development is to reverse the criteria of a diagnosis. For example, Casandra, an 11-year-old African American girl, is experiencing difficulties with her written assignments in class. The teacher expressed serious concerns regarding Casandra's academic progress and laziness and referred Casandra to the counselor to work on her study skills. After two sessions, the counselor realized that something was not right, that this problem could not be construed simply as laziness and poor study skills. By *reversing* the criteria of a disorder of written expression (*DSM–IV–TR*; American Psychiatric Association, 2000), the counselor assumed that at this stage of her life, Casandra's writing skills should be average or above average based on her chronological age, intelligence, and age-appropriate education. Because this was not the case, her current situation merited a *DSM* diagnosis and more specialized interventions.

Counselors who are not aware of developmental and cultural factors often tend to observe behaviors through their adult lenses and therefore pathologize the behaviors of young clients. Rochelle, a 17-year-old, was referred to the counselor because her professional parents believed that there was something wrong with their daughter: She was not particularly interested in going to college, and they knew she had once consumed some alcohol at a party. These behaviors would be considered normal for this adolescent's age and therefore do not reflect a serious disorder. According to Gazda, Ginter, and Horne (2001, as cited in Erk, 2004):

> a period of developmental crisis differs from serious psychopathology in that a child (and other family members) is very likely to move through the crisis eventually, although an accurate assessment and appropriate counseling intervention would move the child and family through a crisis period more quickly and with less turmoil (counseling might even enable those involved to reframe the crisis [or alter some aspect] to achieve higher developmental levels). (p. 5)

Balancing Child Development, Culture, and Psychopathology

According to Ginter and Glauser (2004), an "inaccurate diagnostic label might prove to be little more than a 'scientific slur'—serving to add to the problems confronting the person" (p. 8). Ginter and Glauser noted that the authors of the *DSM* recognize the importance of cultural influences and recommend seeking a cultural explanation for the child's behavior. In other words, prior to pathologizing any behaviors and rendering a *DSM* diagnosis, it is important to understand the developmental and cultural contexts. For example, Ramiro, a 14-year-old immigrant from El Salvador, was referred by the teachers and school principal to a counselor to deal with his oppositional behavior and his "intolerance and outburst of anger and hostility." Before developing any kind of intervention to help Ramiro, the counselor must filter his or her assessment decision through the layers displayed in Exhibit 1.1.

Other factors to consider in the assessment process are environmental and psychosocial stressors (Axis IV on the *DSM–IV–TR*) that may also disrupt a child's progression through normal development. According to the *DSM–IV–TR* (as cited in Ginter & Glauser, 2004), the following examples of stressors must also be factored into a diagnosis: discrimination; family turbulence as a result of parental separation, divorce, or estrangement; removal from a parent's custody; remarriage of a parent; physical abuse; excessive overprotection by parents; neglect; death of a close friend; exposure to an unsafe neighborhood; extreme financial poverty; frequent clashes with teachers or classmates; birth or adoption of a sibling; major life-cycle transition (e.g., moving to a new neighborhood, state, school); and personal exposure to a natural disaster, war, or suicide attack by a terrorist. The maturity level of the child will affect how the child perceives the stressor. In Ramiro's case, exposure to an unsafe neighborhood, family turbulence, his recent immigration, and the normal anger outbursts during adolescence must all be considered before assuming a *DSM* diagnosis of oppositional defiant disorder.

It is unfortunate that psychopathology is relatively prevalent in children, according to Mash and Dozois (1996, as cited in Erk, 2004), who cited statistics indicating that 3%–7% of all school-age children in North America have ADHD, 1%–10% have conduct disorder, and overall estimates for all developmental, emotional, and behavioral disorders in children range

Exhibit 1.1
Assessment Process

Counselor's Personal Biases
What previous experiences or lack of them may *taint the way I see my client*? (i.e., lack of exposure and knowledge about El Salvadoreans, biases transmitted by the media, learned discrimination in family or cultural context)

Think Developmentally
What is the *developmentally appropriate* behavior of a 14-year-old? (i.e., can be impulsive, is slowly transitioning to formal operational thinking but may still exhibit concrete thinking patterns, may be experiencing peer pressure and therefore demonstrates toughness, is on an emotional roller coaster where anger outbursts are not necessarily atypical)

Think Culturally
What is the *culturally appropriate* reaction of a 14-year-old immigrant coming from a country torn by a debilitating civil war? (i.e., history of the country, victims of war, defense mechanisms, frustration against a possible racist environment)

Think on the Basis of the DSM–IV–TR
Is his *negative behavior* extreme, intense, and repetitive? By reversing some criteria, the counselor can render a tentative diagnosis (i.e., the child does not initiate aggressive behavior; he does not bully, threaten, or intimidate others; he is not physically cruel to animals or people; his behavior does not occur in more than one place, etc.)

from 14% to 22%. Given this picture, practitioners must be knowledgeable about the *DSM–IV–TR* and consider it within the context of developmental, cultural, and environmental factors. As Prout (1999) noted,

> Children are not simply "little adults." Their treatment cannot be viewed as scaled-down adult therapy; their developmental stages, environments, reasons for entering therapy . . . necessitate a different, if not creative, approach to therapy. The child/adolescent therapist must have an expanded knowledge base of the human condition and a different perspective of what constitutes therapy or counseling. (p. 1)

Characteristics of Effective Child Assessment

Problem Identification

In problem identification, it is important to distinguish between practical and emotional problems (DiGiuseppe, 1999; Vernon, 2002). Practical problems relate to external or environmental events and typically involve difficulty in managing, adapting to, or solving specific problems in the environment. Examples of practical problems for children or adolescents might include poor study habits, aggressive rather than assertive behavior with a friend, not knowing how to be self-sufficient if left at home alone, or not knowing where to find information about a specific career. Practical problems involve behavioral skill deficits, lack of information, inadequate problem-solving skills, or unrealistic environmental demands.

Emotional problems are undesirable emotions about the practical problem and interfere with the client's ability to solve the practical problem. Examples of emotional problems include feeling guilty about poor grades resulting from bad study habits, feeling angry about mishandling a relationship problem, or feeling ashamed for not readily knowing what to do or where to access information. Emotional reactions add another layer to the problem and must be assessed and addressed for the problem to be resolved.

It is also critical to assess the frequency, intensity, and duration of the symptoms. The Frequency Intensity Duration (FID) Scale (Bernard & Joyce, 1984) is a useful technique for determining the severity of the problem. By identifying the frequency with which the problem occurs, the intensity and duration of the response, and how long the problem has been evident, the practitioner develops a realistic perception of the problem, which in turn is useful in determining the level of further assessment and intervention. This is also helpful for parents, because, as is frequently the case, parents who refer a child for counseling are somewhat anxious and may unintentionally exaggerate the extent of the concern. For example, I (Ann Vernon) recently consulted with an 8-year-old's parents who were convinced that their child was not working up to his potential and would get bad grades throughout school. In probing further, I learned that this above-average-ability child recently had gotten a failing grade on one test, and that was the extent of it. By looking at the frequency of the bad marks, which in this case was one, and comparing it with his other grades and with his potential, I determined that the problem was not occurring frequently enough to warrant further assessment or intervention. It would have been different had this become a pattern in which the child's grades had been declining over a period of time in more than one class. Using the FID Scale is invaluable in obtaining a clear picture of the issue.

Hood and Johnson (2002) emphasized how important it is to consider the possibility of multiple problems. This is particularly pertinent to adolescent assessment, because these clients may well have depression coupled with substance abuse, for example. Assessing the situation as well as the client is also important. Galassi and Perot (1992) noted that environmental factors often interact with individual characteristics and affect behavior in particular situations.

Above all, it is important to make tentative hypotheses and revise as additional data are available. Being aware of cultural or personal biases is critical, as well as using several different methods of assessment to attain a broader picture of the problem (Hood & Johnson, 2002). This point was very evident in the case of a young boy who drew a picture characterized by high degrees of aggression and violence. As the student counselor discussed the case in internship seminar, she voiced concern about this client's rage. Her classmates and instructor encouraged her to probe further by using an anger checklist. During the next seminar meeting, she shared the results of the anger survey and was puzzled by the discrepancy between the rage expressed through her client's picture and the low score on the instrument. However, after discussing this with the client in the next session, she learned that the boy's picture was based on a video that he had seen the night before his session with her. Had she not used multiple assessments, she would have misdiagnosed the problem.

Assessment Relationship

Because children and adolescents often do not "own" the problem, do not refer themselves for counseling, or do not understand the purpose and process of the assessment, they may resist or be reluctant. Furthermore, in some cultures, counseling is not as acceptable or is only considered as a last resort because the family is the primary source of support (Pedersen, 2000). Resistance, reluctance, or discomfort may be manifested in a continuum of behavior from overt unwillingness or refusal to cooperate to acceptance and compliance. Even if the child is in counseling willingly, it is essential to establish a sound working relationship by gearing the vocabulary toward the client's developmental level and to use strategies that are more effective for a younger clientele. Sattler (1993) made the following suggestions:

1. Formulate appropriate opening statements.
2. Make descriptive comments.
3. Use reflection.

4. Give praise frequently.
5. Avoid critical statements.
6. Use simple questions and concrete referents.
7. Formulate questions in the subjunctive mood when necessary.
8. Be tactful.
9. Use props, crayons, clay, or toys to help children communicate.
10. Use special techniques to facilitate the expression of culturally unacceptable responses.
11. Clarify an episode of misbehavior by recounting it.
12. Handle children who are minimally communicative by clarifying the interview procedures.
13. Handle avoidance of a topic by discussing it yourself.
14. Understand silence.
15. Handle resistance and anxiety by giving support and reassurance (pp. 420–424).

Other considerations include the following:

1. Explain to the child how the information obtained from the assessment process can be used to facilitate problem solving.
2. Use humor where appropriate to help establish a more comfortable relationship.
3. Find out about hobbies, favorite athletic teams or musical groups, school activities, favorite pastimes, and family traditions. Use this knowledge to "chit chat" in the first few minutes of the session.
4. Create an inviting, but not overly stimulating or cluttered, environment. If possible, have smaller furniture for younger children. Multiethnic young clients may be more responsive in an environment that is natural, with wooden (not metal) furniture, artwork, plants, soft lights, and soothing music (Clemente, 2004).
5. Be yourself. It is important to be personal but not an overly friendly "buddy."
6. Be warm, empathic, open, genuine, patient, and engaging.
7. Show genuine interest and concern for the client.
8. Take leads from the client. If you sense that he or she is more comfortable on the floor, do not restrict yourself to your chair. By all means, do not sit behind a desk even when conferring with parents, because this creates distance and inhibits a collaborative relationship. At the same time, remember that "personal space" varies, depending on the client's gender, age, and culture, so be observant and flexible.
9. Be sensitive to others' worldview; be respectful.
10. Explain the limits of confidentiality and how the assessment data will be communicated to parents and others.
11. Be flexible and creative; if one approach is not working, try another.
12. Adjust your expectations; sometimes, the harder you push, the less you get.

For specific age groups, consider the following ideas:

The Preschool Child. After introducing yourself to the child and indicating that you are glad he or she is here, it often is effective to share a toy or play a game with a child of this age, particularly if you sense discomfort: "Joshua, if you'd like to, you can hold this cuddly stuffed elephant." Providing a simple explanation of the reason for the visit and "normalizing" the problem also are important to alleviate anxiety: "Joshua, your mom wanted you to come to see me because she knows that it's hard for you to go outside or up to your bedroom because you're afraid of being alone. I've worked with several kids who feel like this." Some informal discussion about family members, pets, or friends also can facilitate rapport building. If the child is extremely shy or reluctant, it may be good to invite the parent(s) into the interview room. Verbal praise or a reward such as a sticker is appropriate at this age for reinforcing cooperative behavior and attention to task.

The Elementary School Child. Following an introduction of yourself and a basic description of what you do, it is important to ask the child if he or she knows why he or she is meeting with you, how he or she feels about it, and if he or she has any questions. If the child seems unclear about the purpose of the visit, it is best to be straightforward: "Your dad told me that you were having some problems adjusting to your new baby sister. He brought you here so that I could learn more about the problem and we could figure out some ways to help you. What do you think about that?" It is also a good idea to advise parents about what to say to the child about visiting with you. For instance, if your title is "Dr." the child may think that you are a medical doctor and that he or she is going to you for a shot, as one 8-year-old client recently shared. If both the professional and the parent can clarify misconceptions, it is easier to establish the relationship.

Playing a board game such as checkers or *Sorry* (Parker Brothers) often is effective. We prefer to use more personalized games or strategies that yield more personal data about the child. Six- to 9-year-olds respond well to a simple strategy titled *Who Are You?* (Vernon, 2002, p. 21):

> *Dr. V.:* Let's play a short game to help us get better acquainted. You can ask me "Who Are You?" and I'll give you an answer. Then I'll ask you, and you can ask me, and we'll continue for awhile until we learn some things about each other.
> *Danielle:* Who are you?
> *Dr. V.:* I'm a dog lover. I have two Springer Spaniels. Who are you?
> *Danielle:* I like pets too. I have a rabbit and two fish. Who are you?
> *Dr. V:* I am someone who likes to read. Who are you?
> *Danielle:* I am someone who likes to ride my bike. Who are you?

The information obtained from this simple game can be used in subsequent sessions to reestablish the relationship. "Tell me something funny that your rabbit did this week" sets the client at ease and shows her that she is important because you remember things about her.

The Adolescent. An adolescent often is reluctant to attend counseling and participate in problem assessment. Do not expect the adolescent to "own" the problem, to be eager to deal with it, or to like you. With adolescents, it is best to be direct and honest about who you are and what you do, and to listen to their feelings about being with you. "Your mom told me that you didn't want to come today. I understand that, but I would like to try and help you work on the problem with your depression. I have several other clients your age, and by working together, they began to feel better. Some of them felt like they were 'sick' or 'crazy' because they were here. . . . Do you feel that way?" Although an adolescent may not raise this concern about being different or sick, it generally is a fear, and bringing it out in the open is often helpful. Acknowledging an adolescent's resistance and indicating that he or she does not have to like coming, but perhaps can tolerate it for at least a few times, is a strategy that seems to work well with this age group. Demystifying the assessment process by avoiding the use of the word *test* is recommended.

The Shy or Hostile Client. It may be too intimidating to begin an interview with a shy client by immediately attempting to assess the problem. A more informal, conversational approach might be best: learning more about the client's interests, pastimes, favorite teams, or musical groups. Playing a game can help a shy client feel more at ease. With this type of client, it is important not to "push" the process. Often the more intense the approach, the more the shy child backs away. Patience pays off in the end.

A hostile client, most often an adolescent, presents a professional challenge. Characteristically he or she denies problems, is unwilling to reveal personal information, and is guarded and suspicious. Remember that fear and anxiety usually underlie the anger and the hostile behavior that protect him or her from being too vulnerable. With this client, it is best to proceed slowly, listen to his or her perspective, and take it seriously. Even though there may be distortions in his or her thinking, a hostile client often can be engaged by helping him or her see that you can intervene in the family system, if that is creating part of the problem, and that you can give specific techniques for dealing with anger, because that is creating further problems. The following case is an example of this approach.

Twelve-year-old Kevin was extremely hostile and had only come for his appointment after his parents had given him the choice of meeting with me (Ann Vernon) or going to the hospital. Knowing that he was very resistant, I told him that I wanted to hear his "side" of the story so that we could determine what was causing his problems. Immediately he volunteered that he should not be seeing me because his parents had the problem. I acknowledged that could very well be true and that I also would be working with them. This seemed to reduce the hostility somewhat. I then indicated that I needed to get some idea of the frequency and intensity of his anger and how he behaved when he was angry. He once again insisted that if his parents knew how to be better parents, he would not have to get angry. "Kevin, I'm sure you're right, but so far you haven't been able to change their behavior by getting angry. In fact, I'll bet it just gets you in more trouble, right?" He nodded his head, but he insisted that he had no other choice. I told him that I understood that but knew from past experience in working with other kids who had similar problems that there were some things he could do to better express the anger so that he would not have to be punished by his parents all the time. Then, once he had accomplished that, he could work on ways to change them. This strategy did de-escalate the hostility, and during the second session we were able to get into the problem assessment process.

Some additional rapport-building activities (Vernon, self-developed) that can be adapted for most age levels include the following. In using them with ethnically diverse youth, remember that they may not be comfortable sharing much personal information, so further adaptation may be necessary.

People, Places, and Things (Vernon, 2002, pp. 22–23). For this activity, you will need a piece of tagboard cut into a 6- to 8-inch circle, divided into three parts, with one section labeled "people," another labeled "places," and another labeled "things." Make a tagboard arrow and attach it to the center of the circle using a brass fastener so that it will move. Then take turns with the client, spinning the arrow and sharing something about yourselves based on where the arrow lands. For example, if it lands on "people," you could talk about a favorite relative, friend, or movie actor/actress.

Alphabet Soup (Vernon, 2002, p. 24). For this activity, you will need a set of index cards with a letter of the alphabet written one per card. Turn the cards face down and put them into a shallow box. Take turns drawing a letter and sharing something about yourselves that begins with that letter. For example, if you draw a C, you might share that you like to color.

Pick Up Straws. Cut paper into very thin strips that could slip inside a drinking straw. On each strip, write a short question or an unfinished statement, such as: What is your favorite food? What do you like to do in your free time? What do you like best or least about school? What is something you don't like to do? and so forth. Slip the strips inside the straws, spread the straws on a flat surface, and take turns picking up a straw and sharing a response to the question.

Which One Are You? You will need 12–15 (or more) 6-inch paper plates, depending on the number of word sets you have. Using a marker, write the following sets of words, one word on either side of a paper plate: saver/spender; athlete/musician; watch TV/play a game; swim/ride bikes; read/play video games; pink/purple; hot dog/ taco; country/city; green/blue; soccer/basketball; summer/winter; go shopping/stay home. Take turns picking a paper plate, looking at both sides, and then sharing which you are most like or prefer.

Fact or Fiction? You and the client take turns making a statement about something you have done, somewhere you have been, or something that has happened to you. After one person makes a statement, the other has to guess if it is a fact or fiction. If it is a fact and the person identifies it as such, the person who made the statement gets a point. Then it is the next person's turn. Giving the points encourages facts as opposed to fiction.

Awareness of Developmental Issues

Developmental issues have a definite impact on the assessment process with school-age children in several significant ways. Ginter and Glauser (2004) explained that practitioners have to guard against what they termed *developmental reference point errors*, which occur when one lacks knowledge or has false information about pertinent developmental factors and therefore draw erroneous conclusions that affect the diagnosis and treatment. It is clear that, without an understanding of what is normal at various stages of development, problems can be misconstrued and even pathologized. The following case illustrates this issue.

Andrew, a high school junior, was referred to a counselor by his parents, who were extremely concerned about his relationship with a young woman. His mother stated, "Andrew is much too preoccupied with this relationship. He limits his hours at work so that he can spend time with her. He never sees his buddies, and he has lost interest in his usual activities." What blew the problem "out of the water" was when Andrew left several notes lying around in his room and his mother happened to glance at one as she put his clothes away. She panicked at the references to sexual desires and immediately limited the amount of time he could spend with his girlfriend. This, in turn, angered Andrew, and a series of intense family arguments ensued. The parents, convinced that he was sexually active on a regular basis, met with the girlfriend's parents, urging them to also restrict the involvement. Jane's parents maintained that this was a normal teenage relationship and had no intention of complying with their request.

When Andrew's parents called to set up an appointment for him, the counselor suggested that the three of them attend the session. After meeting first with Andrew, it seemed as if his parents had blown the problem out of proportion. Yes, he professed to love Jane, wanted to be with her constantly, and was struggling with his desire to be sexual with her. After an open discussion and sharing of one of the notes with the counselor, it was apparent that Andrew was wrestling with normal developmental issues, as were his parents. "Letting go" is a critical task for parents at this stage in an adolescent's development, and exploring a sexual identity and developing an intimate relationship are primary tasks for the teenager. Had the parents been more aware of adolescent development, there might not have been the overreaction. Certainly concern about the relationship was appropriate, but jumping to conclusions based on sexual innuendos in a note definitely distorted the issue.

As this case illustrates, awareness of developmental tasks and stages helps put a problem in perspective and perhaps circumvents extensive assessment and intensive intervention. Several other characteristics of effective child assessment are described subsequently.

Awareness of Cultural Issues

Given that we live in a multicultural society, it is imperative that we consider how culture affects the assessment process. As Whiston (2000) noted, "problems can occur with instruments that do not consider cultural differences" (p. 313). Certainly the practitioner views the situation or information through his or her own cultural perspective, but it is critical to understand the client's worldview because "the less the counselor knows of the client's culture, the more errors the counselor is likely to make" (Hood & Johnson, 2002, p. 344). For example, most North Americans would consider it rude if a parent came to a conference 30 minutes late and might infer negative things about the parent's commitment. To many Latin Americans, this would be normal behavior with no negative implications.

Communication style also is culturally related. In an interview situation, a child might not respond to questions, because, in his or her culture, certain things are not discussed with relative strangers. Sue and Sue (2002) noted that African American families are particularly reluctant to discuss family problems outside the family. Eye contact is another example. Although valued by White middle-class Americans, the Native American culture sees this as a sign of disrespect (Baruth & Manning, 2003).

"The culturally sensitive professional looks for the parallels in the behaviors of children of various groups, while still appreciating the differences between the groups' perceptions of the world" (Garbarino & Stott, 1992, p. 94). These authors noted that although all people share similar problems, different cultures define situations and circumstances differently. For example, they cited an inner-city adolescent who lies to cover for a powerful gang member, contrasted with a suburban child who lives in a safe environment but lies to a friend. Although both lie, one does it in response to a threat for survival and the other to avoid a friend's disapproval. Garbarino and Stott also stressed that practitioners must understand cultural meaning from the young person's point of view as well as from their own.

Gender roles, ethnicity, and social class are other important variables to consider in the assessment process. Each culture defines its gender roles, and what is considered normal in one culture may vary significantly in another. Several other dimensions affect the assessment process as well. Cultural groups have different definitions of such factors as (a) discipline and caregiving: what one culture perceives as abusive, another may see as good firm discipline (Gray & Cosgrove, 1985); (b) health and illness: different groups vary in their ideas about the causes of illnesses and how to treat them; and (c) personal–institutional relationships: maintaining close family relationships is more important than the system (Helms & Cook, 1999). Understanding how different groups experience such factors has direct bearing on the outcome of assessment. More specific information on multicultural assessment follows in chapter 3.

Involvement of Significant Others in the Assessment Process

"Adults are an important source of information in the assessment of childhood problems" (Wagner, 2003, p. 97). According to Wagner, adults can reliably report on overt behaviors, and parents are often asked to provide a developmental history. LaGreca (1990) identified several reasons why promoting a problem-solving approach and mutual participation to address concerns of parents, professionals, and children is an extremely important criterion of effective assessment: (a) The child's behavior may be situation-specific, and it is important to evaluate it within the broader social context; (b) the child generally is referred by parents or teachers, and therefore it is critical to obtain their perspective in addition to the child's; and (c) these significant persons such as parents and teachers typically are involved in some phase of the intervention process, and furthermore, involving them facilitates their understanding of the child. From a cultural standpoint, involving family in the assessment process is essential because in many non-Western cultures, an individual is defined within the context of relationships, connections, and interdependencies; the individual is not separate from the unit (Pedersen, 2000).

Vernon (2002) suggested that practitioners undertake a specific assessment that includes identifying the problem from the parents' perspective, as well as from the perspectives of other individuals who are involved, and evaluating how the problem is affecting those individuals. It is also critical to determine the duration of the problem, any extenuating circumstances or transitions, cultural practices, specific instances in which the problem is manifested, and strategies that have been used to address the problem and how successful they have been.

Not only does one develop a better understanding of the child from the adults in his or her life, but one also obtains a more accurate understanding of the problem. In many cases, although the child manifests the symptom, the problem lies within the environment. For example, consider the child who is referred by the classroom teacher for disruptive behavior. It may be true that the child is disruptive, but unless some assessment is made of the system, the practitioner may try to "fix" the child, never realizing that this child is not the only one who is disruptive in an ineffectively managed classroom.

Involving significant others is important for the reasons stated earlier, but it is also often essential to the assessment process to get an accurate representation of the problem, as the following case demonstrates.

Fifteen-year-old Nina was having problems dealing with her anger. There were frequent, explosive parent–child conflicts that usually occurred when Nina's parents denied her requests to stay out later, do something with friends, spend money, or asked her to assume some responsibilities at home. As an only child, Nina had been used to getting her way, but as she got older and was requesting more freedom, her parents were setting curfews and placing reasonable limits on what she could or could not do. They also had decided that they were no longer going to give in to Nina's demands, and this usually resulted in a temper tantrum.

Initially during counseling sessions, Nina was very open about the conflicts and willingly worked on her anger. Several family sessions were held and things improved. However, knowing that change does not occur overnight, the counselor continued to meet with Nina to develop anger management techniques further. After a session or two, Nina kept insisting that everything was fine and that she had not had problems at all with anger. Therefore, it was rather surprising when the counselor received an urgent phone call from Nina's mother indicating lots of recent conflict and that Nina's anger often was very out of control.

The moral to this story? Children and adolescents may, for a variety of reasons, distort the extent of the problem. This may have to do with shame (What does it say about me if I have problems?), confusion and anxiety (Am I "sick" because I'm in counseling?), hopelessness (This won't help anyway), or ownership (It's not my problem, it's theirs.). It also may reflect the child's inability to specifically express how the problem affects him or her. Whatever the cause, involving others in various aspects of the assessment process results in more accurate problem assessment (Vernon, 2002).

Ethical Considerations

Regardless of what is being assessed and how, practitioners must respect the feelings of young clients and acknowledge that they may be resistant or reluctant because they do not understand the counseling process. Although developmental assessment often tends to be more informal and is tied to the intervention process, children still may be anxious about participating, particularly if the referral comes from the parent or teacher. It is the helping professional's ethical responsibility to establish a good working relationship with the client and to conduct the assessment in a respectful manner.

Although it is not the intent of this chapter to present a detailed coverage of ethics, some specific issues arise when working with younger clients. For instance, the assessment process may have a negative emotional impact on children. If children respond to questions about their worries, fears, or peer relations, will they become more distressed? Although Burbach, Farha, and Thorpe (1986) noted that little empirical data exist to support this concern, practitioners should approach the assessment process in a sensitive manner, carefully explaining the purpose and procedures to the children. This may be a particularly salient caution when working with youth from various cultural groups.

Second is the issue of confidentiality. Ordinarily assessment data are considered professional information and are not disclosed to others without client consent (Hood & Johnson, 2002). However, with minors, parents or guardians also have access to the results of the assessment (Whiston, 2000). Semrud-Clikeman (1995) noted that while the primary responsibility is to protect the rights of the child, counselors also need to maintain professional and legal obligations with parents. Furthermore, school and the court system also may have legitimate reasons for accessing assessment data and can get it without client consent, according to Whiston. Children need to be informed prior to the assessment that the practitioner probably will communicate to some extent with parents and teachers if necessary, because they most likely will be involved in helping the children resolve the problems. Emphasizing to the children that the purpose of the assessment is to gain information to help them deal more effectively with the concern often circumvents this issue. Furthermore, because the developmental assessment process often is not as structured or explicit as other assessments, children may be more receptive to having information shared because there is not a score that categorizes them.

As in any counseling situation, professionals have an obligation to only use those instruments or techniques that they are qualified to administer, and they need to keep assessment results secure. Furthermore, they need to use methods that are appropriate and culturally sensitive for children and consider how the results will be used.

Summary

As the importance of developmental factors becomes more widely acknowledged, professionals will rely more on developmental assessment with children and adolescents for the following reasons.

1. It provides more useful, relevant information. Instead of a test score, which may only confirm a loosely formulated diagnosis, these assessment data can be tied more readily to interventions and problem resolution.

2. It is more culture and gender sensitive, because the instruments and assessment methods are modified more easily.
3. It looks at the problem within the total context of development and helps define what is normal.
4. It can be less threatening to younger clients, because a variety of assessment techniques may be used to determine the specific nature of the problem.
5. It involves significant others in the assessment process, which in turn assures their more active participation in the intervention phases.
6. It encompasses a wide variety of assessment procedures that can be adapted more readily to match the age and culture of the client.

Chapter 2

Methods of Developmental Assessment

✳

Ginter and Glauser (2004) stressed that "thinking developmentally is a prerequisite for rendering a valid diagnosis" (p. 4), and they described the importance of understanding normal developmental deviation, how developmental level affects psychosocial and environmental effects, and how knowledge of human development provides a context to understanding important cultural differences. Their points encompass the essence of developmental assessment, which by definition is qualitative in nature. With this approach, one does not simply give a test and report the results. Rather, there is an interactive element between assessment and the counseling process. A distinguishing characteristic of developmental assessment is its reliance on developmental theory, which describes how individuals change and grow (Bradley, 1988; Drummond, 2004). As Drummond noted, "Developmental assessment is important in understanding cognitive, ego, interpersonal, moral, and psychosocial development as individuals progress through the various stages of their life" (p. 284). Furthermore, it focuses not only on the child but also on the child's environment, taking into account how the child functions in different life areas such as school, family, and peers because behavior can vary across these contexts (Erk, 2004).

✳

Developmental assessment is particularly appropriate with children and adolescents, because, during this period of life, tremendous developmental changes occur (Erk, 2004; Wagner, 2003), which Yule (1993) stressed must be considered in assessment and intervention. Tying the assessment process to the developmental framework provides a more accurate sense of (a) how the child is moving through stages of development and (b) where and to what extent intervention should occur.

The purpose of this chapter is to describe the development of appropriate assessment procedures that can be used with children and adolescents, to identify existing developmental instruments, and to present an assessment model that incorporates a developmentally based approach.

Designing Developmental Assessment Instruments

According to Drummond (2004), "Developmental tests measure typical skills that should be mastered at certain stages" (p. 284). Although commercial developmental assessment instruments exist and can be used as formal evaluation or screening devices, many of these instruments are designed more specifically for infants or very young children and assess a broad spectrum of abilities to determine readiness or placement (Drummond, 2000; Guidubaldi, DeZolt, & Myers, 1991). These instruments emphasize performance in speech and language development, fine and gross motor development, perceptual development, physical development, and cognitive and self-help skills. However, parents, teachers, and children often want to know where children "fit" in relation to more typical developmental problems, such as the things they worry about, the amount of independent behavior they exhibit, or their level of self-esteem. Although instruments measuring social–emotional development exist, many are designed specifically for very young children or do not address appropriately some of the more common questions that parents, teachers, or children have about development. Furthermore, sometimes direct testing is not possible or less useful because of the developmental level of the client or because of a disability (Drummond, 2004). For these reasons, practitioners need to know how to design and utilize more informal assessment procedures that may be less structured but nevertheless provide relevant data about other issues related to growth and development. Chittooran and Miller (1998) proposed that there are a number of advantages to informal assessment, including their belief that it provides "a richer, more complete understanding" (p. 13) of a child's behavior and is also more appropriate with children from culturally diverse groups. Drummond (2004) also pointed out that informal assessment procedures provide a more global perspective of the problem, and Vance (1998) cited flexibility as an advantage of this type of assessment.

Myrick (1997) outlined the value of informal assessments, particularly in the following areas: physical development, including posture, grooming, and energy level; social development, including fluidity of speech, friendships, and attitudes; cognitive development, including values, consequences, sense of reality, and logic; cultural development, including religious and environmental influences and sense of stigmatization; history, including relevant events; and future perspective, including goals, sense of responsibility, and sense of control. These more informal assessment procedures may yield results that can be used for effective intervention, or they may need to be paired with a commercially developed instrument for a more comprehensive picture of the problem. In addition, observing children in their natural environment allows practitioners to see how a child behaves in everyday functioning (Drummond, 2004). Also, it is often necessary to interview parents and teachers to obtain a comprehensive view of the child. Yule (1993) cautioned that assessment results should not be viewed in isolation; instead, findings should be pieced together with other information to look at patterns of adjustment and how these relate to developmental norms as well as environmental factors.

Practitioner-designed procedures may assume a variety of formats, which allows a better fit with the client's learning style, verbal ability, emotional maturity, gender, or cultural background. When developing or selecting assessments for ethnically diverse clients, it is vital that the counselor adopt a culturally reflective position. To be exact, the counselor should develop every assessment tool on the basis of the following questions: (a) Will this be offensive in any way to the client? (b) Can the client relate to the context of the assessment instrument? (c) Is it gender sensitive? (d) Does it take into account the history of the ethnic group? (e) Is it an appropriate assessment tool if English is not the first language of the client? and (f) Does it reflect European values or is it generic enough to fit the value system of non-European American clients? Examples of assessment tools that can be developed include:

1. Checklists or rating scales of developmental characteristics
2. Unfinished sentences
3. Writing activities
4. Decision-making dilemmas
5. Games
6. Art activities
7. Storytelling and bibliotherapy techniques
8. Self-monitoring techniques
9. Role-play activities
10. Play therapy strategies
11. Self-rating scales
12. Music

Checklists or Rating Scales of Developmental Characteristics

Checklists can help practitioners assess adjustment in relation to a set of norms for children of similar ages (Garbarino & Stott, 1992). Depending on the client's age, a checklist or rating scale might be given to parents or teachers, to the client, or to the client and the adult(s). Checklists can be constructed simply by listing characteristics that relate to the initial identified concern. For instance, if parents are questioning whether their 10-year-old is developing appropriate social skills, the practitioner could refer to stages of interpersonal development (Selman, 1980, 1981; Selman & Schultz, 1998), describe social skills characteristic of children at this age, and give the parents a checklist. The checklist may include questions such as:

• Does your child seem to be aware of others' feelings? (Example: My teacher was really mad.)

- Is your child able to see social situations from more than just his or her point of view? (Example: I didn't get invited to the party, but maybe his parents would only let him invite a few kids.)
- Does your child understand that if he or she helps a friend, a friend might in turn help him or her? (Example: If I lend you a book, maybe you'll let me borrow your new video game.)
- Is your child able to recognize and avoid statements that might be potentially offensive to others? (Example: She wears ugly clothes.)
- Is your child able to recognize personality characteristics in others? (Example: He is shy; she is bossy.)

To determine the level of social development, the practitioner would compare the parents' responses with Selman's Level 2 (second-person reciprocal perspective taking, ages 8–10) and Level 3 (third-person perspective taking, ages 10–12) characteristics that describe where 10-year-olds should be with respect to social development (see discussion of these levels in chapter 1). This checklist can be modified to include a rating scale. Rather than responses with a yes or no, a 1–5 scale could represent low to high dimensions of a particular characteristic. Vance (1998) suggested that rating scales can also include category ratings (selecting a word that best describes a person or event) or forced-choice items (e.g., indicate *always* or *never*).

When using a checklist or rating scale with ethnically diverse clients, counselors must be aware of the societal expectations of these clients to effectively assess them. As an illustration, inner-city children and adolescents develop a series of coping skills to deal with aggression and intimidation. Therefore, they may be prone to use more physical force when intimidated than Euro American middle-class children. By middle-class standards, these young inner-city clients may be considered developmentally immature.

Unfinished Sentences

Unfinished sentences elicit responses that help identify concerns and stages of development. If you are attempting to assess an 8-year-old's level of self-worth, sentences based on five areas, in which children evaluate their self-worth (Harter, 2001), could provide useful information:

1. When I don't do well on a test, I feel _____.
2. If my friend runs faster or plays sports better than I do, it means that_____.
3. If I misbehave in class, I feel _____.
4. If I don't get invited to a party, I think_____.
5. When I look in a mirror, I_____.

By designing questions that address the five areas of self-worth (scholastic competence, athletic competence, behavioral conduct, social acceptance, and physical appearance), the practitioner can develop a sense of how the child sees him- or herself. By comparing the responses with what developmental theorists have determined is characteristic of children at this particular age, you have a picture of what is normal as well as areas that need strengthening.

Depending on the child's age, the child may complete the sentences on paper independently or the questions could be read to the child and the responses recorded. Unfinished sentences can also be constructed to elicit more general assessment information, such as feelings about family life, school performance, or relationships with peers. While it may be possible to relate responses to developmental levels, the data will also be useful in assessing specific concerns. For example, consider using unfinished sentences such as the following for assessing a 12-year-old's concern about her family relationships:

1. In my family, I feel I get the most support from my _____.
2. If I could change something about my family life, I would change _____.
3. The person in my family who is most critical of me is _____.
4. Something I appreciate about my family is_____.
5. Something I don't appreciate about my family is_____.

Unfinished sentences are culturally sensitive tools because they address multiple areas of life. However, if assessing for self-worth in highly collective-oriented cultures, and depending on the level of acculturation of the client (e.g., African, Native Indian), the concept of self-worth is based on the well-being of the group and not the individual.

Writing Activities

Through various writing activities, it is possible to identify patterns that can be compared with developmental stages. Diaries, logs, journals, and self-composed poems and stories are excellent sources of information that assist in the assessment and intervention processes. Like storytelling, writing activities allow ethnically diverse clients who have a nonlinear way of thinking to express themselves in a more circular and systemic fashion. Depending on the type of writing activity, this form of assessment may be more appropriate for academically gifted students and adolescents. Examples of writing assignments that can be used to assess a variety of factors include the following:

1. Journal entries illustrating feelings and triggering events that occurred throughout the week.
2. A written analysis of songs that they think describe how they see themselves.
3. Self-composed short stories or poems that identify moral dilemmas or decision-making issues.

4. Self-composed songs that describe personal or social relationship concerns.
5. Letters to significant others or people with whom they have issues, expressing feelings and concerns.

For example, a 13-year-old shared her journal entries with her counselor. On the basis of what she had written, it was apparent that she was still at a very concrete level of cognitive development because she was not able to develop hypotheses or make conclusions about effective ways to solve problems. She was also very immature in her social and emotional development, evidenced by the fact that she only perceived things from her point of view and described interactions with others using very basic feelings. At this age, she should have been able to identify more complex feelings (McDevitt & Ormrod, 2002) and see things from another perspective (Selman & Schultz, 1998).

Another effective writing assessment is to provide children with a short story stem related to family life. These stems can provide valuable information relative to family interaction and conflict, parental acceptance, and behavioral control (Shamir, DuRocher Schudlich, & Cummings, 2001). An example of a short story stem is: "If I were to describe the best and the worst part about living in my family, I would say that . . ." (and the client would finish the rest of the story, which may range from a short paragraph to a much longer story).

Decision-Making Dilemmas

How children and adolescents make decisions is influenced by their stages of moral development. By designing dilemmas that require the young client to make a decision, it is possible to assess the decision-making process, understand why certain decisions are made based on stages of moral reasoning (Kohlberg, 1981), and design intervention strategies to facilitate more effective decision-making skills. In developing effective dilemmas, consider characteristic issues for the targeted client. Colangelo and Dettmann (1985) identified decisions about intervening or reporting; problems with alcohol, drugs, and tobacco; relationship issues; and conflicts about cheating, stealing, and lying as key moral dilemma topics for young adolescents. On the basis of this information, the following describes a decision-making dilemma for an adolescent client.

> You and two friends are in a clothing store looking at sweatshirts. Before going to the mall, one of your friends indicated that she didn't have any money and therefore couldn't buy anything. At school the next day, you notice this friend is wearing one of the sweatshirts that she looked at yesterday in the store. You're sure her parents didn't buy it for her, because she stayed at your house until after the stores closed because her folks were out of town. You also know that the other friend who was with you didn't buy it because she spent all her money in the first store. You remember now that she had on her older brother's

jacket, so it is possible that she had the sweatshirt on under the jacket and took it off when she got back to your house.

After reading the dilemma, engage the client in a series of questions: Assuming that this friend stole the sweatshirt, what do you think about what she did? Should you do anything about it? If so, what are your options?

On the basis of the responses, it is possible to determine the approximate stage of moral development. For instance, most adolescents are in what Kohlberg characterized as the conventional stage of moral development (Santrock, 2000). As such, they believe that stealing is wrong because there are laws against it, but they also use loyalty to others as a basis of moral judgment. Therefore, they may not consider turning in their friend to authorities or telling the parents, because this is not in keeping with what a good friend would do. Once this developmental level has been assessed, interventions can be identified to help clarify the issue and look at alternative ways to deal with the problem. As a word of caution, for many ethnically diverse clients, moral reasoning is strictly based on a divine source (e.g., Koran, Torah); therefore, there is no room for alternative ways of solving a dilemma. This could be interpreted erroneously by the counselor as rigidity and unwillingness to explore other points of view.

Games

For younger children, in particular, various types of simple games can be used in the problem assessment process. Games are also used effectively with resistant children and for those who are not very verbal. Using games as a form of assessment can help reduce anxiety, and the actual material substance of a game (cards, playing board) can help organize the physical relationship with the practitioner (Bromfield, 1999).

Suppose that you want to assess the emotional maturity of a 6-year-old. According to developmental theory (Berk, 1999), 4- to 6-year-olds can identify basic feelings accurately and can communicate about simple emotions but do not realize that feelings can be disguised or that different feelings can be experienced simultaneously. On the basis of this information, a board game could be constructed on a large sheet of tagboard by drawing small circles in a zig-zag manner across the board. Each small circle would be numbered 1–3. These numbers would correspond to short vignettes that would be written on index cards and represent increasingly difficult degrees of emotional development. An example for number 1 could include: "You are at the grocery store and your dad won't let you have a pack of gum when you reach the checkout line. How do you feel?" Number 1 vignettes should be based on identification of simple emotions such as happy, sad, mad, scared. An example for number 2 could include: "You are playing a game with a friend. You see your friend start to frown. Your friend feels_____." Number 2 vignettes should be based on feelings that could be disguised or on emotional expressions that do not always represent true feelings. An example for number 3 could include: "You are starting first grade tomorrow. You feel _____ and _____." Number 3 vignettes should be based on experiencing two feelings simultaneously. Engage the child in the game by giving him or her a marker to move along the board. When the child lands on a circle, read a vignette that corresponds to the number on the circle and invite the child to respond. From the child's responses, the practitioner will gain a sense of where the child is in regard to his or her emotional development. The game can continue until the child reaches the end of the circles.

Art Activities

Art activities often appeal to children and adolescents of all cultures and are an excellent source of information regarding their perceptions and feelings about situations and aspects of their development. According to Kwiatkowska (2001), art facilitates expression and helps clients perceive themselves more clearly. Limited only by one's creativity, the practitioner can involve young clients in drawing cartoons, self-portraits, pictures about events or family, self-concept badges, or lifeline murals. They can also make collages, or do soap and clay sculptures or finger paint activities. Another valuable strategy is to ask clients to draw the ideal self, which not only can reveal rich data about self-perceptions but also can enhance clients' self-understanding (Moran, 2001). Because art activities are easily administered, brief, and relatively nonthreatening, Oster and Gould (1987) advocated using art to learn more about the child to develop therapeutic goals.

Photography also can be used effectively to determine client self-perceptions. As Harter (2001) noted, self-understanding progresses from the concrete to the abstract. Therefore, if asking an adolescent to look at a photograph of him- or herself, the practitioner might expect that the youth would be able to describe him- or herself based not only on physical appearance but also on values, beliefs, and dispositions. Comparing the responses to theories of self-development provides information that can be used to structure interventions to address deficits.

Art is an effective form of assessment with diverse populations because art activities transcend cultural boundaries (Gladding, 1995). Although art activities, like other informal procedures, are invaluable as part of an assessment procedure, they should be used in conjunction with other assessment data (Schmidt, 1996), including instruments, observations, and developmental and cultural background information.

Bibliotherapy and Storytelling

Bibliotherapy is the use of literature as a therapeutic counseling process. Literature serves a variety of purposes in counseling and can be used effectively in the assessment process by providing young clients, particularly those who like to read, with fiction or nonfiction that presents issues similar to those that they might be dealing with at their stage of development.

Bibliotherapy is especially helpful with clients who are reluctant to express their thoughts and feelings. Having a structure such as the reading material to rely on facilitates discussion of issues they may be experiencing, and consequently aids in assessment. Assigning *The Diary of Anne Frank* (Frank, 1963) to an adolescent girl is an effective way to assess feelings and concerns about puberty, for example. Reading and discussing *There's A Monster Under My Bed* (Howe, 1990) to a kindergartner provides information about this child's fear and fantasies. On the basis of developmental theory, the practitioner knows that fear of the dark and fantasy are typical at this stage of development (Bee, 2000; Cobb, 2001) and can compare the child's responses with this information to determine the degree of concern and level of intervention.

Children, especially those between the ages of 9 and 14 (Kottman & Stiles, 1990), benefit from R. A. Gardner's (1979) mutual storytelling technique. With this approach, the counselor and the child tell a story. The counselor begins it with phrases that parallel the child's situation and then has the child tell the story. Used as an assessment device, this procedure is an effective way to determine what the child is thinking or feeling about a situation. Comparing data with developmental patterns assists the practitioner in designing appropriate interventions if needed. This is a particularly effective assessment tool with ethnically diverse clients because many cultures such as the Native Indian, Latino, and Pacific Islander, among others, rely on oral history. Therefore, depending on the level of acculturation of the client, storytelling is part of their daily lives.

Self-Monitoring Techniques

Self-monitoring techniques, which require clients to keep a record of specific behaviors or feelings (Drummond, 2000), are helpful in determining the degree to which a child or adolescent is experiencing a particular feeling, behavior, or concern. However, self-monitoring techniques may not be very effective with some ethnically diverse clients because international students and first-generation immigrants from certain ethnic groups (e.g., African, Asian) may not even have a definition or an understanding of self. Their interactions with and reactions to their social environment are based on the collective experience of their family of origin or extended ethnic group (e.g., tribe). Therefore, even though their behavior may be problematic, their level of awareness or individual perceptions may be lacking.

Self-monitoring techniques can assume a variety of formats and are easy to use.

1. *Feeling charts:* Clients assign a number from 1 to 5 (low to high) to identify the intensity of a particular feeling such as anger, anxiety, or depression at different points throughout the day over a period of a week or more. This gives good baseline data for determining the prevalence of the identified emotion.

2. *Worry boxes:* Clients write worries on small sheets of paper and put them in the worry box. The counselor and clients discuss them to determine the extent of the worries, how they compare with developmental concerns, and where to intervene.
3. *Food, exercise charts:* Clients keep a record of food and exercise to assess eating habits/eating disorders.
4. *Temper/behavior graphs:* Clients monitor their temper tantrums, aggressive or nonassertive behavior, and bullying or cooperative behavior by doing daily charting.
5. *Jellies in a jar:* Clients put a green jelly bean in a jar whenever they take a risk to overcome a fear or phobia and a red one when they are not able to overcome the fear. The ratio of red to green jellies helps both client and counselor determine the extent of the fears and phobias over a given time period.

Role-Play Activities

Given the limited verbal ability of some children, role playing can be used as an assessment device for various kinds of problems. The role-play technique engages the client and counselor in acting out a situation or dilemma. On the basis of the child's responses, the counselor can ascertain the problematic areas more clearly. When selecting a topic or a situation, the counselor must be aware of the level of acculturation of ethnically diverse clients in order for the role-play activity to acquire significance. To structure the role play, select the topic and invite the child to participate: "Let's act out this problem with your friend so that I have a better idea about what's bothering you. I'll be your friend, and you be yourself. Why don't you start and pretend that we're on the playground since that's where you said the problems happen. What happens?" The practitioner can refer to Selman's (1980) and Selman and Schultz's (1998) stages of interpersonal development (see chapter 1), which illustrate the developmental stages, and then compare the client's responses to determine developmental level and target areas for intervention. For example, suppose this 10-year-old client role played a situation in which her friend did not invite her to play kick ball and just sat on a bench throughout recess. The client was mad because she assumed her friend did not like her since she did not want to play with her. According to Selman, children at this age should be developing the ability to see things from another's perspective. Therefore, the client's self-centered response would indicate to the counselor that this client needed intervention that would target this lack of skill.

Play Therapy

Play therapy has been recognized as an exceptionally valuable means of learning about children, particularly those between the ages of 3 and 12 (Kottman, 2004; Landreth, 2002). Because play is a vital way for children to express themselves, practitioners need to "appreciate the value of play in the assessment of children" (Wagner, 2003, p. 89). Used as part of the assessment process, play becomes the medium to communicate concerns and express emotional issues. Dolls, puppets, or family figurines provide insight about family dynamics and physical or sexual abuse. A "magic wand" illustrates fantasies, worries, or wishes. Scary toys such as "fierce" animal puppets (wolf, bear, alligator) or rubber snakes, rats, insects, and sharks help children identify fears, whereas aggressive toys such as bop bags, toy weapons, toy soldiers, and foam bats facilitate assessment of aggression (Kottman, 2004). Dress-up clothes can yield information about gender role awareness, family interaction and roles, and social play and development issues. The practitioner must be able to translate what the children are saying through play into meaningful data that can be used in conjunction with developmental norms and cultural considerations to help them understand the level of concern and select appropriate interventions.

Self-Rating Scales

Self-rating scales can be adapted for children of all ages by substituting pictures or symbols for words. Self-rating scales help assess children's perceptions of themselves relative to various dimensions. For example, to learn more about how a preadolescent sees herself, the counselor could develop a scale such as the following in which the items reflect issues about puberty and appearance:

1. I like the way my body is changing
    A lot _____ A little _____ Not at all _____
2. In comparison to others my age, I like the way I look
    A lot _____ A little _____ Not at all _____
3. I feel more grown up as a result of my changing body
    A lot _____ A little _____ Not at all _____
4. I think/worry about how my body isn't/is changing
    A lot _____ A little _____ Not at all _____
5. Now that I am older, I think I look better
    A lot _____ A little _____ Not at all _____

As mentioned previously, the counselor must exercise caution when dealing with the concept of self with ethnically diverse clients, especially first-generation immigrants and international students. In some cultures, the self as a concept is not consistent with the well-being of the group.

Music Activities

Music can be used to increase awareness and intensify understanding as well as reduce anxiety (Jensen, 2001). For these reasons, music is an effective form of assessment as well as intervention. Furthermore, music appeals to, and is an important part of, most cultures, so utilizing music as a form of assessment can work well with diverse groups because it allows them to freely express themselves and validates their sense of aesthetics and beauty. Music is also a particularly good form of assessment to use with nonverbal youngsters.

There are various ways to incorporate music into the assessment procedure. Clients can compose their own songs about issues that are troubling to them. They can also select pieces of music that reflect a problem or concern they are dealing with. Developmental themes can be identified, which in turn can lead to further data gathering and intervention. For example, an adolescent male was not able to verbalize much about the issues he was struggling with, but he was willing to share a tape of his band performing at a coffee-house concert that included songs he had written for the group. After listening to these songs, the counselor was able to identify several themes that reflect developmental tasks of adolescence: struggling for independence, anxiety about the future, and relationships with the opposite sex. Sharing these themes with the client, and introducing writing activities because he was not very verbal, elicited more data about the problems so that interventions could then be developed.

Developmental Assessment Instruments

It is critical for professionals to know what type of information can be gained from various assessment techniques and instruments. As Yule (1993) noted, "Assessment is not and should not be merely the application of available tools or techniques. It should always be undertaken for a stated purpose" (p. 16). A clear conceptualization of the purpose of the assessment helps determine whether a test is the best method for gathering the information. In many instances, the what and how of assessment is a judgment call of the practitioner. For instance, if you were assessing acting-out behavior, you probably would get a more accurate perspective from the teacher or parent. On the other hand, if you wanted to know how depressed a child was, asking the parent alone would probably be insufficient. A comprehensive assessment generally will include both formal and informal assessment techniques, with information obtained from multiple sources. Drummond (2000) stressed that although using multiple measures might be more time consuming, getting information from a number of different sources, individuals, and occasions is very beneficial.

Developmental tests or screening instruments often are given to infants, toddlers, and preschoolers to assess developmental status. The Bayley Scales of Infant Development—Second Edition (Bayley, 1993) give indication of early signs of behavioral problems. The McCarthy Scales of Children's Abilities (McCarthy, 1972) provide a general cognitive index, and the Miller Assessment for Preschoolers (Miller, 1982) measures sensorimotor and cognitive abilities as well as fine and gross motor skills. Garbarino and Stott (1992) indicated that, although tests of this nature are useful for assessing cognitive delay, they do not predict later cognitive abilities, and therefore should be considered only descriptive of current developmental status. Furthermore, developmental tests often fail to assess social and emotional functioning comprehensively, so testing may not be the best method for learning about the child's ability to interact and form relationships. Increasingly, direct observation in structured and unstructured settings is recommended (Drummond, 2000; Yule, 1993).

In the emotional area as well, practitioners rely heavily on structured and unstructured observations and interviews with significant adults in the child's life rather than on a formal test. Greenspan (1981), Greenspan and Lieberman (1980), and Greenspan and Porges (1984) developed a procedure for assessing emotional functioning in young children. By integrating developmental theory and information from clinical case studies, Greenspan formulated the clinical developmental structuralist approach to assessment and diagnosis. Through this approach, it is possible to determine whether the child has completed tasks at each developmental level and whether the emotional patterns are adaptive or maladaptive.

Developmental assessment instruments usually are used to assess both biologically based and socially developed skills and provide an evaluation of a child's cognitive, socioemotional, language, and motor abilities (Garbarino & Stott, 1992). Some authors, such as Garbarino and Stott, distinguished between developmental screening tests and developmental assessment tests. They noted the purpose of developmental screening is prevention through early intervention, whereas developmental assessment tests provide a more comprehensive evaluation that results in a diagnosis from which remedial recommendations can be made. In either case, this type of assessment can be used to help identify how normally children are developing or in what ways they are not. With this information, prevention, intervention, or appropriate placement can be determined.

Drummond (2000, 2004) identified several standardized tests to help professionals assess language development, cognitive stages, psychosocial development, and moral development. These are discussed below.

Language Development

The following tests help practitioners assess qualitative as well as quantitative differences: The Reynell Developmental Language Scale assesses slow development in expressive and receptive language in children ages 1–7; the Houston Test for Language Development measures verbal and nonverbal communication from birth to age 6; and the Test of Language Development measures such methods as picture identification, grammatical completion, and word discrimination to assess receptive and expressive vocabulary and expressive grammatical structure.

Cognitive Stages

Assessments in this area are based on Piaget's theory of cognitive development. Drummond (2000, 2004) identified two tests that focus on how children think and reason. Although they do not give norms and standard scores, they are useful in instructional planning and also provide a reference point for looking at emotional and social development. The Concept Assessment Kit contains three forms that measure cognitive development of preschoolers and primary grade children. Conservation, number substance, weight, and conservation using length and area are some of the specific areas included in this assessment. The Wach Analysis of Cognitive Structures is a culture-free, nonverbal test that assesses development of learning ability in young children. It is used with children who have mental, language, or hearing deficits.

Psychosocial Development

Drummond (2000, 2004) identified the Measures of Psychosocial Development (MPD) as one of the major instruments to assess this area of development. The MPD, a 112-item self-report inventory, consists of 27 different scales based on personality theory: 9 positive scales (trust, autonomy, initiative, industry, identity, intimacy, generativity, ego integrity, and total positive), 9 negative scales (mistrust, shame and doubt, guilt, inferiority, identity confusion, isolation, stagnation, despair, and total negative), and 9 resolution scales (one for each stage) and a total resolution scale. This test is for adolescents and adults who respond on a 5-point scale ranging from *not at all like you* to *very much like you*.

Moral Development

Drummond (2000, 2004) described the following instruments that measure moral reasoning. The Defining Issues Test is a paper-and-pencil instrument consisting of dilemmas from which the client selects preferred responses. The Ethical Reasoning Inventory is a paper-and-pencil inventory of six dilemmas that includes questions from Kohlberg's Moral Judgment Inventory. The questions are followed by two responses and sets of reason that correspond to stages of Kohlberg's theory. The Moral Judgment Interview uses a structured interview technique. Raters match the client's responses on a minimum of 21 questions regarding three moral dilemmas against Kohlberg's stage criteria.

Several other examples of developmental assessment instruments appropriate for use with children and adolescents include the following.

Physiological System Survey

Developed by Fadely and Hosler (1980), the Physiological System Survey is an extensive checklist that identifies developmental characteristics for children from ages 2 to 5 in several different dimensions: physical, social, personality, cognitive, language, sensorimotor, auditory perceptual, visual perceptual, and psychosocial development. Questions such as the following are used to identify developmental progression:

Social Development (3 years)
_____ Begins to wait for turn

_____ Distinguishes between boys and girls
_____ Loves to be with other children
_____ Does not share willingly
Social Development (4–5 years)
_____ Swearing and silly words
_____ Imagination varied and vivid
_____ Endless questions of how and why
_____ Cooperative play with rapid change in friends
Language, Personality, and Cognitive Development (3 years)
_____ Begins to show self-control
_____ Temper tantrums at a peak
_____ Enjoys praise
_____ Imaginary worries; fears dark, dogs, death
Language, Personality, and Cognitive Development (4–5 years)
_____ Name calling added to tantrums
_____ Acts out if he or she does not get his or her way
_____ Boastful, dogmatic, bossy
_____ Difficulty in separation of fantasies and reality

The complete checklist can be found in *Developmental Psychometrics: A Resourcebook for Mental Health Workers and Educators* (from J. Fadely & V. Hosler, 1980, pp. 15–36. Copyright 1980 by Charles C Thomas, Springfield, Illinois. Reprinted with permission).

Washington University Sentence Completion Test

Developed by Loevinger, Wessler, and Redmore (1978) to assess stages of ego development, the Washington University Sentence Completion Test is a paper-and-pencil test consisting of 36 unfinished sentences that can be completed in 30–45 minutes. The responses to the items are matched with those listed in *Measuring Ego Development II* by Loevinger et al. (1978). Other unfinished sentence tests for youngsters are the Rotter Incomplete Sentence Blank (Rotter & Rafferty, 1950), which contains 40 items that assess attitudes toward family, peers, school, work, anxiety, guilt, and physical disability, and the Hart Sentence Completion Test for Children (Hart, 1972).

Bender Visual-Motor Gestalt Test

Generally administered to children between ages 5 and 11, the Bender Visual-Motor Gestalt Test is used to measure visual-motor integration. The test consists of abstract designs that are presented one at a time on cards. The child is asked to reproduce these designs. Koppitz (1982, as cited in Drummond, 2000) designed a development scale to accompany this test with the following 12 emotional indicators:

1. Confused order—represents confusion, poor organization
2. Wavy line—represents emotional instability, poor motor coordination
3. Dashes instead of circles—represents impulsivity, lack of interest

4. Increase in size—represents low frustration tolerance, explosiveness
5. Large size—represents impulsivity, acting-out behavior
6. Small size—represents anxiety, withdrawal, constriction, timidity
7. Fine line—represents timidity, shyness, withdrawal
8. Careless overwork, reinforced lines—represents impulsivity, aggressiveness, acting-out behavior
9. Second attempt at drawing figures—represents impulsivity, aggressiveness, acting-out behavior
10. Expansiveness, two or more pages—represents acting-out behavior
11. Box around one or more figures—represents attempt to control impulsivity, weak inner control, need for outer limits and structure
12. Spontaneous elaboration or additions to designs—represents unusual preoccupation with own thoughts, fears, anxieties, serious emotional problems

Draw-a-Person Test

This Draw-a-Person Test was originally developed to assess intelligence but was later expanded to evaluate personality variables, according to Drummond (2000). Originally known as the Draw-a-Man Test, it consists of drawing three figures—a man, a woman, and a self-portrait. The child is asked to draw the figures as completely as possible, and there are no time constraints. The scoring manual describes how credits are given to such factors as inclusion of body parts, detail, and accuracy of proportions of the figures. For example, Koppitz (1982) noted that poor achievement might be reflected in omission of body, arms, or mouth, or that depression might be revealed by tiny figures with short arms and no eyes.

Family Drawings

Drummond (2000) indicated that both the House-Tree-Person Test (HTP) and the Kinetic Family Drawing Test (KFD) can give insight about how children perceive their place within the family. The KFD instructs the child to draw a picture of the family doing something together, and according to Drummond, the assessor looks for who is present or omitted from the drawing, as well as position, distance, and interaction of the family members. The HTP consists of the child drawing a house, a tree, and a person. The house may symbolize how the child sees the home situation and family relationships; trees represent more subconscious personal feelings based on the size, shape, and quality of the trunk, branches, and leaves; and the drawing of the person is a representation of how the child perceives his or her environment.

Personal Orientation Inventory

The Personal Orientation Inventory was developed by Shostron (1974) and can be used for self-awareness and evaluating mental health for high school students. It is based on Maslow's (1998) hierarchy of needs. There are 150 questions that yield 12 scores: time competence, support ratio, inner directedness, self-actualizing value, existentiality, feeling reactivity, spontaneity, self-regard, self-acceptance, synergy, acceptance of aggression, and capacity for intimate contact.

Social Recognition Skills Checklist

The Social Recognition Skills Checklist, developed by Fadely and Hosler (1980), consists of 25 specific areas of social abilities that provide an extensive amount of information. Questions such as the following, directed to the child's parents, are rated on a 1–10 scale:

1. *Rights of others:* awareness and acceptance of the rights of other people as distinct from the child's: (a) Does your child respect the ownership of toys and objects by others? Does your child ask permission to play with them rather than merely taking them? (b) Does your child accept and abide by the rules at school and home designed for group management?
2. *Empathy:* the awareness of the feelings of others and a willingness to attempt to understand their needs: (a) Does your child display appropriate concern and feelings of understanding toward situations and events that affect others? (b) Does your child feel the happiness and pain of others with true empathy followed by comforting behaviors?

Other dimensions addressed include internalization of social values, expressiveness, assertiveness, listening skills, leadership, cooperation, and altruism. The complete checklist can be found in *Developmental Psychometrics: A Resource Book for Mental Health Workers and Educators* (Fadely & Hosler, 1980).

16 Personality Factors for Adolescents

The 16 Personality Factors test, developed by Cattell, Eber, and Tatsuoka (1970), is an objective assessment of personality characteristics. There is also a children's version called the Children's Personality Questionnaire, which includes two forms: the Early School Personality Questionnaire, for young children ages 6–8, and the High School Personality Questionnaire. Sample factors in these tests include reserved or outgoing personality characteristics, identification of cognitive style, stability and emotional maturity factors, inactive versus overactive behavior, and social dependence versus self-sufficient behavior.

The Denver Developmental Screening Test II

The screening tools from the Denver Developmental Screening Test II (Denver–II), developed by Frankenburg, Dodds, Archer, Shapiro, and Bresnick (1992), are designed to identify developmental delays. There are 105 test items that assess personal/social (interpersonal and self-help behaviors), fine motor (eye-hand coordination), language (receptive and expressive), and gross motor (sitting, walking, jumping) abilities. The Denver–II is used with children from birth to 6 years of age, and the newer profile can be used with beginning adolescence to assess developmental change.

Interviewing Techniques

Interviewing is an important way to learn about children, and even young children can share helpful perspectives of their own experiences and perceptions. According to Whiston (2000), practitioners begin the interview process by talking with the child and using a structured, semistructured, or unstructured approach. Because children have various levels of cognitive understanding and verbal ability, this must be taken into consideration to make the process worthwhile. Likewise, it is important to take into account cultural differences such as eye contact or proximity preferences that may affect the interview process (Semrud-Clikeman, 1995). In conducting interviews with children, counselors need to take extra care that the child fully understands what is being asked and to rely on communication methods familiar to the child. Using props such as dolls, toy telephones, human figures, or other manipulatives also can facilitate discussion during an interview, which should be conducted in an environment that is comfortable but not overstimulating (Thompson & Rudolph, 2000).

Adults need to avoid asking questions that go beyond children's abilities to respond. Garbarino and Stott (1992) cautioned that young school-age children are sensitive to what they perceive as adult expectations and may respond to these regardless of whether they have real information. Thompson and Rudolph (2000) pointed out that direct questions are appropriate for gaining factual information but that open-ended questions generate more data, as well as fewer contradictions (Lamb & Fauchier, 2001). Children younger than age 10 are less likely to know what they do or do not know.

Hughes and Baker (1990) described questioning with children as "a subtle art" (p. 35). Questions asked during an interview must be appropriate to the child's developmental level, and Barker (1990) suggested relying on simple questions and avoiding multiple questions in a single statement, why questions, and negatively phrased terms. The following suggestions (Boat & Everson, 1989) may be helpful:

1. Rephrase, rather than repeat, questions the child does not understand.
2. Avoid asking questions that involve time sequence.
3. Use names instead of pronouns.
4. Try to use terms the child would use.
5. Acknowledge comments, but do not respond to every answer with another question.
6. Avoid long sentences.
7. Refer to familiar routines to stimulate recall.

8. Ask the child to repeat what you have said, rather than ask, "Do you understand?"
9. Use caution in interpreting responses to specific questions; children can be very literal.

Ivey (2000) created a model for assessing client developmental level during the interview process and matching counseling interventions with client needs. Ivey's model is an extension of Piagetian theory, but he emphasized that clients represent a mixture of several developmental levels, although one usually predominates in the interview session. Ivey described the following as characteristic of lower developmental levels: incongruous verbal and nonverbal behaviors; negative "I" statements; negative, confused, and inappropriate emotions; passive and negative descriptors; external locus of control; and dependence or excessive independence. Conversely, higher developmental levels are characterized by congruent verbal and nonverbal behavior; positive "I" statements; positive emotions that are contextually appropriate; ability to deal with mixed feelings; active, positive descriptors; internal locus of control; and interdependence.

To assess cognitive functioning, Ivey (2000) suggested the following questions, adapted from Weinstein and Alschuler (1985):

1. *Preoperational stage:* Where did it happen? When? What were you doing? What did you do? How did you look?
2. *Middle concrete operations stage:* What were you feeling? What were you saying to yourself during this time? What did you think would happen?
3. *Early formal operations stage:* How did your response remind you of other situations? Is this a pattern? Do you feel the same way in other situations?
4. *Late formal operations stage:* When you feel that way, can you do anything about it? What could you do or say to yourself that would change what you are feeling or thinking? (p. 23)

It is apparent that higher levels of thinking are characterized by more emphasis on feelings and abstract thinking. Ivey (2000) suggested that these questions can assess developmental level but also pointed out that clients are a mixture of several levels, depending on the topic. Careful attention to the clients' nonverbal behavior will assist the interviewer in determining the client's developmental level, as will attention to the characteristics of lower and higher developmental levels. Shifting the interview style to meet developmental needs as described enhances the effectiveness of the assessment process, providing the practitioner with information that can be used to structure appropriate interventions that match developmental level.

A Comprehensive Assessment Model

Increased emphasis is placed on utilizing a variety of assessment approaches with children and adolescents to form a comprehensive picture of developmental progress and to target areas for intervention or prevention (Garbarino & Stott, 1992; Vernon, 2002), including obtaining information directly from the child (Keat, 1990). Likewise, there is a trend toward mutual participation in the assessment and problem-solving process: involvement of the child, practitioner, and significant other adults.

One model of counseling that includes a multiple assessment focus, as well as mutual participation, is the BASIC ID, a multimodal approach developed by Lazarus (1976) and applied to children by Keat (1979, 1990). The BASIC ID is an acronym for Behavior, Affect, Sensation, Imagery, Cognition, Interpersonal relationships, and Drugs or physiological considerations. The HELPING model, which Keat adapted for children from the BASIC ID, includes the following dimensions: Health, Emotions–feelings, Learning–school, People–personal relationships, Imagination–interests, Need to know–think, and Guidance of actions, behaviors, and consequences. As assessment models, both emphasize a holistic approach that helps the practitioner organize what is known about the young client from a variety of sources, including the parents, teachers, and child. Starr and Raykovitz (1990) developed the Multimodal Child Interview Schedule (MCIS) based on the HELPING model. The MCIS consists of several questions for each mode. The practitioner selects questions that are relevant to the child's presenting problem and then summarizes the information from the child, parents, and significant others in order to design appropriate multimodal interventions to address areas that need strengthening.

The comprehensive nature of these models is particularly important, because it is easy to overlook a dimension of a problem during assessment. It is often this missing piece that sheds light on the real issue, as in the case of Darrien.

Darrien, a third grader, was brought to the attention of the counselor by his teacher, who was concerned about his aggressive behaviors, which were most evident in his destruction of property. After the counselor interviewed Darrien and also discussed the problem with the teacher and parents, they agreed to try some behavior modification techniques to address the situation, because the problem did not seem to be emanating from excessive anger, poor peer or parental relationships, or academic frustration. However, after a period of time, it was apparent that the situation was not getting better. Particularly after lunch, Darrien became rather hyperactive, carving on the desk with his pencil, tearing pages out of books, or kicking things out of his way. One day, after a discussion with the school nurse, the counselor asked Darrien what he usually ate for lunch. "Jelly sandwiches and candy bars" was his reply. Some stories do have happy endings. In this case, once his parents started packing a more nutritious lunch, the behavior subsided. Had the counselor systematically assessed all areas of development, including health issues, this dimension would not have been ignored inadvertently.

The models presented by Lazarus (1976) and Keat (1979, 1990) both addressed dimensions critical to child development and provided an effective means of targeting developmental concerns. A variety of both formal and informal assessment approaches can be used in conjunction with these models. The helping professional can ask directed, developmentally and culturally appropriate interview questions; make use of art or play mediums that may appeal to children who are kinesthetic learners; or design checklists or use commercially produced tests to determine specific areas of concern. Because of the flexibility, these models can be effectively adapted for use with clients of all ages and cultures. The following case study illustrates this approach.

HELPING Assessment With Jesse

Jesse, a fourth grader, presented several concerns to the counselor. First of all, she worried about fatal car accidents, damaging storms and tornados, and fires. In addition, she and her 12-year-old brother fought constantly. Jesse's parents questioned her frequent minor illnesses and school absences as a result.

In applying the HELPING model, first determine what you already know or infer about each dimension. In Jesse's case:

- *Health:* Frequent minor illnesses and school absences.
- *Emotions:* Anxiety about events related to natural disaster.
- *Learning/school:* Possibly behind in school because of absences.
- *Personal relationships:* Conflict with brother.
- *Imagination, interests:* Vivid imagination about fearful events in which she sees herself as powerless.
- *Need to know–think:* How to overcome helplessness; how to deal more directly with issues rather than through avoidance (illness).
- *Guidance of actions, behaviors, consequences:* Lacks conflict resolution strategies; exhibits avoidance (school) behavior.

After this initial overview, you as the practitioner decide what additional data need to be collected to get a comprehensive view of the problem(s). With a child this age, it is logical to involve the parent(s), who can provide information about when these problems began, whether anyone in the family or neighborhood had actually been in a bad accident or fire, how frequently Jesse experiences the anxiety and school avoidance behavior, whether she has had a physical exam and the results, and more about the specifics of the relationship with her brother. You also would want to interview the teacher to learn more about the effect of her absences on her academic performance and if there seems to be any pattern to the absences.

Checklists could be developed to get a more concrete representation of these data.

In interviewing Jesse, you know that as a 9-year-old she is probably in the concrete operations stage of cognitive development, and therefore is capable of more logical thought patterns. She also is able to anticipate and explain cause-and-effect and can, to some extent, assume the viewpoint of others. Drawing from Ivey's (2000) work, the following types of questions should be appropriate for Jesse; if not, she may be operating at a lower cognitive level and the focus would need to shift: "Jesse, you mentioned that you are afraid that something bad might happen to your family, like a tornado that would rip your house apart or a bad car accident. When you think about those things, what feelings do you have? Can you tell me some of the things that you say to yourself when you get scared like that?" To further assess her anxiety, you could have her draw a picture of what she thinks might happen in these events and keep a chart that shows how often she gets anxious.

To evaluate the conflict with her brother, which is a relatively normal developmental issue, Jesse could be asked to keep a list of the different events that trigger the conflict, to see how often it occurs, and to rate it on a 1–5 scale in terms of intensity. Role playing also would be helpful in demonstrating the nature of the conflict and how each party reacted.

To assess the problems related to her frequent illnesses, you could develop a checklist with questions such as the following:

- When I go to school, I feel _____
- If I don't feel well and stay home from school, I usually _____
  _____
- One of the reasons I don't want to go to school is because _____
  _____
- When I stay home from school, my parents_____
- When I stay home from school, my teachers _____

When the information from all sources has been gathered, it can be evaluated for patterns, specific problems, areas that may need to be assessed further, and areas of strength. A multimodal approach does not assume that there are problems in every dimension. But by identifying strengths or deficits in each area, a comprehensive assessment occurs. Following the assessment, specific interventions can be targeted for each area as needed. As with the assessment process, interventions may engage parents, siblings, teachers, or other school personnel in addition to counselor-directed strategies with the child.

Summary

Childhood and adolescence are the formative periods when change is most dramatic. Helping professionals are frequently asked, "Is my child doing

OK?" Children and adolescents express concern, "Am I normal?" These questions only can be answered by accurate assessment of the problem that uses a multifaceted approach, including information from a variety of sources. In this chapter, information on how to develop informal assessments such as checklists, unfinished sentences, writing activities, games, and decision-making dilemmas was presented, as well as descriptions of numerous formal assessment instruments. A comprehensive assessment model, the HELPING model, was discussed, followed by a case study to illustrate application of the concepts.

As a young client in her 8-year-old wisdom stated, "I know my friend is sad and I want to help her, but unless she tells me what's wrong, I don't know what to do." This is the concept of assessment. Until more is known about the problem and how it interfaces with developmental stages and cultural and environmental contexts, appropriate interventions cannot be determined.

Chapter 3

Methods of
Multicultural Assessment

✳

The assessment process with children and adolescents becomes more challenging when one considers race and ethnicity, which are often overlooked and mistaken for typical as well as atypical behaviors. This conceptualization is due to a lack of cultural awareness and knowledge regarding cultures (Erk, 2004). To overcome this problem, counselors need to develop cultural awareness as well as skills to interact success-fully with young clients from diverse backgrounds. The ability to do this is called diversity competence, *a term that implies the underly-ing qualities of awareness, understanding, and interpersonal skill (Hogan-García, 2003).*

✳

Because of constant ethnic and racial changes in the fabric of U.S. society, being culturally competent is imperative. Without cultural awareness and competency, the assessment process of ethnically diverse clients is impaired. This chapter addresses the multidimensional areas of diversity that should be considered during the evaluation process, including ethical issues, instruments, and culture, race, and ethnicity as fluid constructs.

Ethical Issues and Diversity

Multicultural and diversity issues should be regarded as critical elements of the evaluation process of children and adolescents, not as options but as obligations for an ethically and professionally competent counselor. The code of ethics of the American Counseling Association (1995) addresses the issue of diversity in numerous sections: Sections A.2.b. (Respecting differ-ences), A.4.b. (Personal values), A.2.a., C.5.a. (Nondiscrimination), E.8. (Diversity in testing), F.2.i. (Diversity in programs), and G.1.f. (Diversity). The American Counseling Association has established that diversity issues are instrumental aspects of the code of ethics and should be carefully con-sidered in every counseling area. Consistent with the code of ethics, the Multicultural Counseling Competencies and Standards were developed to operationalize these diversity principles (Sue, Arredondo, & McDavis, 1992; Sue et al., 1998). The operationalization of these principles allows counseling professionals to have an articulated foundation that serves as a guideline for which they can strive.

Personal Exploration of Cultural Sensitivity and Competency

Political correctness has affected the behavior of helping profession-als. However, being politically correct does not necessarily imply be-ing culturally sensitive. Acting according to the established social and political conventions for the sake of keeping the status quo does not pro-mote personal change, growth, or insight. Typical comments such as the following reflect the fine line between political correctness and genuine cultural awareness:

> "I don't see color, I just see a human being."
> "You are just like me; I only see your skills and not your race."
> "I came from a very accepting family; my parents never talked about race and discrimination. All people were valued for who they were."
> "I treat all my clients the same regardless of where they come from."

To a certain extent, the aforementioned comments sound admirable; however, the majority of these statements are most likely not based on gen-uine affirmations of differences that promote self-assessment. Rather, these comments stem from the fear of sounding discriminatory, narrow-minded, and intolerant. To address this, the first step in becoming culturally compe-tent is to self-assess one's level of cultural awareness and knowledge (Clemente, 2004). The following scale (see Table 3.1) serves as a prelimi-nary indicator of the level of biases, prejudices, and stereotypical percep-tions held by counselors. Readers are encouraged to respond to the items instinctively without rationalizing every response.

Table 3.1
Counselor's Self-Assessment of Cultural Awareness Scale

1 = (very much)   2 = (somewhat)   3 = (not at all)

1. I grew up in a neighborhood in which the majority of the people were:			
(a) Hispanic/Latinos	1	2	3
(b) African Americans	1	2	3
(c) American Indians (Native, First Nations)	1	2	3
(d) Asian Americans	1	2	3
(e) European Americans (Whites)	1	2	3
(f) Middle Easterners	1	2	3
2. Most of my friends are:			
(a) Hispanic/Latinos	1	2	3
(b) African Americans	1	2	3
(c) American Indians (Native, First Nations)	1	2	3
(d) Asian Americans	1	2	3
(e) European Americans (Whites)	1	2	3
(f) Middle Easterners	1	2	3
3. I have dated, or my significant other is:			
(a) Hispanic/Latino	1	2	3
(b) African American	1	2	3

(continues)

Table 3.1 (*Continued*)
Counselor's Self-Assessment of Cultural Awareness Scale

	1 = (*very much*)	2 = (*somewhat*)	3 = (*not at all*)
(c) American Indian (Native, First Nation)	1	2	3
(d) Asian American	1	2	3
(e) European American (White)	1	2	3
(f) Middle Easterners	1	2	3
4. At home we speak:			
(a) Spanish	1	2	3
(b) English	1	2	3
(c) An Asian language (i.e., Mandarin, Thai, Vietnamese, Hindi, etc.)	1	2	3
(d) Arabic	1	2	3
(e) Other	1	2	3
5. I am comfortable if my daughter or son dates (if you have children):			
(a) Hispanic/Latinos	1	2	3
(b) African Americans	1	2	3
(c) American Indians (Native, First Nation)	1	2	3
(d) Asian Americans	1	2	3
(e) European Americans (Whites)	1	2	3
(f) Middle Easterners	1	2	3
6. Most of my clients are:			
(a) Hispanic/Latinos	1	2	3
(b) African Americans	1	2	3
(c) American Indians (Native, First Nation)	1	2	3
(d) Asian Americans	1	2	3
(e) European Americans (Whites)	1	2	3
(f) Middle Easterners	1	2	3
7. I feel comfortable working with:			
(a) Hispanic/Latinos	1	2	3
(b) African Americans	1	2	3
(c) American Indians (Native, First Nation)	1	2	3
(d) Asian Americans	1	2	3
(e) European Americans (Whites)	1	2	3
(f) Middle Easterners	1	2	3
8. I routinely read professional literature (i.e., books, journals, magazines, periodicals) about:			
(a) Hispanic/Latinos	1	2	3
(b) African Americans	1	2	3
(c) American Indians (Native, First Nation)	1	2	3
(d) Asian Americans	1	2	3
(e) European Americans (Whites)	1	2	3
(f) Middle Easterners	1	2	3
9. The counseling outcome would be favorable if I had to work with:			
(a) Hispanic/Latinos	1	2	3
(b) African Americans	1	2	3
(c) American Indians (Native, First Nations)	1	2	3
(d) Asian Americans	1	2	3
(e) European Americans (Whites)	1	2	3
(f) Middle Easterners	1	2	3

(continues)

Table 3.1 (*Continued*)
Counselor's Self-Assessment of Cultural Awareness Scale

1 = (*very much*)   2 = (*somewhat*)   3 = (*not at all*)

10.	I feel comfortable developing a counseling relationship with:			
	(a) Hispanic/Latinos	1	2	3
	(b) African Americans	1	2	3
	(c) American Indians (Native, First Nation)	1	2	3
	(d) Asian Americans	1	2	3
	(e) European Americans (Whites)	1	2	3
	(f) Middle Easterners	1	2	3
11.	At least once a day I think about my own race or ethnicity:	1	2	3
12.	At least once a year I participate in a diversity/ multicultural experience regarding:			
	(a) Hispanic/Latinos	1	2	3
	(b) African Americans	1	2	3
	(c) American Indians (Native, First Nation)	1	2	3
	(d) Asian Americans	1	2	3
	(e) European Americans (Whites)	1	2	3
	(f) Middle Easterners	1	2	3
13.	I am an advocate for _____ in the form of social, political, and educational advocacy.			
	(a) Hispanic/Latinos	1	2	3
	(b) African Americans	1	2	3
	(c) American Indians (Native, First Nation)	1	2	3
	(d) Asian Americans	1	2	3
	(e) European Americans (Whites)	1	2	3
	(f) Middle Easterners	1	2	3
14.	I know the cultural, ethnic, and racial history of my family:	1	2	3
15.	I and/or my family invite people of diverse ethnic backgrounds for dinner or social activities:	1	2	3
16.	Due to the ethnic diversity of my clientele I have to consider culture and ethnicity when developing my interventions:	1	2	3

	Total score	Ratio
Hispanic/Latinos	_____	_____
African Americans	_____	_____
American Indians (Native, First Nation)	_____	_____
Asian Americans	_____	_____
European Americans (Whites)	_____	_____
Middle Easterners	_____	_____

Interpretation of the Scale

The Counselor's Self-Assessment of Cultural Awareness Scale should not be used as a parameter of success or failure as a counselor but as a measure of cultural self-awareness. The results should be examined with honesty and a willingness to challenge one's personal and professional growth. The use of formal or informal assessment instruments is meaningless if the counselor is insensitive to the cultural needs of the clients or unaware that the assessment measure he or she is using may be biased and inappropriate. For that reason, we are not providing an interpretive scale that determines what is or not acceptable. For instance, James, a Euro American school counselor with 10 years of experience, always refers "all the students of color" to Tristan, an African American counselor in the same school. James argues that Tristan can relate better to the students of color because he is one of them. However, James is only keeping a distance from students who belong to underrepresented ethnic groups. He is not willing to take risks and learn to be truly open and sensitive to their needs.

Personal Culture and Cultural Awareness

In the past, ethnic and racial differences were viewed as challenges experienced by members of underrepresented ethnic groups. However, the cultural, ethnic, or racial gap is a two-way street that Euro American counselors have to experience to ensure mutual understanding and respect. Personality, which is defined as the individual paradigm that addresses assumptions about reality, meanings, and beliefs, must not be mistaken for personal culture and used as an excuse to behave in a culturally insensitive manner (Green, 1999). In fact, personality or personal identity is an intricate part of the personal culture, often referred to as the *core identity* (Merry, 2001). For instance, if Barbara, a community agency counselor, is selectively abrasive against adolescents whose first language is not English, then her attitudes are discriminatory and not based on personality.

Personal culture is a dynamic entity that underlies one's individual behavior and includes everything an individual finds meaningful: beliefs, values, perceptions, assumptions, and explanatory frameworks about reality itself. "This personal culture develops in and through our social interactions with family and others who belong to our sociocultural milieu" (Hogan-García, 2003, p. 16). The counselor's personal culture, like that of his or her clients, does not develop in a vacuum and is not exempt from being influenced by his or her surroundings. For example, if Bob practices counseling in a community that has gone through socioeconomic segregation, his current attitudes are influenced by those experiences. Furthermore, the mainstream culture (the national culture of the United States) influences the way we develop a sense of self. For instance, the U.S. culture promotes the values of independence, self-control, personal freedom, assertiveness, and individualism. At the same time, these monocultural assumptions and policies that influence the schools, the media, and other institutions and organizations may not reflect the values and beliefs of many of the clients we serve (Delgado & Stefancic, 1997). For example, the educational system encourages students to engage in dialogues and debates with teachers and peers to develop assertiveness. However, parents of Asian American and Latino students discourage their children from being assertive, especially with people in power positions such teachers or school principals, because their belief is that one should respect people in such positions. Therefore, the passivity displayed by some ethnically diverse students may be interpreted as an unwillingness to participate or a lack of independence.

Most racial identity models address the dynamics of ethnic and racial awareness from the client's perspective (Atkinson, Morten, & Sue, 1998). But the majority of these models place the counselor in a different dimension of self-awareness. Specifically, counselors are typically portrayed as highly objective professionals who are impartial and unbiased. The White identity development model (Helms, 1989, 1995) mentions the impact of racial self-awareness with the assumption that the majority of helping professionals belong to the Euro American majority. However, this model does not directly address the consequences of a culturally and ethnically unaware counselor. For instance, it is typically assumed that if a counselor belongs to an ethnically diverse group, that condition by itself will make him or her automatically an unbiased and unprejudiced individual. That is a false premise that stems from the assumption that ethnically diverse individuals are automatically open and unbiased.

The best way to increase the level of success when working with ethnically diverse clients is to promote personal cultural change. The identity-change model (Hogan-García, 2003) provides a foundation of awareness for counselors to explore their current level of cultural awareness and competence. Like any other model, the stages should be approached in a nonlinear and nonsequential way. The model can be conceptualized with the case of Tammy.

The Case of Tammy Wisely

Tammy is a female Euro American counselor who is an example of a person who is progressively developing cultural awareness. Her growth through the stages of identity change and cultural awareness is discussed in the following stages.

Stage 1: Conformity. Preconceptions, stereotypes, confusion, stress, denial, and nonrecognition of sensitive issues related to diversity are the common characteristics of this first stage of conformity (Loden 1996; Morrison, 1992). Individuals have a monocultural perception and are blind to the current and historical reality of cultural diversity (Sleeter & McLaren, 1995). For example, Tammy likes to use standardized tests with her young clients. She believes that all tests have good reliability and validity. Furthermore, she thinks that there is no need to interpret the results of a test if the young client has a different ethnic or racial background, or to explore the possibility of using some projective or qualitative test or inventory. In fact, she does not think about those issues at all. She sees all assessment and intervention techniques as universal and objective. In other words, "one size fits all."

Stage 2: Resistance. In this second stage, resistance, individuals question and resist concepts, ideas, or principles that seem to contradict the mainstream culture's assumptions and beliefs about ethnicity, diversity, and multiculturalism. Feelings of anger and embarrassment are commonly experienced (Tatum, 1993).

After having been exposed to some seminars and interactions with professional counselors of color at a national conference, Tammy resists the idea of "revising" all her current assessment and intervention processes with her young clients. She argues that it is an exaggeration and that if she tries to accommodate all the individual needs of everyone, there is no way that she can get anything done. Tammy thinks that children are children regardless of their color. She cannot understand why some children from the other side of the town are so loud and cannot follow through with her correctional behavioral plans.

Stage 3: Redefinition. As a result of the growing awareness of and sensitivity to information regarding diversity and multiculturalism, individuals start making personal changes and transforming the lives of those close to them in this third stage, redefinition. As an illustration, their awareness of social phenomena such as racial profiling of African American and Middle Eastern men provokes a need to keep learning and growing as a fully aware and responsible individual in order to overcome their biases.

Tammy is now beginning to understand that some of her behavioral interventions were too rigid and impractical for some her nontraditional adolescents. For instance, some of her African American male clients made fun of her when she suggested that the use of "I" statements could help them be more assertive in order to stop others from harassing them. They told her that in their neighborhood this approach does not work. She is now realizing that there is room for personal and professional growth.

Stage 4: New identity. In this fourth stage, individuals develop a higher degree of ethnic and multicultural awareness and are comfortable with their new identity. Their understanding and continuous study of ethnic and cultural dynamics in the United States facilitates and maintains their growth.

Tammy joined two community organizations and proactively reached out to individuals from diverse groups. As a result of her growing sensitivity, her counseling interventions now reflect the culture and reality of her young clients. For example, instead of using books with Caucasian characters, she now selects books that reflect the young client's culture. She includes people from the community as consultants or facilitators when conducting group activities with ethnically diverse students.

Stage 5: Diversity competence. In addition to acquiring knowledge and information with respect to social and cultural dynamics experienced by individuals in the United States, counselors in this fifth stage are able to reach out and develop effective relationships with people from ethnically diverse groups (Helms, 1989; Winkelman, 1999).

Tammy opens her house to her new friends from the community and genuinely wants to know how to be more sensitive to their needs. She does not wait for her supervisor to recommend culture sensitivity workshops; in fact, she registers for seminars and culture-related activities on her own. Her reading repertoire now includes autobiographical literature by ethnically diverse authors. She continuously examines her counseling interventions in light of the client's culture.

To further understand these concepts of cultural awareness and development, Mary's case below provides a framework of reference. Her subtle lack of cultural self-awareness tends to be more typical than blatant discrimination, which can be easily identified.

The Case of Mary Blindly

Mary is a 48-year-old White Euro American female from the Midwest who has been a professional counselor for 20 years. She takes pride in being an open-minded individual with a distinct dislike for racism, oppression, and discrimination. Throughout the years, her performance evaluations have been excellent.

Because of the installation of a meatpacking plant, the demographics of her midsized community have changed dramatically. As a consequence, the student population is looking more "brown" because of the Mexican and East European immigrants. Some of Mary's neighbors have sold their houses and moved to the suburbs, and a large number of her coworkers have left the school, claiming that the work conditions were not the best and that they were incapable of performing their job duties appropriately.

Lately, Mary has had to rely on interpreters to counsel some of her students, and the administration is requiring that all employees, regardless of their job description, take sensitivity training and basic Spanish. Although Mary initially welcomed this idea, she now insists that she is too old to learn a new language. Lately, Mary has been experiencing some discomfort after learning that her older son is in a serious dating relationship with a young Mexican woman and is talking about marriage. She told her son that it is perfectly acceptable to have multiethnic friends, but when it comes to interracial relationships he should reflect more on the social consequences. Her son labeled her a hypocrite for "not walking the walk."

Mary adamantly rejects the idea of being racist or discriminatory, stating that it is the reality of life and she wishes that other people were more understanding. However, after the cumulative effect of these situations, Mary has been considering a transfer to another school district to keep the family together and to expose her children to better educational standards.

Unfortunately, Mary's situation is not atypical and is more prevalent as the country's demographics change. Mary represents the stereotypical well-educated counselor who is "book smart" about multicultural and diversity issues. She intellectually comprehends the dynamics of prejudice and racism but has not fully integrated her knowledge base into her daily behavior. Because of the limitations of living geographically isolated in an area populated by one ethnic group (Euro Americans), her book knowledge lacks meaning because it has never been tested under real conditions. Taking international trips to experience another culture is not sufficient if the intention is to be knowledgeable and open minded, because tourists often have minimal interactions with the local population.

Mary is experiencing cultural dissonance as her beliefs regarding multi-ethnic groups acquire a different meaning when personal areas such as work and family are affected. Her principles are tested as her comfort level is altered. It is intriguing that she blames society for not being open enough when it comes to interracial marriages, but she has not realized that she is perpetuating social dynamics and myths to maintain the status quo in her own life. In addition, the opportunity to learn a new language constitutes more than an intellectual challenge; it could be an opportunity to reduce the communication barriers. However, instead of learning another language, Mary continued to force her clients to accommodate to her linguistic and cultural realities. The truth is that Mary was not as open-minded and pro-multiethnic as she professed to be.

Mary's case is an illustration of how practitioners must be aware of the subtleties associated with discrimination as opposed to blatant racism, which is easily identified. Most importantly, one's cultural filter has to be reexamined when working with ethnically diverse clients.

Integrating Culture and Ethnicity
Into the Assessment Process

Over the last 40 years, the counseling profession has revisited traditional assessment tools and theoretical conceptualizations with regard to culture, race, and ethnicity. As a result of Wrenn's (1962) article about the encapsulated counselor, studies have indicated the importance of including culture during the assessment process (Barth, 1998; Goode, 2001). Many behavioral traits were typically considered to be "deviant or abnormal behaviors" prior to the inclusion of ethnically diverse individuals in research studies. Traits such as collective thinking, cooperation, and the display of emotions were considered to be a lack of independence, dependency, and emotional instability, respectively. Those myths were later debunked by understanding how cultures alter the psyche, emotions, and behaviors of individuals.

When the words *evaluation* and *assessment* are used, the automatic assumption is that there must be something "wrong" with the client. As a result, it is very likely that the counselor will be looking for areas of deficiency that need improvement. To avoid this mindset, the counselor must be grounded in normal developmental theory, as well as systemic and multicultural principles. Children are not referred to the counselor as a reward for appropriate behavior or for positive feedback unless there is an academic-related activity that involves awards. Instead, students hold the belief that they are referred to the counselor when they get in trouble or when there is something wrong with them. Therefore, the assessment process becomes a two-way street in which the previously held perceptions of the counselor and the young client alter positively or negatively the outcome of the evaluation. In a multiethnic society, the evaluation of young clients becomes more complex and forces the counselor to consider variables that historically have been ignored.

Ignoring the importance of culture during the assessment processes can be detrimental to the psychological and educational progress of young ethnically diverse clients. Prior to utilizing the *DSM–IV–TR* or any other formal or informal assessments, the counselor must consider the appropriate developmental stages and the ethnic and cultural background of the young client.

An example of a culturally responsive assessment follows. I (Roberto Clemente) adapted Paniagua's (1998) Cultural Formulation Concepts and Aspects of Culture or Ethnicity (Hogan-García, 2003), adding or deleting concepts to accommodate the unique needs of young ethnically diverse clients, and renamed it the Extended Cultural Evaluation Form. The case of Raúl, an 8-year-old Mexican America boy, helps to illustrate these concepts, integrating assessment considerations and providing some suggestions for appropriate cultural interventions.

Raúl is an 8-year-old Mexican American boy experiencing learning and adaptation difficulties. The teachers report that he is inattentive, talkative only with his Mexican peers, and uninvolved during recess. The homeroom teacher has sent him home several times because after routine health checks, she found lice. His parents were notified by mail and were called several times, but there was no response. The homeroom teacher claims that the parents do not care because they are uninvolved.

Extended Cultural Evaluation Form—1st Part

- History and social status
  Cultural assessment: Mexican Americans have been traditionally discriminated against in the United States. They have been misunderstood and secluded as a marginal class.
  Intervention: The teachers and counselors must learn more about the Mexican American struggle in the United States. They must expose themselves to successful Mexican Americans who have contributed to U.S. society. Raúl can be empowered by integrating Mexican cultural aspects in the curriculum and by bringing Mexican group facilitators or speakers to the class. Also, a peer helper of Mexican descent from high school can help Raúl adapt to his current school context.
- Social group interaction patterns, value orientations, and family
  Cultural assessment: Mexicans, like most Latinos, have a collective view of the world. As a group, the present is more important than the future. The family is the core of their society. The assessment process should reflect this value.
  Intervention: The counseling interventions should also take into account the position of the family. Counseling interventions with Raúl are futile if they are done in a vacuum. Individualistic and

behavioral interventions that stress independence and assertiveness separate from the family of origin lack effectiveness. The parents need to be aware of the counselor's plan.

- Language and communication
  Cultural assessment: Spanish is the first language for many Mexican Americans and is usually spoken at home. An interpreter may need to be involved in the assessment process.
  Intervention: It is possible that Raúl's language proficiency has not been properly assessed. Raúl seems to be talkative with his Mexican peers but inattentive in class. He is only exercising his right to communicate with those who can fully understand him. Raúl needs a bilingual assistant to help him adapt to the class activities. To develop more culturally sensitive interventions, the counselor needs to have a cultural formulation of the case (Paniagua, 1998).

Extended Cultural Formulation Form—2nd Part

- *Cultural identity of the client:* Is Raúl a first-, second-, or third-generation Mexican? Does he relate better to Mexicans than to children of other ethnicities?
- *Cultural factors related to psychosocial environment and level of functioning:* Is Raúl's behavior a result of his culture or a cultural clash? How well does he behave in his own cultural context?
- *Cultural elements of the relationship between the client and the counselor:* As a counselor, what could I be doing that is impeding the development of a healthy relationship with Raúl?
- *Overall cultural reaction:* As a counselor, do I think that there are cultural issues involved? Is Raúl's behavior typical or atypical within the Mexican culture?

Assessment Guidelines for Ethnically Diverse Children and Adolescents

To successfully evaluate ethnically diverse clients, the counselor has to be aware of areas that are commonly ignored and consider them as instrumental in the assessment process. An inviting multicultural environment could make the difference between a valid assessment outcome and an unreliable result. The following guidelines will help counselors be more culturally sensitive during the assessment process:

1. Create an inviting multicultural environment. Decorate the office with symbols that reflect diverse cultures and ethnicities. Create a delicate balance between professional emblems such as diplomas and professional certificates and art and natural elements such as plants and fish tanks (Clemente, 2004).
2. Have games, artifacts, books, pamphlets, and literature and dolls from various countries and cultures in your office.
3. Explore your own biases, think developmentally and culturally, and, as a last resource, think with reference to the *DSM–IV–TR*.

4. Before working with a client from a cultural–ethnic group with which you are not familiar, develop a list of all the stereotypes, biases, and negative concepts you may hold against this group. Research the history of the ethnic group in the United States. Before meeting the client, evaluate your counseling assessments in light of the negative biases you developed.

5. Explore the level of acculturation of the young client avoiding stereotypical assumptions. For instance, what is the language spoken at home? What is the first language of the client? How is the client's command of the English language? Primarily, who does the client socialize with—members of his or her own ethnic group or members of the majority group?

6. Allow extra time for the assessment process, especially if English is not the client's first language.

7. Develop a pool of interpreters from the area who are native speakers and sensitive to the unique particularities of young clients. Avoid using relatives or friends as interpreters. Like any other paraprofessional, the interpreters must be aware of issues related to confidentiality and ethics.

8. Think collectively and systemically. Be open to inviting family members at some point during the initial or follow-up evaluation. Most ethnically diverse clients do not operate individually; therefore, the chances of obtaining a more positive counseling outcome increase with the inclusion of relatives during the counseling process.

Culturally Sensitive Assessments

The selection of culturally sensitive assessments is instrumental in influencing the outcome of counseling and the ultimate success of young multiethnic clients. More importantly, the level of acculturation of the young client can be a strong indicator in ruling out "dysfunctional" behavior as established by the standards of the majority culture (Kim & Abreu, 2001). Also, misconduct or inappropriate behavior could be a result of acculturation difficulties and not necessarily be a reflection of cultural differences or abnormal behavior. Especially with children, the process of constructing an ethnic identity in a different cultural context could be one full of frustration and disappointments (Roysircar-Sodowsky & Frey, 2003).

Multiple acculturation scales have been developed that can serve as sources of information, clarification, and rationalization of distinct behaviors and attitudes. Table 3.2 lists some examples.

Table 3.3 lists examples of culturally appropriate books to use in the assessment process.

The Latino culture uses *cuentos* (short stories) and *dichos* (popular sayings) as vehicles to teach values, morals, and social principles to children. These cuentos and dichos are especially relevant to Latinos because they are ingrained in a cultural context that has unique meaning to

Table 3.2
Acculturation Scales

Scale	Focus	Age Level	Author
For use with Latinos/Hispanics			
Short Acculturation Scale for Hispanic Youths (SASH-Y)	Acculturation	Adolescents	Barona & Miller, 1994
Acculturation Rating Scale for Mexican Americans–II (ARSMA)	Acculturation	Young Mexican adolescents	Cuellar, Arnold, & Maldonado, 1995
The Bidimensional Acculturation Scale for Hispanics (BAS)	Acculturation	Young adolescents	Marín & Gamba, 1996
A Children's Hispanic Background Scale	Acculturation	Young children	Martínez, Norman, & Delaney, 1984
For use with Native/American Indians			
Rosebud Personal Opinion Survey	Acculturation	Adolescence	Hoffman, Dana, & Bolton, 1985
For use with Asian Americans			
The Asian Values Scale	Exploration of Asian values and worldview	Adolescence	Kim, Atkinson, & Yang, 1999
The Suinn–Lew Asian Self-Identity Acculturation Scale (SL-ASIA)	Self-identity and acculturation	All ages	Ponterotto, Baluch, & Carielli, 1998
Na Mea Hawai'I: A Hawaiian Acculturation Scale	Acculturation of Hawaiians	All ages	Rezentes, 1993
For use with African Americans			
Developmental Inventory of Black Consciousness	African American identity	Adolescence	Milliones, 1980
A Scale to Assess African American Acculturation	Acculturation	Adolescence	Snowden & Hines, 1999
The African American Acculturation Scale	Acculturation	Adolescence	Landrine & Klonoff, 1994

Table 3.3

Culturally Appropriate Books

Assessment—Title	Issue/Concern	Age or Grade Level	Author
For use with Latinos/Hispanics			
Storytelling, metaphors, and images	Gender issues and abuse	Late adolescence (females)	Bracero, 1998
Cuento therapy (Spanish short stories)	Adjustment issues and ethnic identity	Young children	Constantino, Malgady, & Rogler, 1986
Cuento and hero/heroine modeling therapy	Adjustment issues and ethnic identity	All ages	Constantino & Malgady, 1996
Dichos/Metaphor	Cultural transitions and adaptation	All ages	Zuniga, 1992
For use with Native/American Indians			
Powwow	Developing ethnic pride	Grades 2–5	Ancona, 1993
Indians: An Activity Book	Cultural knowledge	Grades 5–6	Artman, 1981
Dancing Colors: Paths of Native American Women	Sexuality—young adolescents	Adolescence	Brafford, 1992
Lightening Inside You and Other Native American Riddles	Motivation—boys	Grades 4–6	Bierhorst, 1992
Go Indians! Stories of the Great Indian Athletes of the Carlisle School	Inspirational	Late adolescence	Hall, 1971
For use with Asian Americans			
American Eyes: New Asian American Short Stories for Young Adults	Racial discrimination and bicultural identity issues	Grades 8–12	L. Carlson, 1999
The Japanese Americans	Pride and Japanese cultural history	All ages	Lee, 1996
Peacebound Trains	Cultural history	Grades 4–6	Balgassi, 1996
The Moon Bridge	Internment camps in the United States	Ages 8–12	Savin, 1995
For use with African Americans			
Through My Eyes	Gender and race equality	Ages 8–12	Bridges, 1999
A Picture Book of Frederick Douglass	Meaning of freedom	Grades 4–5	Adler, 1993
The Watsons Go to Birmingham—1963	Impact of violence and inequality	Ages 9–12	Curtis, 1997
Invisible Man	Social injustice and prejudice (classic)	Grades 10–12	Ellison, 1982
Let the Circle Be Unbroken	How to overcome injustice by using the system	Grades 9–12	Taylor, 1981

them. Although there are certain cuentos that carry the same themes among Latin American countries, it is advisable to select cuentos and dichos that have been specifically written in the country of origin of the young client. A short story developed in Mexico may have no significant meaning to a young client from Argentina, for example. The best resources for cuentos and dichos are the English as a Second Language (ESL) teachers and Spanish instructors in schools. The same standards for using bibliotherapy as an assessment tool apply when using cuentos and dichos.

In addition to acculturation scales, and the informal assessments described in the previous chapter, bibliotherapy is a particularly useful assessment tool to use with ethnically diverse clients. In using this technique, the counselor must consider the cultural background of the client and avoid using normative standards of behavior established by the majority. The following are some guidelines in using literature, short stories, fiction, or poems as assessment tools:

1. Young clients see characters as projections of their own lives. Therefore, the counselor must use the characters as personality assessments, targeting three different aspects: how the clients perceive themselves, how they perceive the world, and how they interact with their environment.

2. There are some representative questions to use when assessing self-concept, self-esteem, and quality of perceptions and interactions with people, including the following:
   a. Which characters look like you?
   b. Which character thinks like you?
   c. What do you think the character had in mind when he or she did that?
   d. If you were this character, what would you do in this situation?
   e. What do you dislike the most about the character? Like the most?
   f. Which character is the most attractive? Intelligent?

3. Counselors can use inanimate objects or animals in a short story as vehicles to assess a "filtered" opinion or perception by young clients by asking questions such as the following:
   a. If you were the house, what would you say is going on with the family?
   b. If the dog, cat, or fish could speak, how would they feel about the character in the story?
   c. If the tree in front of the house could see, what do you think he or she is seeing?

4. Another way of assessing the intimate wishes of young clients is to let them complete the end of the story, alter the beginning, or add or eliminate characters of the story to make it "better."

5. The counselor could isolate one or two characters from a story and let the clients create a new story in a new context (i.e., house, neighborhood, country).

Summary

Assessment with children and adolescents who belong to ethnically diverse groups is a complex and fluid process. Similar to the rapid changes occurring in U.S. society, ethnically diverse children and adolescents do not remain culturally fossilized but change as they interact with children of European American descent. Counselors must be culturally sensitive and competent to serve this population in an ethical way. The conceptualization of ethnicity and culture must be at the forefront when evaluating the behaviors of children from different ethnic backgrounds.

Chapter 4

Designing Developmentally and Culturally Responsive Interventions

✳

Several counseling students were discussing a case study during practicum class. "I just wish there was a recipe to follow so that I would know exactly what to do, how, and when," said Noriko. "I always wonder if I'm doing the right thing, and sometimes I can't even think of an intervention." Sound familiar? On the down side, it is frustrating when you cannot come up with the right intervention; on the up side, this is where the counseling process is a challenging and creative endeavor.

✳

Although there is no recipe as such, the purpose of this chapter is to share some specific information that will assist in the intervention phase of the counseling process. A four-stage process for designing interventions is outlined, including specific considerations in designing developmentally appropriate interventions. Examples of a wide variety of interventions that are particularly applicable for school-age children also are described.

The Design Process

Counseling with children and adolescents must not be a "fly by the seat of your pants" endeavor. Interventions must be developed and selected after careful contemplation, taking into account the developmental level of the child, his or her learning style, cultural considerations, and the appropriateness of the method for the particular problem.

In designing an effective intervention, both the counselor and client need a sense of direction and purpose that can be achieved through a planned change process (Reynolds, 1993). Adapted from Reynolds' model, four stages integral to this process are described below: planning, design of intervention, implementation, and evaluation.

Planning Stage

Following problem assessment, in which the presenting concern is explored in detail to determine when it began, under what conditions it occurs, and with what degree of frequency and intensity, the counselor and client can proceed to the planning stage of the intervention design process. This stage consists of the following five substages:

1. *Vision:* Compared with how things are now, what could be different? How could things be better? What would be ideal?
2. *Goal setting:* What is going well? What needs to be worked on? What are the goals for change?
3. *Analysis:* What is enabling or interfering with achieving these goals or this vision? What is getting in the way of resolving the problem?
4. *Objective:* What specifically would the client (or the parent or the teacher) like to change? The objective should be stated measurably and succinctly, such as "to identify five ways to control anger."
5. *Exploration of interventions:* What already has been tried and how did it work? How does the client learn best? Where is the child in relation to developmental stages? Will parents or significant others be involved in the process? What research has been done on the most effective types of interventions for this specific problem? Are the interventions being considered appropriate for the client developmentally and culturally? What is the counselor's skill level in relation to design and implementation of various interventions?

Designing the Intervention

Rather than prescribe an intervention, it is generally more effective to collaborate as much as possible with the young client and parents as appropriate in the intervention design process. Not only does this reduce resistance, but frequently clients or significant others can contribute ideas that increase the effectiveness of the particular intervention and, in turn, the likelihood that it will be successful. I (Ann Vernon) recall working with 4-year-old Nick, a bright and verbal youngster who was aggressive and impulsive with peers as well as adults. Although I had identified several interventions after a thorough assessment of the problem, I met with his parents to solicit their input as to what might be most effective, because they also would be working with him during the implementation stage. As I shared some ideas with role playing, his father indicated that Nick liked to play dress up and that one of his favorite activities was to accompany his dad to the community theater when Dad was rehearsing for a play because he liked to try on costumes. Through brainstorming, we developed a specific intervention, using dress-up clothes to act out appropriate and inappropriate behaviors in different situations with different people. Had I not involved the parents, I would not have had the information needed to personalize an intervention to increase its applicability.

The following guidelines should be useful in designing and selecting developmentally appropriate interventions for children and adolescents.

1. Children's thinking progresses from concrete to abstract. Use concrete analogies, props, pictures, and drawings as part of the intervention with young clients. Example: "We've talked about how you feel and what you can do when someone calls you a name. Now, if you

could draw a picture of a solution in each of these squares, you can tape it to your desk to help remind you what you can do."

2. Younger children's attention spans are more limited, so integrate the assessment/intervention process as much as possible, including a variety of approaches. Example: Counselor to 6-year-old Katya, "First I'd like you to draw a picture for me that shows what scares you so much that you go to that secret hiding place you have been talking about. Then I'll read you a story about a little girl your age who gets scared like you do. Maybe you can get some ideas from the story about what helps her when she feels scared."

3. Children's ability to remember concepts from session to session may be limited. Making use of short homework assignments that reinforce or introduce interventions that the young client can be working on throughout the week is helpful. Example: "Pedro, this week when you feel like you're so frustrated that you're ready to explode, try taking a deep breath and mentally picturing a big stop sign in front of your face. STOP stands for: Stop, Think, Overcome, and Proceed."

4. Use concrete, simple explanations with children who are at the concrete operational stage of cognitive development. Demystify the counseling process so that it seems more like problem solving rather than analyzing. Example: Rather than saying, "Marta, you seem to have a problem with anxiety; let's see what we can do about that," phrase it as, "Marta, I understand that you are worried about how you'll get along in third grade. Would you be willing to make a list of the things you worry about and bring them next time? Then together we can figure out some things you can do so that you won't have to worry as much."

5. Children and adolescents need to see a reason for counseling. Engaging them in a discussion of their goals and explaining how the particular intervention can help them achieve that goal is important. Example: Tom, an 18-year-old, shared that his goal was to terminate a long-standing relationship with his girlfriend, but he was worried about how to tell her and did not want her to become violent or out of control. The counselor explained concepts of assertive versus aggressive communication to him, noting that while Tom could not control or even predict her response, his best chance of getting a calmer reaction would occur if he was assertive. After outlining the steps of an assertive message, the counselor invited him to practice this communication skill through role play to help him explain his position more effectively to his girlfriend.

6. Younger clients learn best if interventions are specific and personal. Interview them about their interests, talents, heroes, favorite television shows, and musical groups, as well as how they like to learn. Use this information in structuring personalized interventions. Example: Ten-year-old Maggie loved to draw cartoons. One of the interventions used to help her develop more positive peer relation-

ships was to have her make a cartoon book illustrating positive ways to maintain friendships.

7. Using relevant examples and interventions contributes to the effectiveness with adolescents. Invite them to share yearbooks and pictures of friends and relatives so that examples and interventions are meaningful. Example: After Carol shared her pictures from camp, the counselor utilized examples in her intervention. "Carol, you told me that you had a miserable time at camp and that you never did anything with anybody. But when I look at this picture that shows you and several others laughing as you are canoeing together, I wonder if maybe you did have some fun after all? Do you think that you might have been overgeneralizing just a bit about the negative aspects of this experience? Let's backtrack and make a list of specifically what was really good, what was somewhat unpleasant, and what was absolutely awful. Maybe that will give you a different perspective."

8. Children and adolescents retain concepts more readily if they are involved in selecting meaningful analogies, activities, and interventions. Example: Nine-year-old Felipe got frustrated easily when he could not do things right. He and the counselor worked on some self-statements that he could use in these situations, and the counselor asked him if he could think of something that would help him remember not to get so upset and to use his self-statements. She shared an example with him that an older boy had used for a similar problem. He had pretended that his head was a giant bug zapper and that those frustrating thoughts would just be "fried" before they got inside his head. Felipe said that he would pretend that his head was a giant eraser and he could just erase the thoughts that caused his frustration.

9. It is critical to structure age-appropriate interventions. For instance, most adolescents are "wired" to their compact disc players, and young children respond well to games. Example: Invite adolescents to make a music collage, tape recording segments of songs that they think illustrate positive ways for them to solve their problems. With young children, make a game such as *Give a Little* (Vernon, self-developed game), in which students roll dice, move a given number of spaces, select a conflict card, and identify effective conflict resolution strategies.

10. Consider the client's learning style. Although counseling traditionally has been characterized by a verbal orientation, Myrick (1987) cautioned that some clients "may feel hopelessly inundated with words when being 'counseled.' They may feel overwhelmed, insecure, or lost in the intellectual efforts that seem to form the basis of most school counseling and guidance" (p. 131). Rather than limit the effectiveness of the intervention with clients whose learning styles are not primarily auditory, a wide array of interventions that access a

variety of learning styles should be considered: art activities, drama and play, music and movement, games, imagery, and bibliotherapy. Example: Seven-year-old Melinda literally bounced off the walls during counseling sessions. Drama and play interventions were more effective than verbal approaches for a child with limited attention span and a tactual, kinesthetic orientation.

11. The timing of an intervention is critical. Do not rush the process or try to implement interventions that are too advanced for the client at this stage in the counseling process. Example: Although 17-year-old Marcos wanted to begin dating, the counselor needed to work with him to develop more self-confidence and overcome his fear of rejection before encouraging him to ask out someone. After this step, small interventions could be tried: talking to a young woman on the school bus, calling her on the phone, meeting after school for a soda, and, finally, asking her for a date.

12. What works with one child might not work with another, even if it is the same problem. If an intervention does not work, swallow your pride, and do not be afraid to try another. Counselors do not have crystal balls and cannot always predict what will or will not be effective. Although it is important to be on target as much as possible, sometimes an intervention will not work because of the client's readiness level or state of being at the time. Be flexible and consider varying your approach. Example: A 14-year-old boy felt inadequate in social situations. Previous interventions such as role playing and self-concept activities had not alleviated the problem. The counselor decided to obtain permission from this client to invite another teenager who also had had similar problems to share with him his feelings and how he had worked on the issues. This intervention was very effective; the client began to take more risks as he observed a peer modeling these behaviors to age-appropriate dilemmas.

13. Use language that is appropriate to the age of the child; rephrase as necessary. Be sensitive to the fact that English will not necessarily be the client's first language. Learn the "lingo" of the young client to facilitate better communication, but do not do this if it does not seem natural. For example: To Ishan, age 6, "Could you use these toy figures and act out something that shows what you can do when you have your 'yucky' feelings at school?" Using the word yucky would be appropriate and descriptive for Ishan, but trying to connect with a delinquent adolescent by using the language of the "hood" would probably seem fake.

14. Develop a good rapport and a sense of trust with the child, adolescent, and significant others before designing an intervention that might be too threatening or too unusual. Example: Carla and her mother were constantly at odds, with Carla desperately trying to gain power and control of the relationship. Carla discovered that what

really "got" to her mother was her foul mouth; and although this resulted in being grounded to the bathroom for various periods of time, it did not bother this 13-year-old. After meeting with the mother alone and explaining the obvious power struggle, the counselor invited the mother to try structuring a 10-minute swearing time each day. The mother was a bit reluctant to try this rather unorthodox intervention, but at the same time, she trusted the counselor's judgment and was willing to try it. Once this was initiated, the swearing stopped because Carla could see that her behavior was not affecting her mother; it was no longer a viable way for her to be in control.

15. Have a good rationale for the selection of a given intervention. As stated previously, counseling is not a "fly by the seat of your pants" endeavor. There should be a clear connection between the assessed problem and the intervention. Example: Shenika does not know how to express her anger appropriately. Instead of focusing on this skill, the counselor had her complete the *One of a Kind* activity (Vernon, 1998a, pp. 23–25) to help her identify ways in which she was unique. Although this certainly would be appropriate if the problem related to self-concept, with an issue as specific as expression of anger, the counselor can address this skill more directly.

16. Do not be gimmicky. In other words, do not use interventions because they may be appealing to the client or fun to try. There needs to be a reason for choosing the intervention. Example: Antonio loves to play checkers, so he and the counselor play a game during each counseling session and chat about how things are going. Although this may be a good rapport builder, it does not address the assessed problem. It would be possible to adapt the checkers game by having Antonio share ways to stay tuned to a task after a move if paying attention was his problem.

17. Do not overstructure. Beginning counselors have a tendency to rely on a plan that includes specific interventions for each counseling session. Although it is important to structure interventions based on the assessed problem, it also is important to have latitude to go in a different direction if new information is presented. Do not lock yourself in. Example: In the previous session, Emily had completed an unfinished sentence checklist that indicated that she had some problems with her mother. The counselor selected a book to read to Emily about relationships with parents, but Emily seemed distracted during the session and said that she needed to talk about her grade on a test. Allow some flexibility; remember that children sometimes have a problem one week, but it may be gone the next; judge accordingly. A good rule of thumb is to begin each counseling session by briefly summarizing the last session and the identified problem, then asking the client if that is something he or she would like to continue working on or if there is a new issue.

*

18. Consider your own knowledge, comfort level, and abilities in select-ing interventions for young clients. If you are uncomfortable using art or play media, for example, do some research, observe another counselor, or take advantage of continuing education opportunities to learn more. It is easy to get into a rut and not try new things, and part of the adventure in working with children and adolescents is to find effective interventions that address their issues.

19. Use culturally appropriate interventions that incorporate art, music, and storytelling. Avoid using paper-and-pencil procedures that may involve extensive reading and writing in a language different from their own. Be sensitive to the fact that some clients will be intimi-dated by activities that require expression of feelings (Pedersen, Dra-guns, Lonner, & Trimble, 2002). Group activities can be very effective.

20. Continually assess your level of cultural competency in selecting interventions for culturally diverse young clients, and remember that some of the traditional concepts associated with counseling vary depending on culture. For example, in some cultures, the counselor is more of a special teacher, and it is honorable to accept help from a teacher. Therefore, it might be helpful to explain the role of counselor as a teaching–learning interaction (Pedersen, 2000).

Implementation Stage

After the intervention has been selected, the next stage is implementation. This stage occurs in several ways: (a) immediately following the design of the intervention, within the same session; (b) as a homework assignment for the client to implement between sessions; (c) as a step-by-step imple-mentation, in which a segment of the intervention is worked on, followed by additional steps after successful completion of the first; and (d) a combi-nation of all of these.

In working with younger clients, it is important to remember that, because their sense of time is so immediate, it may be necessary to identify one aspect of a problem, design an intervention, and move directly to implementation in a short period of time. The advantage of this approach is that it shows the children and their parents that something can be done, which makes the problem seem less overwhelming. The possible disad-vantage is that the entire process is more piecemeal. However, as a 10-year-old once said, "I need help now! Maybe my friend won't be mad at me tomorrow, but I can't wait till then to make things better." Thus, one needs to consider with whom one is working and adapt the process accordingly. Furthermore, after this intervention has been selected and implemented, the counselor and client can recycle into further problem assessment and then reenter the planning stage to target another issue.

Furthermore, helping professionals must use their judgment to deter-mine how much of the problem to address and at what pace to proceed with interventions. To some extent, this depends on the age of the client and on the magnitude and degree of intensity of the problem. If the problem interferes a lot with daily living and is causing a great deal of distress to the client or to others in the system, it is advisable to work on portions of the problem and intervene sooner, recycling back as necessary.

Interventions also can be implemented successfully as a homework assignment. Homework helps clients change more quickly and profoundly (Ellis & MacLaren, 1998). Not only does this reinforce concepts discussed during the counseling session, but it also is particularly helpful for younger clients whose recall ability from session to session is often limited. Homework assignments are also empowering for youngsters and can be a good way for young clients to share what they are working on with parents and teachers (Vernon, 2002). Homework can assume a variety of formats:

1. Reading: biographies, fiction, nonfiction, poetry, magazine or newspaper articles.
2. Writing: journals, diaries, poetry, fiction, letters to express emotions or clarify thoughts.
3. Behavioral tasks: risk-taking exercises, task completion, learning new skills.
4. Observing/viewing: specific movies, television programs, ways in which others behave or approach situations.
5. Activities: practicing coping self-statements, conducting short surveys or experiments.

It is important to invite the young client to participate in the homework assignment. The counselor can explain the purpose of the task and how this will help the young client achieve identified goals. If the tasks are creative and engaging, there is greater likelihood that the client will complete them, but if not, do not make an issue over it. And, because children and adolescents often have a negative connotation with the word *homework*, it may be preferable to use the term *experiment*.

Working on segments of an intervention also contributes to its effectiveness. For instance, with an anxious child, behavioral interventions need to be developed and implemented in a carefully structured hierarchy by breaking the ultimate goal into manageable steps appropriate to the child's developmental abilities. If too much is initiated too soon, the child may get discouraged and the entire procedure may fail. Although dividing the intervention into successive parts takes careful planning and patience, it is well worth the effort in the long run.

Evaluation

Did the intervention work? This is the key question to ask during the evaluation stage. Characteristically, when problems are not resolved, there has not been adequate evaluation. However, time constraints, lack of commitment, and lack of momentum often interfere with this critical step. The intervention may be implemented, and things may temporarily improve, but unless a systematic evaluative procedure is exercised, the implementation process is incomplete. Inevitably, without a deliberate assessment of what did or did not work, the problem increases in severity and intensity, which prompts the client or others to seek assistance again. Unfortunately, by allowing the problem to become more severe, subsequent change efforts become more difficult, as illustrated in the following case study.

Darnell, age 12, saw his school counselor on several occasions for help in adjusting to a recent physical disability. During problem assessment, it became apparent that Darnell was experiencing some mild depression and felt very self-conscious about having to wear a hearing aid. After identifying several interventions, Darnell, his mother, and his teacher implemented the plan. During the first few weeks when the counselor and Darnell discussed his progress, things were going well. Darnell's mother and teacher also confirmed this. However, as is frequently the case with school counselors, more immediate needs arose, and the counselor stopped seeing Darnell on a regular basis. Not surprisingly, after a month, Darnell's mother called the counselor to say he resisted going to school and had withdrawn from his friends in church and scouting activities. By this time, Darnell was more depressed. He and the counselor started over again to determine what to do about the initial problem and these subsequent symptoms.

Naturally, it is not always possible to prevent a situation like this from occurring, given the nature of the problem and the reality that things sometimes get worse before they get better. However, ongoing evaluation and gradual termination are recommended as a means of avoiding this situation. Involving parents or teachers in the evaluative process also is critical, because too often a child is ready to say "everything's okay" when the teacher or parent sees little or no improvement. In Darnell's case, after several weeks of progress, a short evaluation session with Darnell, his mother, and his teacher could have determined what had worked and what issues still needed to be addressed. A phase-out process could have been established to provide further evaluation and support. By considering evaluation an integral part of the intervention process, a feedback loop is established. That is, on the basis of the evaluation, it may be necessary to recycle back to the planning stage, or even to the assessment stage if new problems emerge, then to designing and implementing new strategies to address various aspects of the problem.

The Four-Stage Design Process: A Case Study

The case of Sandra, a 14-year-old Caucasian girl from a lower-middle-class single-parent family, illustrates the application of this four-stage model. Sandra was referred to the school counselor by her mother because of her defiant behavior and low grades. During the assessment process, which included both Sandra and her mother and teachers at separate times, it was determined that this client was of above-average intelligence with several other problems: inferiority feelings and lack of friends, some experimentation with alcohol and tobacco, jealousy toward her baby sister, and rebellious actions and attitudes, which created frequent and intense conflict with her mother and her mother's live-in boyfriend.

Because there were several problems in this case, the counselor and client needed to agree during the planning stage about which problem to address first. Although Sandra was not overjoyed to be in counseling, she was tired of the conflict and was willing to participate. In Sandra's opinion, the reason she was starting to drink, smoke, and get low grades was because she was angry at her mother and did not like her mom's boyfriend. Because she expressed her anger defiantly, which increased conflict between mother and daughter, the counselor agreed that this issue was of more immediate concern than the inferiority, friendship, and sibling issues.

During the planning stage, Sandra was asked about her vision: Compared with how things are now, how could they be different or better? She identified it would be better if she and her mother did not fight as much. Next, they discussed goals: What things were going well? Sandra was a pretty unhappy adolescent and could not identify much that was going well. Her goals for change included to feel happier and get along better with her mother. Next, the counselor and Sandra discussed what was interfering with achieving the goals and resolving the problem. In her opinion, she would feel happier if her Mom's boyfriend did not live with them, but she admitted that she and her mother had had problems even before that had occurred. As Sandra described their conflicts, the counselor drew a circular pattern of interaction to help explain what happens when one person reacts to another: If Mom refused to let Sandra do what she wanted to do, Sandra yelled, cursed, and called her names, which made Mom angry and resulted in Sandra's being grounded, which in turn prompted her to be more rebellious. In this way, it became clear to this young client that the way she and her mother responded to each other created more problems.

Next, specific objectives were identified: (a) to learn how to deal with anger in constructive rather than destructive ways and (b) to establish a more positive relationship with her mother by utilizing positive communication techniques. After exploring what Sandra had tried in relation to the targeted problem, the counselor was ready to design and implement interventions to address the first objective. Sensing that this client was tactual, the counselor invited Sandra to beat a plastic bat on a pillow and verbalize what angered her. The counselor took notes so that Sandra could also see what she had expressed. He also encouraged her to keep a journal or use a tape recorder to identify how she had felt so that this could be discussed in the following session. Next, he adapted an activity called *Healthy/Unhealthy Expression* (Vernon, 1989b, pp. 191–192) to help Sandra distinguish between positive and negative ways to express anger and to identify advantages and disadvantages of both kinds of expression. This was followed by an intervention called *Chain Reactions* (Vernon, 1989a, pp. 33–34), which illustrated the chain effect of negative emotions resulting in negative behaviors.

Before addressing the second objective, the counselor and Sandra discussed results of a weekly log, in which Sandra recorded the number of times she felt angry and acted defiantly and the ways in which she had expressed anger positively. This was a concrete way to determine any progress.

To deal with the second objective, the counselor and Sandra reviewed concepts from the book *The Mouse, Monster and Me* (Palmer, 1977), discussing the difference between assertive, aggressive, and nonassertive communication. They also role played, with Sandra assuming each of these communication styles in situations pertaining to issues with her mother and the boyfriend. Sandra read *How to Control Your Anger* (Potter-Efron, 1993) as a homework assignment to learn more about anger management and to complete an anger checklist. The counselor also involved her in several small-group counseling sessions with other teenagers about getting along with parents. When he felt Sandra was ready to apply what she had learned, he encouraged her to invite her mother in so they could work on goals for improved communication.

As part of the evaluation process, the counselor asked Sandra to complete the anger checklist again to compare her current responses with previous ones. Meeting with the mother also became part of the evaluation session: Was there less conflict and tension? If there was conflict, was it resolved in a healthier way? Were they better able to discuss issues? Sandra also had kept a weekly log to monitor progress. After determining that things had improved, the counselor continued to meet with Sandra to address the other issues, gradually decreasing the number of visits. A final "checkup" session for evaluation was held with Sandra and her mother.

Progression through this four-stage implementation model is enhanced by a repertoire of various interventions, as described next.

Types of Interventions

When I (Ann Vernon) wrote the earlier edition to this book, we had recently added another golden retriever puppy to our family. Whereas our previous golden retriever was mellow and required little obedience training, Tawney was more of a challenge. We labeled her behavior "spirited" and used a variety of techniques to help her develop a calmer nature. It did not take us long to realize, however, that what worked with one dog would not necessarily work with another, and if one strategy failed, there was always another one to try. It is much the same with counseling interventions. What works with one client will not necessarily work with another, but there are always new things to try. Similarly, there are no generic multicultural approaches to intervention. For example, African American clients from the inner city versus from a middle-class background may approach the world differently despite the fact that they belong to the same ethnic group; socioeconomic and racial experiences make every client unique. This same principle applies to ethnically diverse clients from different acculturation levels. The point is, interventions must be specifically tailored to the *individual*. In terms of interventions, art, music, and storytelling are universal experiences that are systemic, circular, and collective in nature. Therefore, ethically diverse clients respond most readily to these interventions that acknowledge their way of thinking and interacting with the world.

In the following sections, specific examples of tried-and-true interventions appropriate for use with children and adolescents are described. Although several of these categories already were described in the assessment section, their purpose here is different: The assessment process provides the diagnostic impression, whereas the intervention addresses the problem. As is true with assessment instruments, interventions for a school-age clientele cannot be scaled-down versions of what works with adults. Rather, careful consideration needs to be given to (a) the age, gender, cultural background, and developmental level of the client; (b) the types of interventions that might be most meaningful and appropriate for this particular client; (c) the intervention(s) that will yield the best results and lead to problem resolution; and (d) interventions that the practitioner is competent to administer.

Writing Activities

Writing is used to help individuals develop perspective. When using writing activities, consider whether these are an appropriate intervention for the client. For children who find writing laborious, for children whose first language is not English, or for those who are more auditory or kinesthetic in their learning styles, this may not be the best intervention. The following are examples of writing activities described in relation to a specific problem(s) to clarify the procedure.

Journaling. Journaling, either structured or unstructured, is a form of expressive writing that helps clients reflect on their personal experiences and discover how much growth has taken place (Gladding, 1998). Kincade and Evans (1996) noted that journaling may be particularly appropriate for Asian Americans because culturally, they are often less willing to share feelings or discuss family relationships with a counselor. Journaling provides insight, is a good form of catharsis, and is an especially effective intervention to use with adolescents on such issues as self-awareness, relationships, values clarification, or decision making. Gladding identified several forms of journaling, including the period log, which encouraged clients to reflect on a specific period of their lives; the daily log, which is similar to a diary and is a subjective record of one's experiences; or the dream log, in which clients write about their dreams.

If the journaling is unstructured, the counselor simply invites the young client to record thoughts and feelings that occurred during a given period of time, suggesting that if he or she chooses, elements of the journal may be shared with the counselor. If the journaling is structured, the counselor provides a list of suggestions to guide the writing, as the following example describes:

Marissa, a 16-year-old, was invited to journal about her ambivalent feelings in a relationship. The following suggestions were offered:

When I'm with this person I usually feel _____.
What I like best about this person is _____.
What I like least about this person is_____.
When I think about ending the relationship I feel_____.
What I've learned most from this relationship is _____.

Clarification can come through journaling of this nature and can be followed with more specific interventions that address the concerns.

Stories. Writing personal stories with different endings is an effective way to help clients make a decision when it is difficult to select an alternative. Clients of all ages can participate in this type of intervention, although the counselor most likely will serve as the scribe for younger clients. This strategy was used with Jeremy, a seventh grader who was forbidden by his parents to associate with two of his classmates. For Jeremy, writing the stories with different endings that anticipated consequences helped clarify his decision about whether to obey his parents. Stories can also be used to help clients see situations from other perspectives. For example, Lori was invited to write a story about a conflict with a friend, first from her own perspective, and then from what she thought might be her friend's viewpoint. In so doing, she was able to look at the problem more objectively, which in turn resulted in her being able to calmly discuss the incident with her friend and mend fences.

Poetry. Writing poetry results in increased sensitivity and insight. Whether reading or writing it, poetry is a way to express emotions, healing and identifying aspects of self (Gladding, 1987) and helping children "sift through the layers of their lives in search of their own truths" (Sloan, 2003, p. 35). Some younger children may need poetic stems, such as "I used to . . . but now I . . . ," as well as an illustration to get them started (Gladding, 1987, p. 308), whereas others need less structure. This intervention is especially helpful with adolescents who are depressed. Usually they need no prompting; they have been using poetry as a way to express themselves on their own. In a supportive counseling relationship, the catharsis through poetry is one way to help the client feel better. Recently, a 16-year-old shared in her counseling session a series of poems she had written over the course of a year. Rereading these poems helped her see that even though she was still depressed, her level of hopelessness and pain was much less than it initially had been, which in turn helped her see that she could continue to get better.

Limericks. Limericks, a form of poetry written with precise rhythm (Sloan, 2003), can be a fun and engaging way for clients to think "outside the box" and discover their own ways to solve problems. In writing limericks, the first and second lines rhyme, the third and fourth lines rhyme, and the last line rhymes with the first. The following limerick was written by a young client, with help from his counselor, about how to handle teasing:

> You can throw your sticks and stones
> But they will not break my bones.
> What you say is not okay
> And you are wrong in every way
> So stay away and don't invade my zones.

The client can post the limerick inside a locker or desk top to serve as a visual reminder about how to handle classmates' teasing.

Letters. Writing letters can be very cathartic and therapeutic. Letter writing is especially effective for helping children deal with loss, such as loss of a friendship or romantic relationship, loss connected with transitions such as moving or graduation, or loss associated with a disability or disease. An adolescent recently shared a letter she had written to her Cron's disease, in which she expressed anger about the pain, the way the disease made her feel different from her peers, and how it could affect her future. This intervention was therapeutic for the client, but because she chose to share it with her parents, it was an excellent way for them to gain insight into how she was feeling about her illness. Writing letters is also very therapeutic for children dealing with the death of a loved one. Orton (1997) suggested that children write letters describing both happy and sad memories about the deceased. When clients are willing to share their letters, the practitioner not only can validate the feelings but can also help the client identify effective coping strategies.

Autobiographies. Because the purpose of an autobiography is to reflect on one's life, this intervention is more limited and perhaps most appropriate for high school juniors or seniors. According to Gibson and Mitchell (1990), writing an autobiography "lets a person express what has been important in his or her life, emphasize likes and dislikes, identify values, describe interests and aspirations, acknowledge success and failures, and recall meaningful relationships" (p. 278). Through writing an autobiography, clients can clarify concerns and develop insight about how to address them.

Autobiographies generally are written one of two ways: describing a particular segment or aspect of one's life, such as school, family, or relationships; or writing a chronicle that covers all of one's life history (Bradley, Gould, & Hendricks, 2004). Once the client provides the written material, the counselor helps the client clarify the issues by asking questions, probing for feelings, confronting discrepancies in the writing, identifying specific concerns, and setting goals for change (Vernon, 2001).

This intervention was used with a high school senior who needed to, in his words, "pull together the pieces so that I know where I'm going." A life-line activity that directs the client to identify specific major events using symbols or words for each year (or specific years) of life also can be incorporated into the autobiography and often facilitates the writing process.

Advice Column. Children, and adolescents in particular, are always offering advice to their peers. An effective intervention is to have the client write a short synopsis of a problem he or she has, as in a "Dear Abby" column. Then invite the client to reply, offering advice about what to do about the problem. It is interesting to see how easily an individual can generate possible solutions when it seems like he or she is giving advice to someone else.

Therapeutic Fairy Tale. Gladding (2005) described the therapeutic fairy tale as a means to help adolescents deal with problematic issues. Clients are asked to imagine a scene that is far away from the present in both time and space, to include a problem in the setting, and to identify a positive solution to the problem. They are given 6–10 minutes to write the story, beginning it with the standard fairy tale opening, "Once upon a time." Clients can learn about themselves by looking at the qualities of the characters, what contributed to the solution, and how the story was created.

Activity Sheets

Activity sheets can be used with children of all ages, but the counselor is advised not to overuse them because they tend to not engage clients as effectively as some of the more creative interventions. Nevertheless, depending on how they are introduced and processed, they can be very effective. Colorful graphics enhance the appeal and can help break up the format so it is more inviting. Activity sheets are generally used as part of an intervention introduced by a counselor, and it is very important to process the activity sheet with the client to clarify concepts and reinforce learnings. Some examples follow.

D Is for Decision (Vernon, 1998b, pp. 73–74). This activity sheet helps young adolescents learn more about the decision-making process.

A difficult decision for me was _____

In making this decision, I:

Discussed it with friends	Yes	No	To some extent
Discussed it with a parent	Yes	No	To some extent
Discussed it with a teacher	Yes	No	To some extent
Considered the risks	Yes	No	To some extent

Thought about it a long time	Yes	No	To some extent
Considered the consequences	Yes	No	To some extent
Worried about it	Yes	No	To some extent
Felt good about the decision	Yes	No	To some extent
Would make the same decision again	Yes	No	To some extent

The thing I think is most important in making a decision is _____
For me, the hardest decisions are/will be about _____
For me, the easiest decisions will be about _____
The most challenging thing about making a decision is_____
Advice I'd give others my age about making decisions is _____

Gain With Goals (Vernon, 1998c, p. 135). This activity sheet helps high school students learn more about goals setting. Clients need to circle R for realistic goals, U for unrealistic goals, ST for short-term goals, and LT for long-term goals.

R	U	Getting ready to go jogging the first time, you set your goal for 3 miles.
R	U	You got 75 out of 100 points on your last Spanish test. Your goal for the next test is to get 80 out of 100 points.
R	U	You are a sophomore in high school, taking your first drama course. Your goal is to become a famous actress by the time you are 20.
R	U	Your goal is to buy a car by the time you turn 16 next month. So far you have saved $100.
R	U	Your goal is to go out with three girls before the end of the school year. It is March, and you have gone out with two so far.
ST	LT	Your goal is to move up from second-chair to first-chair saxophone in the high school band.
ST	LT	Your goal is to be rich.
ST	LT	Your goal is to own a car that runs.
ST	LT	Your goal is to get married and live in the suburbs.
ST	LT	Your goal is to pass algebra.

Therapeutic Games

It goes without saying that games are appealing to children in particular, but they are also appealing to adolescents depending on the specific activity. Because they are nonthreatening, enjoyable, and make children feel comfortable (Bromfield, 1999), games are also very effective with resistant or verbally deficient children. According to Bradley et al. (2004), games can be used to teach new behaviors, facilitate problem solving, and encourage verbalization, as well as help children gain a sense of mastery. Kottman (2001) suggested that games help children enhance their communication and social skills, as well as learn rules. Games are useful in addressing specific topics (Schaefer & Reid, 2000) and can facilitate the counseling process.

We prefer to develop our own games or to use commercially produced materials that relate specifically to the problem areas being addressed, as opposed to more generic games that may target communication skills or self-awareness, for example, but are not appropriate when the client needs to work on behavior management. Shapiro (1996) stressed the importance of developing the game according to its intended purpose. For example, a self-esteem game should include questions that facilitate client self-disclosure and personal successes, and a social skills game might involve role playing to help children practice communication skills. In designing games, it is important that the content and wording of questions matches the client's developmental level and that they are visually appealing (Wagner, 2003). Bilingual games or games in the target language should be considered for culturally diverse clients. Several original games (developed by Vernon) are described first, followed by a selected list of games that can be purchased to address various typical issues. The games are designed for use in individual counseling but can be easily adapted for small-group work.

Fact or Belief? Students of all ages readily confuse facts with beliefs (assumptions) about a given situation, so this game can be used with most school-age children if the examples are age appropriate. Unless children learn to distinguish between facts and beliefs, they frequently distort the reality of the situation, which may have negative ramifications. To develop this game, draw a "tic-tac-toe" configuration on a sheet of tagboard. Next, on strips of paper, develop samples of facts and beliefs/assumptions appropriate to the problem and the age and culture of the child with whom you are working. Examples for a fourth grader who routinely gets caught up in friendship misunderstandings might include: Tanya is in my class; Tanya doesn't like me; if LaTiesha sits by someone else, it means she hates me; there are nine girls in my section; everyone except me got invited to the birthday party, and so on. Examples for an eighth grader about school performance could include: I got a bad grade on this test, so I will probably fail this class; the teacher didn't call on me, so he must think I am stupid; not matter how hard I try, I won't do well on the assignment. The game is played like tic-tac-toe; the client can be X and you can be O; each time either of you makes a mark, draw a strip and identify it as a fact or belief. Discussion follows, with the client coming up with his or her own examples and identifying how to check out assumptions as a way to clarify friendship issues.

Options. Designed to help with decision making, this game can be adapted for elementary and middle school students. Materials include a set of cards that contains decision-making dilemmas. Examples include: (a) You are at the shopping center with your friend. You see her take a pair of earrings from the rack and put them in her pocket. What do you do? (b) Your parents are gone for the evening. One of your friends comes over, and instead of getting a can of soda out of the refrigerator, he takes a beer. What do you do? (c) During the spelling test, one of your classmates looks over your shoulder and copies your work. What do you do? (d) Your parents grounded you for the week, but one of your friends encourages you to sneak out through the window after they are in bed. What do you do?

In addition to the cards, you need a tagboard "wheel" that lists a wide variety of options, such as (a) confront your friend, (b) do what they do to fit in, (c) don't do anything, (d) do what you think is right. The wheel has a spinner attached. After the client has read the situation on a card picked from the stack, he or she spins the dial to the option that seems best and tells how he or she arrived at that decision.

Move It! A variation of the commercially produced game *Twister* (from Milton-Bradley), this is popular with elementary students who need to work on social skills. You need a large plastic tablecloth. Use a magic marker to section off 12 squares, and color them different colors. Next, make a set of instruction cards with situations such as the following: (a) Your best friend makes fun of what you are wearing. What do you think, feel, and do? (Move on the board: right hand blue, left foot yellow); (b) The boy sitting behind you is spreading untrue rumors about you. What do you think, feel, and do? (Move: left hand green, right knee orange); (c) One of your classmates teases you about what you are wearing. What do you think, feel, and do? (Move: left foot red, right elbow purple); (d) Someone pushes you in line. What do you think, feel, and do? (Move: right foot green, left hand orange). This is a fun way to elicit discussion and problem solve about typical developmental situations. Cards can be tailored for a specific child's problem.

Fish for Feelings. This is a good game to use with 4-, 5-, and 6-year-olds to help develop awareness and expression of feelings. You need a set of tagboard fish labeled with feelings such as mad, sad, happy, scared, or worried. Each fish should have a hole in the nose. You also need a fishing pole (a short stick with a string attached to the end and a paper clip tied to the string). Lay the fish on the floor. As the child snags one, read the feeling word attached to the paper clip and ask the child to describe a situation in which he or she felt that way. Also focus discussion on how the child expresses the feeling and how to constructively handle negative feelings. A note of caution: Acknowledging and expressing feelings may not only be a difficult challenge for some ethnically diverse youth but may also be embarrassing for them if they are unable to do this. For instance, in some Asian, African, and Middle Eastern groups, the acknowledgment of feelings is viewed as a sign of weakness; therefore, feelings are typically ignored or repressed.

Adios Anger. This is a game that targets anger and is played like hopscotch. It is appropriate for elementary students or possibly some middle schoolers, depending on developmental level. For this game, you will need a plastic table cloth or an old sheet with a hopscotch board drawn on it. Prior to playing the game, have the client make a list of all the things he or she has been angry about in recent weeks, identifying specific thoughts he or she had about the anger-provoking incident. Ask the client to give you the list, and you read the first anger-provoking incident out loud. Invite the client to describe something he or she could have done to reduce the anger and hop to the first square. Read the second item on the list and, once again, have the client think of something he or she could have done to eliminate or reduce the anger and hop to the next row on the hop scotch board, and so on. This game can also be used for anxiety.

The Road to Achievement. This game addresses underachievement in a concrete manner and is therefore effective with elementary students. You will need a small toy car and a "road" that can be made by drawing a line marked off into individual spaces across a sheet of tagboard. You will also need to make a set of cards with topics such as the following: the assignment looks hard, so you just give up; the assignment is boring, so you watch television instead; you study hard for tests; you write sloppily and don't proofread; you ask for help if you don't understand something; you stuff all your papers in the same folder; you do all your homework each day. To play the game, the client takes the car, draws a card, and decides if the behavior written on the card is a good study skill. If it is, the client moves one space along the Road to Achievement. If it is not a good skill, he or she moves back one space. The game continues in this way, with discussion focusing on the difference between good and bad study skills, which ones the client uses most often, and which behaviors he or she would like to change or maintain.

Behavior Toss. For this simple but engaging game that addresses behavior management, you will need a rubber ring, a blindfold, and three inexpensive plastic tablecloths: red, yellow, and green, cut into 2 feet × 2 feet squares. Place these colored squares randomly around the room, leaving a space in the center for the client to stand. Explain how the game is played: blindfolded, the client tosses the ring. If it lands on, or closest to, a red square, he or she has to identify a negative behavior that has gotten him or her in trouble at home, with peers, or in the classroom. If it lands on a yellow square, he or she describes a behavior that sometimes is troublesome and sometimes is not. If it lands on or near a green square, the client identifies a positive behavior that helps him or her get along well with others at home, with peers, or at school. This game can also be adapted to use with clients who need to eat more sensibly. Red can represent foods they should not eat, yellow can represent foods that are appropriate in moderation, and green can be "go foods—those that are good for you."

Flip for Feelings. Designed for use with elementary-age children, this game helps them distinguish between positive and negative feelings and sensitizes them to how others might be feeling, which helps develop social perspective taking. You will need a coin, two potato chip cans, one labeled "heads" and the other labeled "tails." Inside each can, place feeling strips such as the following: (a) Your teacher calls on you and you don't know the answer. How do you feel? (b) Your mother lost her job. How do you think she feels? (c) You studied hard for a test and got a perfect score. How do you feel? (d) Your brother tried out for the high school play but didn't get the part he wanted. How do you think he feels? (e) You don't get invited to a party but most of your good friends did. How do you feel? To play the game, you and the client take turns flipping the coin, selecting a feeling strip from the appropriate can, depending on the coin flip, and identifying one or more feelings. Discussion about good ways to handle negative feelings can also be a focus of this game.

✳

Selected examples of commercially produced games include the following, available from Childswork/Childsplay (2003; www.childswork.com):

- *Stop, Relax, and Think.* This game, for children ages 6–12, is designed to teach impulsive children self-control. By moving a marker to four areas on the board, children learn to verbalize feelings, relax, and then problem solve to move ahead.
- *The Crisis Intervention Game.* This game is designed to help children ages 6–12 explore feelings, identify and understand normal reactions to crisis situations, and learn to focus on good things in their life.
- *The Good Behavior Game.* This game is recommended for 4- to 10-year-olds and teaches them the importance of good behavior as well as recognizing the consequences of their behavioral choices.

The following games are available from the Self-Esteem Shop (2003; www.selfesteem.com):

- *Bully Busters.* Players learn to identify goals of bullies and ways to thwart them. They also learn how to take a stand against bullies and practice communication skills. This game is suitable for children in Grades 5–8.
- *Breaking the Chains of Anger.* This game, suitable for young adolescents ages 10–14, teaches them how to control anger and identify potential causes and consequences of anger.
- *Family Happenings.* This game is appropriate for children of all ages and addresses divorce, birth, abuse, relocation, and school issues.

✳

Literature

Bibliotherapy, the use of literature as a therapeutic counseling process, can help children understand and cope with developmental as well as situational conflicts. According to J. T. Pardeck and Pardeck (1993), it also helps children explore personally relevant thoughts and feelings. These authors noted that "good fiction can provide clients with models to help them deal with presenting problems" (p. 1). Bibliotherapy has been used successfully for a wide variety of problems, such as divorce, promoting self-development, career awareness, and behavior change (Gladding & Gladding, 1991), parental alcoholism and death (Krickeberg, 1991), enhancing interpersonal relationships (J. T. Pardeck & Pardeck, 1993), as well as for abuse and neglect, adoption, illness, and coping with disabilities (Orton, 1997). It can be used with individual clients, as well as in a classroom setting or with small groups. Furthermore, it can be used for prevention as well as for remediation; literature selections can reflect typical developmental concerns and can be used with children who do not present major issues or be applied more therapeutically with individuals who have varying degrees of emotional or behavioral problems, as well as to those who have specific situational concerns such as being in a blended family or dealing with a chronic illness.

Fiction, nonfiction, poetry, self-help books, autobiographies, or fairy tales are examples of the types of literature used for bibliotherapy. Gladding and Gladding (1991) identified two types of bibliotherapy: reactive and interactive. In the reactive format, the client is asked to read certain pieces of literature. It is assumed that, through character identification, the client can release emotions and gain new insights and ways to behave. The interactive model stresses guided discussion that occurs between the counselor and client concerning the literature, in an effort to help integrate the client's thoughts and feelings in response to the material.

For bibliotherapy to be effective, the counselor must have knowledge of appropriate literature. Materials cannot be too simple or too difficult. They should reflect the client's culture, gender, and age for identification to occur. The counselor needs to have a good relationship with the client and know the child well to match the book to the child. According to Orton (1997), a good match will "help the child experience identification, catharsis, and insight. These experiences are necessary for problem resolution, growth, and change" (p. 303). J. T. Pardeck and Pardeck (1993) emphasized the importance of discussion and other counseling techniques such as art, music, writing a diary from a character's point of view, or role playing (J. A. Pardeck, 1995) in conjunction with the reading of a book to promote self-examination, insight, and problem-solving skills.

An especially effective form of literature is to have clients read true stories, essays, or poems that have been written by others their own age. Based on experience, clients readily identify with this type of literature. Ethnically diverse clients are particularly empowered by reading success stories of children and adolescents who experienced difficult situations and succeeded. And, because these stories are based on a culturally sensitive context, clients can easily relate to them.

Examples written by adolescents about depression, anger, anorexia, issues with parents, and relationship breakup can be found in *The Passport Program* (Vernon, 1998b, 1998c). For further information on appropriate selection of materials, consult *Bibliotherapy for Children Catalog (K–5)*, *Working With Pre-Teens Catalog (6–8)*, or *Working With Teens (9–12)*, all published by Paperbacks for Educators, (www.any-book-in-print.com), the Self-Esteem Shop's *Playtime* catalog (www.selfesteemshop.com), or the Children's Literature Comprehensive Database (www.childrenslit.com).

Activity-Based Interventions

For lack of a better term, activity-based interventions describes a category of strategies that are designed to help children and adolescents deal with an aspect of a problem concretely. With this approach, the client performs an activity that provides insight or clarification or is a behavioral intervention that teaches mastery. The following examples are a few of the activities that I (Ann Vernon) developed.

Interviews. The interview is a strategy that enables the child or adolescent to obtain information to expand his or her understanding of an issue. It can be used to help the client "normalize" the problem as well as be used rather paradoxically. For example, adolescents are prone to believe that their parents are the strictest, most old-fashioned, and stingiest of any they know. This viewpoint often creates a barrier between adolescents and their parents. By inviting the client to develop interview questions and "check out" other parents, he or she often comes to the realization that things are not as bad as they seem. The key is to work with the client to develop the questions in the session. Whether the adolescent actually does the interview is immaterial; the intervention has served its purpose by providing the youth with another perspective, as the following situation illustrates.

Fourteen-year-old Nicole was convinced that her parents were the worst of all. Having met with her parents on several occasions, the counselor did not find this to be the case. However, rather than jeopardize the relationship with Nicole by "taking sides," the counselor acknowledged Nicole's feelings and suggested that perhaps if she interviewed other parents she would have some concrete data to share with her folks in the hopes that they would change. Nicole did not think she should have to do any chores around the house or that she should have such an early curfew, among other things.

Nicole and the counselor developed several questions to ask her friends' parents: Does your son or daughter have to do any household chores? If so, what do they have to do? Do they get paid to do them? Are they grounded if they do not? Does your son or daughter have to be home at a certain time? What time? What happens if they are not? Nicole interviewed parents and found to her amazement her situation was not all that bad.

Other ideas include having children with disabilities interview others who have had to learn to cope with a disabling condition, interviewing parents or grandparents about fears they had when they were young and what they did to overcome them, and interviewing students who graduated the previous year to learn more about how they coped with the opportunities and challenges associated with this significant transition.

Tape-Recorded Activities. This is an intervention best used with younger clients who still enjoy pretending. To help teach independent problem resolution, the counselor invites the child to first imagine that he or she is the child with the problem, and then to imagine being the counselor who is helping the child find a solution. This worked successfully with 6-year-old Leslie, who first pretended to be herself, explaining that she was worried about not doing well in school. She then switched roles and, as the counselor, asked if she was dumb, if she had not gotten good grades last year, and if she could ask for help if she needed it. Although this is similar to role playing, the advantage is that the tape can be replayed and the learning can be discussed and reinforced more readily. Taping regular counseling sessions and giving the tape to the client to listen to during the week also is a good way to review concepts.

Using the Media. Media can be incorporated readily into activity-based interventions. For example, middle school and high school clients can monitor television shows to look for such things as (a) positive versus negative expressions of feelings, (b) consequences of decisions, (c) aggressive versus assertive behavior/communication styles, or (d) rational and irrational patterns of thinking and behaving. In this way, television can be used positively to expand a client's level of understanding, which in turn can be followed by the teaching of skills.

The newspaper can be used in a similar manner. Adolescents can be invited to cut out newspaper articles about problem events. They can bring the articles to the counseling session and engage in a rank-order activity, placing their particular problem in perspective along with the problems depicted in the newspaper articles. This helps those clients who seem to perseverate on the "awfulness" of their problems and do not seem to want to do anything to change.

Find Someone Who . . . This simple intervention is especially good for clients who lack social skills. Oftentimes these individuals do not know how to initiate conversations, make eye contact, express opinions, or show interest in what someone else is saying, for example. However, they often are aware of who is able to do this. Directions for this intervention include asking the client to find someone who demonstrates one or more of these skills well, to observe the individual(s), and to take notes after the observation about what he or she learned. The next step is for the client to try and imitate a skill to help improve his or her social functioning.

Art Activities

A distinction is made between using art techniques in counseling as opposed to pure art therapy, which focuses much more on artistic eloquence as opposed to creating art and looking at the symbolism (Kramer, 1998). Art activities can be used in a developmental, preventive, and remedial context (Orton, 1997), and they can engage clients in a process that helps them clarify and rectify problems. As part of the intervention process, Brems (2002) suggested that art can be used for catharsis (free expression of feelings and needs, expression and recreation of past and current events, and release and mastery of feelings and conflicts) as well as for growth (exploration of problem-solving alternatives, skill development, increased self-esteem, and increased goal-directedness).

Orton (1997) described developmental stages in art expression. Scribbling begins at about age 2, which is followed by making patterns, shapes, and designs. At about age 4 or 5, children begin making pictures that at first are simple figures that may have distortions or omissions, but by age 6 and 7, their pictures are more refined and recognizable. Between the ages of 7 and 9, drawings reflect the child's psychological growth; their human figures are more complete and they include landscapes in their drawings. From ages 9 to 11, children can draw in two dimensions, with greater emphasis on detail. Children between the ages of 11 and 13 draw humans in greater detail and can capture body movement, as well as draw in two and three dimensions.

Of course, counselors are not restricted to using drawing and painting with clients. Other forms of art media are also appealing, including clay and play dough; finger painting; and making masks, puppets, collages, cards, or books that combine illustrations with writing. Listed below are a selected few art activities that have been found to be effective and are original (developed by Vernon) unless noted.

Masks. For young children who are afraid of the dark or monsters, having them make a scary mask to hang on the bedroom door or window has proved successful. As they create the mask, they can discuss their scary feelings with the counselor. Completing the activity can result in a feeling of power; they are in control of the situation.

Body Outlines. The body outline can be used in a variety of ways: to facilitate self-awareness, to expand one's view of self to represent more global characteristics, or to help identify a variety of strengths and weaknesses to develop a realistic self-concept. The body outline is made by tracing the individual's body on paper. The way the outline is used depends on the purpose and the child's age level. For instance, the client can be invited to label and color in body parts or to draw arrows and identify strengths or weaknesses represented by various body parts, or in a group setting, the outlines can be used to illustrate how children come in "all different shapes and sizes."

Cartoons. Cartooning is used effectively to help identify possible solutions to conflict situations (Gladding, 1995). Once the problem is identified, the young client can draw a cartoon strip or fill in ballooned parts of cartoon scenarios to illustrate various solutions. This technique also can be used as a means of catharsis and expression of feelings, in which the cartoon figures simply represent the dilemma the child or adolescent is facing.

Graphics. Graphics—stick figures, lines, sketches, or marks—can be useful in the intervention process, both for the client and for the counselor. For the client, graphics help them "see" the components or the factors that block their effective functioning. For the counselor, graphics offer another way to communicate with the client when words may be insufficient to explain a concept. Graphics can be used to illustrate complex relationships, generate alternatives, teach responsibility, and set goals (Nelson, 1987).

Family Drawing. While having children draw a picture of their family is an excellent assessment tool, a family drawing can also be used as an intervention, with some modification. If a client has expressed difficulty with family relationships, he or she can first draw a picture of the family, including all members. After discussing factors such as where the members are in relation to each other, who appears to have the most and least power, and any feelings each person might be expressing, the client can then draw a picture of how he or she would like this family to look. Follow-up discussion can focus on what would need to change, what changes the client has control over, and what is realistic, with the counselor helping the client develop skills to bring about these changes or cope more effectively with the existing situation. These questions are more suitable for older children and adolescents but can be modified for use with younger clients.

Paper Dolls. Young children readily engage in this intervention that involves making paper dolls to represent peers or family members. As they are making the dolls, the counselor and client can converse about a specific problem the youngster experienced recently. Then, using the paper dolls, the client can engage the dolls in a dialogue that is geared toward resolving the problem.

Art Artifacts. Art artifacts is a term that refers to involving the client in making something tangible to serve as a reminder to practice new behaviors or learn a new skill. For example, an angry client can make an anger alarm out of cardboard, and instead of putting numbers on the clock face, he or she writes things that trigger anger. Then, on the back side of the clock, the client can draw a symbol that represents setting the alarm, indicating that it is time to let go of the anger. Around this side of the clock face the client should write reminders about how to do this.

Another example to help clients deal with teasing is to have the client make a radio using a card board box. Instruct the client to make a dial and attach it to the box. Then ask the client to identify several ways to deal with the teasing and write them on the sides of the radio. The next time someone teases him or her, he or she can think about the box and "change the channel" to tune out the teasing.

This Is My Bag. This art intervention is helpful for adolescents who are struggling to learn more about themselves, a key developmental task at this age. For this intervention, you will need a lunch-size paper bag, magazines, scissors, glue, and a marker. Invite the client to find pictures or words that describe how he or she appears to others (the "outside self") and glue these on the outside of the bag. Then instruct him or her to find words or pictures that symbolize the inner self—the self that others may not see—and place these inside the bag. Discuss with the client what he or she learned and invite sharing of any or part of the bag.

Music

"Music is more than just a medium of entertainment. It is a powerful tool that can capture attention, elicit long forgotten memories, communicate feelings, create and intensify moods, and bring people together" (Bowman, 1987, p. 284). Music is a form of communication that promotes positive mental health (Gladding, 1995), helps clients become "more aware, able, confident, and social" (Gladding, 1998, p. 17), and helps nonverbal clients express themselves (Newcomb, 1994). Because music is a universal, multicultural experience (Gladding, 1998), the applications are numerous. As Bowman reported, music can be used with children and adolescents to reduce anxiety, raise self-esteem, motivate slow learners, reduce disruptive behavior, and promote future planning. Furthermore, it can be used to bring about changes in children who are developmentally delayed (Aldridge, Gustorff, & Neugebauer, 1995), and it is very effective with traumatized children because it is self-affirming and relaxing (Mayers, 1995).

According to Gladding (2005), the effectiveness of this intervention depends on the client's involvement with music. In other words, if a youngster is passionate about music and readily identifies with a certain type or artist, the greater the likelihood that he or she will be assisted by this intervention. Gladding (1998) also distinguished between music therapy, which is more direct and implemented by music therapists who are specialists in music and human behavior, and using music in counseling, which may be done in individual, small group, or classroom guidance and involves listening and improvising, as well as performing and composing. Six musical activities are described.

Self-Composed Music. Inviting young clients to compose lyrics/musical accompaniment to depict their own issue(s) is a powerful intervention. Through this medium they learn to express feelings, gain insight about problems, and identify ways to resolve dilemmas. Encouraging the child or adolescent to share his or her creation allows for a more direct discussion and clarification of issues.

Music/Mood Collages. Music is popular with children, and adolescents in particular. Because many of them listen to the radio or compact discs for hours, they are very familiar with a variety of songs and learn to identify with specific songs in relation to a given mood or feeling. One activity that has proved helpful is to have clients make a tape of several of their favorite songs for a definite purpose: to relax, to feel happy, to be reflective, to be carefree, or to feel hopeful. They can play these taped selections when they want to experience that mood.

Silly Songs. Composing their own silly songs (Vernon, 2002, p. 129) is a good way to help elementary and middle school children deal with sad or depressed feelings, as well as giving them a concrete way to remember important concepts. For this activity, the client will need a sheet of paper and a pencil. Instruct the client to pick out a favorite childhood tune and change the words so that they convey a message about how to deal with sad or depressing feelings. For example, this is a song to the tune of *Three Blind Mice*:

> Three sad kids,
> Three sad kids,
> See how they cry,
> See how they cry,
> They all got tired of crying so much,
> They ran around and made faces and such,
> You've never seen these kids laughing so much,
> The three happy kids, the three happy kids.

Take a Sad Song and Make It Better. This intervention is especially appropriate for adolescents who often listen to sad music when they are depressed, which only exacerbates the depression. When a client describes the music he or she listens to, invite him or her to write the lyrics to some of these songs and highlight the irrational concepts and depressing themes (Vernon, 2002, p. 135). Discuss these and then suggest that he or she rewrites the lyrics, using more rational and less depressing words.

Song Lyrics (Line Savers). The lyrics of some songs are meaningful and can provide direction for clients. In using this intervention (adapted from Gladding, 1995), invite clients to find examples of songs that are inspirational or provide powerful, positive suggestions about how to overcome difficult experiences. If the client writes out the lyrics and selects specific lines that are particularly significant, he or she can refer to these messages for support in overcoming his or her own difficulties.

Mad Music. Music can also be used effectively to help clients deal with anger. Invite an angry client to make a list of words that he or she associates with anger. Then invite him or her to make mad music, using drums, empty waste cans, brooms, or other concrete items, to help express the angry associated with the words on the list. Finding musical selections that reflect these words is another alternative.

Drama

Gladding (1998) referred to the relationship between drama and life, noting that "healthy people . . . are able to change their behaviors in response to environmental demands. They are open and flexible and communicate in a congruent manner. Sometimes they become 'stuck' and 'dysfunctional' too, but in these cases they seek assistance" (p. 102). Gladding noted that, through drama, individuals can get "unstuck," gaining greater understanding of their roles and a clearer perspective on life.

Drama is especially appropriate for children and adolescents, who by their very nature love to pretend or be dramatic. As an intervention, drama allows young clients to assume different roles, try out new behaviors, rehearse new skills, clarify and express feelings, problem solve, and gain insight into themselves. Drama also encourages social interaction, creativity, and spontaneity (Edwards & Springate, 1995).

Gladding (1998) noted that using drama in counseling can be powerful, but counselors should make sure that the clients feel connected with this approach and that they can benefit from it. Gladding also stressed that counselors should be sensitive to developmental levels of their clients so that the drama activity will have maximum impact.

Examples of dramatic activities to use with children and adolescents include the following.

Video Drama. Although this cannot be done in an individual counseling setting, adolescents who have access to video cameras can be invited to make a video with a group of friends. A short play based on an issue relevant to their age group or a series of skits depicting ways to solve problems are examples of video productions. Gladding (2005) cited several advantages of video therapy: Adolescents receive feedback about their behavior, they learn more about who they are through objective self-observations, they feel in control by operating equipment, and they are less resistant to adults because they focus on the equipment.

Another version involving the use of video is to use children as their own models of appropriate behavior. To implement this intervention, you would videotape the child during a given period of time, select incidents of positive behavior, then rerecord these as an edited version and show them to the client so that he or she sees his or her own examples of positive behaviors, which in itself can be reinforcing (Wagner, 2003).

Role Playing. Equally effective as an assessment strategy, role playing allows children to rehearse skills, learn new behaviors, act out events in their lives metaphorically (Kottman, 2001), view situations from multiple perspectives, gain confidence, and express feelings. It can "help children learn about cause and effect and experience the consequences of their behavior in a relatively safe setting" (Thompson, Rudolph, & Henderson, 2004, p. 248). Thompson and colleagues also pointed out that role playing helps children develop empathy and modify their egocentric view of the world, and that negative role playing helps children identify what not to do.

To structure the role play, the counselor can invite the client to play his or her own part while the counselor plays the part of the significant other person. It is best to use a very specific situation. Seventeen-year-old Robert used the role-play technique to practice telling his father that he had been fired from his job. The first time he delivered the message, the counselor noted that he seemed defensive, which could invite an argument. They discussed ways to modify the message so his father might react more calmly. After more practice, Robert felt more competent and comfortable and later reported that he was able tell his father that he had been fired without his father getting angry.

Empty-Chair Dialogue. A variation of the role play is the gestalt empty-chair technique (Gladding, 2005), which is excellent for dealing with guilt, indecision, anger, and other disturbing emotions. The client sits in one chair and has a dialogue with the empty chair about an issue (Gladding, 2005). When he or she feels like it, or as suggested by the counselor, the child shifts to the other chair and "talks back" to the first chair. A variation of this for younger children is to carry on a dialogue with a stuffed animal in the opposite chair.

Role Reversal. Another variation of the role play is role reversal, which can be effective when there is a communication breakdown or interpersonal conflict (Thompson et al., 2004). To structure this intervention, have the client play the role of the significant other such as a teacher, parent, or peer while the counselor assumes the client's role. An advantage of the role reversal is that the client often gains insight and perspective about the significant other, which in turn facilitates problem solving and communication.

Play

Play is a universal experience that children of all cultures enjoy. It is the natural language of young children, according to Kottman (2003, 2004), which is why Thompson and Rudolph (2000) stressed play therapy as an essential method for counseling children 12 years of age and younger. Through play, children are able to act out confusing or conflicting situations and learn to know and accept themselves, as well as express thoughts and feelings, hopes and fears, likes and dislikes (Orton, 1997). Kottman indicated that children develop self-efficacy and competence through play, as well as learn how to solve problems and make decisions. As Landreth (1991) noted, "Toys are children's words and play is their language" (p. 116). For this reason, play is an exceptionally appropriate intervention for children, although the information they give us through play has to be interpreted in light of their current life situation and their developmental status (Garbarino & Stott, 1992).

Although play therapy "has its roots in the traditional psychoanalytic model" (Orton, 1997, p. 221), more recent trends include the application of play to other theoretical orientations. O'Connor (1991) noted that many play therapists now integrate theories and techniques, which allows them to use a variety of techniques that have broad application across several theoretical orientations. Kottman (2004) identified four theoretical approaches to play therapy, including child-centered play therapy, which is nondirective; Adlerian and cognitive–behavioral approaches, which combine directive and nondirective elements; and Theraplay, which is directive. According to Kottman, the main role of the counselor in child-centered play therapy is to communicate acceptance and belief in the child; this activates the child's ability to solve problems. In Adlerian play therapy, the counselor gains an understanding of the child's lifestyle and how the child sees him- or herself, others, and the world. Through a variety of techniques, the counselor helps the client develop insight into his or her lifestyle and then reeducates the client, which helps him or her learn new skills. Cognitive–behavioral play therapy is problem focused, and the counselor helps the child develop more effective problem-solving strategies and adaptive thoughts and behaviors by combining cognitive and behavioral strategies with play activities. Theraplay is directive, intensive, and brief. Parents and children both are involved in the sessions, with one counselor working with the child and another with the parents. As the parents observe the child playing, the counselor assigned to the parents interprets what is happening between the counselor and the child and shares with the parents how they can use these techniques in their interactions with the child. During the last part of the session the parents are invited to practice the Theraplay dimensions with the child while the counselors supervise.

Materials for play therapy should be selected to facilitate expression of a wide range of feelings and thoughts (Orton, 1997), aid in developing insight, and provide opportunities for reality testing. Landreth (1991) suggested that the toys and play materials capture the interest of the child and encourage mastery. Kottman (2001) identified five categories of play materials: (a) family/nurturing toys, such as dolls, doll houses and furniture, play dishes, baby clothes and bottles, and people puppets to help children explore family relationships; (b) scary toys, such as plastic snakes, rats, monsters, and insects to help children express their fears and learn to deal with them; (c) aggressive toys such as play guns, toy soldiers, rubber knives, bop bags, handcuffs, a foam bat, or a pounding bench to encourage expression of anger or explore need for control; (d) expressive toys for creative expression and mastery, such as crayons, clay, paints, newsprint, and pipe cleaners; and (e) pretend/fantasy toys that encourage expression of feeling and help children explore roles and experiment with different behaviors and attitudes. Toys in this category could include costumes, jewelry, hats, block, trucks, purses, telephones, and other items that would help children act out real-life situations and relationships. Although equipping a playroom can be expensive, puppets, dolls, games, and play dough can be handmade, and suitable toys can often be found at garage sales. Parents may also be willing to donate items.

Play therapy has been applied successfully to a variety of problems, including nighttime fears (Knell, 2000), encopresis (Knell & Moore, 1990), attention-deficit hyperactivity disorder (Reddy, Spencer, Hall & Rubel, 2001), and aggressive, acting-out behavior (Fischetti, 2001). According to Kottman and Johnson (1993), many elementary counselors routinely use play techniques as an integral part of their counseling. Play therapy is one of the few therapeutic interventions specifically developed for children, and Wagner (2003) stressed that regardless of theoretical orientation, all counselors should be able to incorporate play into their work with children. As Wagner noted, "play . . . offers young clients a developmentally appropriate medium for the expression of clinically relevant thoughts and feelings" (p. 128).

While practitioners working with youngsters are encouraged to use play techniques such as art, puppets, dolls, games, and other media, this is different from using play therapy, which necessitates further study and training. For a more thorough coverage of play therapy, the reader is encouraged to read *Play Therapy: Basics and Beyond* (Kottman, 2001), *The Play Therapy Primer* (O'Connor, 2000), or *Handbook of Play Therapy: Vol. 2. Advances and Innovations* (O'Connor & Schaefer, 1993).

Puppets

Puppetry is a recommended technique with children and adolescents, because it provides a safe, comfortable way for children to share feelings (Bromfield, 1999). According to Brems (2002), puppets are excellent because they not only allow clients the opportunity to express needs but also facilitate opportunities for problem solving and skill development "without the child ever having to own directly any of the material that is being expressed" (p. 15). Orton (1997) posited that "puppetry enables children to tell stories rich in symbolism and to 'play out' their fantasies" (p. 230). James and Myer (1987) shared a variety of ways in which puppets have been used: (a) to establish trust and acquaint children to the counselor's role; (b) to teach positive attitudes about tasks; (c) to help children understand and express feelings about a traumatic event; (d) to act out relationship problems; and (e) to enhance their ability to express feelings, particularly anger and hostility.

Puppets can be selected to represent different personality types, such as the mischievous child, the perfect kid, the mean parent, the aggressive bully, or the fun-loving friend. Orton (1997) suggested including puppets that represent different racial groups and providing a variety of puppets that includes family hand puppets, finger puppets that can be made from paper or cloth, cardboard cutouts of the family, and animal hand puppets. Through identification with these fantasylike persons or animals, children can act out and begin to express feelings and thoughts that are difficult for them to accept as their own. The counselor works with them to help them learn to cope with their real-world problems.

Not only is puppetry an excellent technique to use in individual counseling, but it is also effective with small groups of children. Jenkins and Beckh (1993) suggested using puppetry for children between the ages of 5 and 11.

Summary

Without thorough problem assessment, appropriate interventions cannot be implemented. Likewise, without an intervention design process and knowledge about how to identify developmentally and culturally appropriate strategies, the counseling process is weakened. Understanding what needs to be done and knowing how it can be accomplished are complex challenges that are simplified with an understanding of the developmental process and models that guide the design and implementation of intentional interventions. As Wagner (2003) stressed, flexibility is key in working with children and adolescents. It is imperative that counselors "adjust their interactional style and treatment strategies to suit their clients' physical size, thought process, social skills, emotional awareness, moral understanding, and plans for the future" (p. 7). Wagner also noted that the developmental challenges of childhood pose significant challenges for helping professionals in the selection of intervention strategies, because most interventions were originally conceived for adults. The intent of this chapter and the following ones is to provide the reader with interventions specifically geared to young clients.

Part II

Application of Developmental and Multicultural Theories: Typical Problems, Assessment, and Intervention

✳

Although dividing human development into age periods is somewhat arbitrary, it nevertheless is the most common way to look at what occurs at various stages of development. The following four chapters describe development across the life span of the school-age child in these areas: self, social, emotional, cognitive, and moral development. Each chapter outlines developmental characteristics of a specific period: early childhood (ages 4–5), middle childhood (ages 6–10), early adolescence (ages 11–14), and mid-adolescence (ages 15–18). Following these descriptions, six case studies illustrate problems typically experienced during this stage of development. The intent is to identify more of the normal problems that helping professionals routinely encounter with children and adolescents as opposed to more serious, diagnosable disorders. An overview of the problem, rather than a session-by-session account, is presented, along with a detailed description of developmental and cultural assessment and intervention strategies. Implicit in each example are the considerations for identifying appropriate assessment techniques and the four-stage intervention design process described in the first three chapters.

✳

In addition to the case studies, other typical problems are identified for each developmental period to portray the range of concerns experienced by children and adolescents. Certainly what is presented has to be considered in light of several factors: the youngster's environment, cultural values and expectations, socioeconomic status, parental support, coping responses, and prior success in mastering other developmental milestones. For some, typical concerns might be far more serious than those listed. For example, children who are sexually abused might not have the energy to worry about whether they are the last to be selected on a team. Teenagers living in alcoholic families might be more concerned about protecting their siblings from violent behavior during drinking episodes than about whether they have to undress in front of peers in physical education class. On the other hand, many young people experience these typical concerns, in addition to the more serious problems within the family or the environment, making their maturation process even more complex.

Helping professionals must be prepared to assist young people with the spectrum of concerns they experience while growing up. In this contemporary society, life is increasingly more complex and there are more challenges for children and adolescents: parental divorce and remarriage; AIDS; physical, sexual, or emotional abuse; poverty; parental drug and alcohol abuse; and homelessness. Unfortunately, many young people cope with these issues in self-defeating ways, through pregnancy, substance abuse, violence, or suicide, which in turn creates another layer of problems. Because these problems have become quite prevalent for far too many young people, professionals naturally have tended to overfocus on these major concerns and perhaps slight the normal, developmental concerns, which also need to be addressed for the youngsters to master developmental tasks successfully. The purpose of the following chapters is to provide practical strategies that address developmental problems of school-age youngsters in a diverse culture.

Chapter 5

Early Childhood:
Assessment and Intervention

✳

Five-year-olds Eric and John had been playing well together most of the afternoon, but Eric's mother could tell that things were beginning to deteriorate. She suggested that perhaps they needed to find a new activity. She volunteered to help them, stating that if they could each come up with several ideas, she would write them down and they could decide what to do. They each identified two or three things, and Eric's mother read the lists back, fully expecting that they would first choose an activity from one list and then try one from the other. Instead, they combined their ideas. John wanted to play "pets" and Eric suggested "store," so they decided to play pet store, quickly transforming the playroom into a store for their stuffed animals.

✳

It is amazing to see young children develop rudimentary problem-solving skills, use their imagination, and acquire more advanced conversational and social skills. During these formative years, so many changes occur that affect later development. For some children, there are developmental delays; others progress normally.

This chapter focuses on how to determine what is normal for the 4- and 5-year-old preschooler. Descriptions of developmental characteristics in the areas of self-development, social development, emotional development, physical development, cognitive development, and moral development are included. This information provides the practitioner with a basis for assessing development and designing developmentally appropriate interventions for children who are experiencing varying degrees of difficulty with their growing-up process.

Characteristics of Young Children

As you think back to your preschool years, you may recall having a favorite stuffed animal you slept with every night or an imaginary friend. You might remember engaging in make-believe play or going to school for the first time. As a 4- and 5-year-old you were learning new things every day. At the same time, you may have had negative experiences associated with abusive or other dysfunctional family circumstances. What you experienced during this period of development contributed to who you are today.

Because the early childhood years are so influential, increased attention has been focused on early education and intervention with this age group. This is based on the recognition that, from a developmental perspective, the earlier the interventions are initiated, the higher the likelihood of success and the prevention of more serious difficulties (Hohenshil & Brown, 1991). If parents and educators understand what characterizes development during these formative years, they will be better equipped to help young children successfully navigate this period in their lives.

Self-Development

A child's self-concept, or understanding of who he or she is, changes systematically with age (Cobb, 2001). For instance, 4- and 5-year-olds have begun to define themselves. They know their name, can tell if they are a boy or girl, and can tell whether they are big or little. Although they have a good idea of their competencies, such as being able to count, tie a shoe, solve a puzzle, or have lots of friends, they do not have a global sense of their self-worth (Bee, 1992), nor are they able to make a clear distinction between different areas of competence, such as being good in school but not in physical skills (Rathus, 2004). At age 4, children are very concrete and often describe themselves in terms of visible physical characteristics, such as what they look like or what they can do: "My name is Adam. I am 5 and I can ride a bike." According to Cobb, by age 5 they begin to characterize themselves in terms of their relationships as well as their psychological makeup.

Preschoolers tend to be very egocentric, assuming that everyone thinks and feels as they do (Cobb, 2001). Their self-esteem is generally quite high, and they tend to overestimate their abilities, thinking that they are competent in everything (Berger, 2003; Seifert & Hoffnung, 1997). Given the fact that they have so many new tasks to master during this period, this belief in their abilities is advantageous. As their sense of competence increases with mastery, so does their initiative. When their self-concept moves from factual to evaluative, it becomes self-esteem—or pride in oneself (Davis-Kean & Sandler, 2001). Children who have relatively high self-esteem as 5-year-olds are better accepted by other children.

During this period of development, preschoolers develop more self-control. They are better able to control their impulses and not be as frustrated if their needs are not met immediately (Berk, 2003).

In terms of gender, preschoolers identify themselves as a boy or a girl and realize that there are two sexes. However, they do not understand that this is permanent—that girls do not become boys if they cut their hair and wear boys' clothes, for example (McDevitt & Ormrod, 2002). They do tend to have very specific, stereotypical ideas about what is gender appropriate.

Social Development

Play serves an important role for children, both in their own skill development and also in relation to others. Associative play, in which children interact and share but do not actually seem to be playing the same game, characterizes 4-year-olds. At this age, children may talk about what they are doing and may be engaged in a similar activity, but there is not any common purpose (K. B. Owens, 2002; Seifert & Hoffnung, 1997). By age 5, they begin to be more cooperative: They take turns, create games, and elaborate on an activity. Usually, only one or two leaders organize activities, and children take on different roles within the group (Berk, 1999).

By the time they are in preschool, children begin spending more time with other children, and through these interactions, children learn how to share, cooperate, take turns, and deal with conflict. They also learn how to lead and how to follow (Rathus, 2004). With regard to friendships, Selman (1980) found that preschool children are most likely to be in Stage 0, momentary playmateship, or Stage 1, one-way assistance. In Stage 0, children are egocentric and cannot see another child's point of view. They have difficulty separating themselves to see a physical action and the intention behind it. If someone takes a toy, they cannot understand that the other child thought he or she had a right to take it. Friends are chosen on the basis of a physical characteristic, such as "I like her because she has long hair," or because of what the friend has, such as a toy or candy.

At Stage 1, children do not understand give and take; they may see that a friend can help them but do not necessarily see that they can help the friend. They are beginning to differentiate between their point of view and that of others. Friendships are characterized by one person taking the lead and another following, and the friendship ends if the follower does not follow.

Children at Stage 1 prefer same-gender playmates and show noticeable gender differences in play behavior. For example, boys take up more physical space in their play and are more interested in being rough and noisy: wrestling, running, climbing, or engaging in rough-and-tumble play (Rathus, 2004). Girls are more inclined to engage in nurturing activities, such as playing house, cooking, playing with dolls, and helping each other. Girls' play is more cooperative, whereas boys' activities are more aggressive. Girls also prefer to play with just one child or a small group, whereas boys engage in more competitive play with more children (Berger & Thompson, 1991; Crombie & Desjardins, 1993).

Emotional Development

Throughout the preschool years, children become increasingly adept at understanding their emotions (Laible & Thompson, 1998). Not only are they able to talk about their feelings, but they can also incorporate them into pretend play, which helps them develop a better understanding of their feelings and how to express them in acceptable ways. Although they gradually develop a better understanding of others' emotions, initially they are quite literal and confuse overt emotional expression with what someone may be feeling (Cobb, 2001). According to Berk (1999), children at this age have difficulty understanding that they can experience different emotions about a situation simultaneously, even though they can understand the idea of experiencing different emotions at different times.

Although they will have made progress managing their emotions by the time they are in preschool, it is important to remember that this progress may be very uneven. Their emotional vocabularies are expanding and they are beginning to understand which emotions are appropriate to specific situations (Izard & Ackerman, 2000). However, because they often lack the ability to accurately verbalize their feelings, young children tend to express them directly through action (Elkind, 1991).

Emotional development in early childhood is influenced by cognitive development as well as experience (Siegler et al., 2003). For example, they may experience more fear as their imaginations develop and they start to be afraid of imaginary creatures. And, as they become more aware of others' intentions and motives, they become better able to regulate negative emotions. During the preschool years, children generally are less emotionally intense and not as emotionally negative (Murphy, Eisenberg, Fabes, Shepard, & Guthrie, 1999).

Physical Development

Significant physical changes occur in early childhood, but by the preschool years growth is slower. The child loses baby fat and becomes slimmer, and by age 6, body proportions are similar to those of an adult. Normal weight for a 6-year-old is 46 pounds and normal height is 46 inches (Berger & Thompson, 1991), but this varies depending on genetic background, nutrition, and health care. Boys tend to be more muscular and have less fat than girls. During the preschool years, it is not uncommon for children to have smaller appetites.

Although influenced by heredity and environment, age-related patterns of activity level are linked to brain maturation. It generally is acknowledged that activity level decreases each year after the first 2 years of life, but research suggests that it is a mistake to expect young children to be still for long periods of time. Because activity level also is associated with the ability to concentrate and think before acting, it is important to take this into account when structuring activities or behavioral expectations for the preschool child (Eaton & Yu, 1989).

Gross motor skills that involve large body movements such as running, jumping, hopping, throwing, swinging, and climbing improve markedly during early childhood (Berger, 2003). Whereas a 2-year-old is clumsy and falls down frequently, 4- and 5-year-olds can climb ladders, throw and catch a ball, jump and hop, and ride a tricycle. They also engage in a typical gross motor activity, *chase* play (Steen & Owens, 2000, as cited in

McDevitt & Ormrod, 2002), in which a young child runs after another and pretends to be a type of predator. Campbell and Eaton (1999) noted that there are some gender differences in the activity level associated with gross motor skills. Boys are generally more active and slightly ahead of girls in skills involving force and power (Berk, 1999). Berk also noted that body build influences gross motor skills.

Fine motor skills also improve dramatically during early childhood (Berk, 1999), although according to Berger (2003), fine motor skills such as drawing, using scissors, writing, or tying a bow are harder to master than gross motor skills because they involve small body movements, particularly with the hands and fingers. These skills gradually improve with experience and practice, in addition to normal neurological development. Four- and 5-year-olds can draw rudimentary pictures (Beaty, 1998), and Berk noted that as their cognitive and fine motor skills improve, their drawings are more realistic. There are some cultural variations in the development of drawing; children in cultures in which artistic expression is emphasized produce more sophisticated drawings, whereas children in remote areas who do not go to school may not have the opportunity to develop drawing skills, according to Berk. Although many 5-year-olds can write the letters of the alphabet (Graham & Weintraub, 1996), it is important to remember that there are considerable individual differences in the rate at which fine motor skills develop. Some research suggests that certain kinds of fine motor skills may be easier for girls than for boys (Cohen, 1997).

Cognitive Development

Preoperational thought patterns characterize the cognitive development of 4- and 5-year-olds (Berk, 2003; McDevitt & Ormrod, 2002; Santrock & Yussen, 1992). Because they are able to represent objects and events mentally, they can think and act more flexibly than during the sensorimotor stage. The fact that they can recall past events and envision future ones allows them to connect experiences and results in more complex understandings (McDevitt & Ormrod, 2002).

Although they become increasingly adept at relating symbols to each other in meaningful ways, there are some definite limitations. First, they have preoperational egocentrism, which is the inability to see things from another's perspective. They might, for example, play games with others but never check to see that they are all playing by the same rules (McDevitt & Ormrod, 2002). Second, they may confuse external physical objects with internal thoughts; a child who is afraid of monsters and the dark may think that a doll would feel the same way. Third, children of this age also have problems understanding the idea of reversibility (Berk, 2003). If they always walk to school and are asked for the first time to walk home, they most likely will not understand the process of walking to school simply needs to be reversed.

Also characteristic of their cognitive style is what Piaget described as *centration* (Berk, 2003; McDevitt & Ormrod, 2002). Centration refers to the tendency to focus on one aspect of a situation rather than on a broader view, thus neglecting other important features. Berger and Thompson (1991) cited an example of centration: If the sun is shining through the bedroom window, it is time to get up even if it is 5:00 a.m. on Saturday morning. Because of this tendency to center on one idea, preschoolers understand things in terms of an either-or framework. For example, it is very difficult for a parent to explain to a child this age that the child is not good or bad but, rather, is a person who sometimes acts good and sometimes acts badly.

Centering on one aspect, rather than on the relationship of situations, also interferes with preschoolers' ability to understand cause and effect. For instance, instead of realizing that they fell down because they were running too fast, they might blame someone else (Berger & Thompson, 1991). Centration also affects children's ability to take a perspective other than their own and their ability to see that the same object or situation can have two identities, one real and one apparent (Flavell, 1985). For instance, preschoolers have difficulty understanding that their mother could also be a doctor; to them, a person is either one or the other but certainly not both simultaneously.

Language progresses rapidly during this period of growth, but the children's vocabulary reflects their concrete stage of development. By age 5, children can understand almost anything explained to them in context if the examples are specific (Bjorklund, 2000). And although they can introduce new topics into a conversation, they have difficulty maintaining a sustained conversation about one idea (R. E. Owens, 1996). They also have difficulty with concepts such as time and space, asking "are we there yet?" 5 minutes after the car has left the driveway for a 2-hour trip. Elkind (1991) cautioned that although young children may be verbally precocious, they may not be as advanced cognitively. It is important to be aware that a discrepancy may exist. For example, although they can use the word *dead* accurately in a sentence, their understanding of death is that someone went away for awhile. It is not uncommon for a 5-year-old to ask when his dog is coming inside when he has just seen it buried.

Young children's ability to recall past events is more limited, and they are more likely to omit details (Garbarino & Stott, 1992). However, the more relevant the experience is to them, the more likely they are to recall it with greater accuracy. Concrete props can assist with memory recall, such as use of anatomically correct dolls with child sexual abuse victims. Garbarino and Stott also suggested asking specific questions such as "Did you play with blocks at school?" rather than simply asking what they did that day, which likely will be answered with "nothing" (p. 58).

Imaginative play and vivid fantasies characterize this period of development. By age 4, preschoolers often have imaginary friends and engage in pretend play by themselves and with others, assuming different roles as they act out familiar routines such as going to the store or to the doctor.

According to Cobb (2001),

> Preschoolers chatter to themselves when alone, talk to their stuffed animals, tell their troubles to their pets, assume the identities of their action figures, and spend hours in make-believe play, enacting fantastic adventures as well as the more familiar routines of their lives. (p. 297)

Cobb also noted that at this age, children tend to readily transform objects into other things. A stone can become a turtle or a rocket ship, for example. According to Nicolopoulou (1993), this type of play contributes to children's cognitive and social skills. Berk (1999) concurred, summarizing research indicating that make-believe or imaginative play strengthens memory, logical reasoning, language and literacy, creativity, and the ability to take another's perspective.

Animism and artificialism also characterize preschoolers' thinking. *Animism* refers to the attribution of lifelike qualities to inanimate objects, such as thinking that boats go to sleep at night. *Artificialism* is the belief that people cause natural phenomena, such as believing that wind occurs because a man is blowing (Rathus, 2004).

Moral Development

Preschool children are in what Kohlberg defined as the preconventional level of moral judgment (Berk, 2003; Berndt, 1992). In this stage, they assume that adults determine what is wrong and right. Their moral reasoning is dominated by concerns about the consequences of their behavior; behaviors that result in punishment are considered bad, whereas behaviors that result in rewards are seen as good (Berk, 2003). Newman and Newman (1991) emphasized that children need to understand the consequences of their behavior on others to develop a basis for making moral judgments. Although many 4- and 5-year-olds struggle with this concept, it is nevertheless important to begin relating behaviors to moral principles (telling the truth, respecting others' feelings, and respecting authority) so that these are integrated into the children's concepts of right and wrong.

Several authors (Berk, 2003; Newman & Newman, 1991; Turiel, 1983, 1998) have cited an important distinction between moral rules or imperatives and social conventions, emphasizing that social conventions differ across cultures and are customs determined by consensus, such as table manners or social interaction rituals. According to Berk, a moral imperative is a standard that protects people's rights and welfare. Stealing another child's toy would be an example of a moral imperative, whereas a social convention would be whispering during sharing time or wandering away during large-group time. Newman and Newman indicated that 4- and 5-year-olds are able to understand that moral transgressions are wrong because they affect others' welfare and are more consistent across settings, whereas social transgressions are disruptive and may depend on the situation. In other words, at home it might be permissible to get up from the table during dinner, but there is a rule against leaving the table during snack time at school. Berk suggested that children in Western as well as many non-Western cultures distinguish between moral and social conventions.

According to Turiel (1998), young children learn the difference between a moral offense and a social convention violation by observation. For example, if a child starts to hit a classmate, peers may try to stop the behavior or tell a parent or teacher who will offer support for the victim. But in the case of a social convention, others would most likely not react.

Berk (2003) described a third domain in addition to morality and social convention: matters of personal choice. These do not involve the rights or welfare of others, nor do they directly affect the functioning of a system; they are up to the individual child. For instance, if the parent of a 5-year-old says he or she cannot play with a friend, this child would not assume automatically that the parent was correct, as Kohlberg's stages of moral development indicated. Because the child distinguishes a personal issue from a moral rule, he or she does not automatically consider this a fair decision. It is important to know a child's personal domain when assessing the child's moral development.

The remainder of this chapter discusses special considerations in working with parents of 4- and 5-year-olds, followed by a variety of problems typically presented by preschool children or reported by parents and significant others. Examples of assessment procedures are identified, followed by specific developmental and culturally appropriate interventions.

Parental Involvement With Young Children

When parents of young children bring them to counseling, the parents frequently feel inadequate and guilty: "We should have been able to prevent this problem from occurring. What's wrong with us?" They also may feel powerless: "Why does our child act this way? Nothing we do seems to help?" Parents may be particularly vulnerable as their children reach the preschool years. As children spend more time away from home, it becomes more difficult to control other environmental factors that may affect them. The helping professional may need to work directly with parents on some of these issues if their negative emotions interfere with their ability to implement appropriate interventions. Krista's situation illustrates this point.

According to her parents, 4-year-old Krista was the perfect only child until she started preschool the previous month. Since then, there had been dramatic behavior changes: temper tantrums or tears when it was time to leave for school, resistance about sleeping alone in her room, and refusal to leave the yard to play with friends. After ruling out possible abuse or any other trauma, the counselor explained to the parents that these behaviors indicated some separation anxiety problems that were quite typical for 4-year-olds and that there were a number of things that they could do to help Krista through this transition. However, the parents continued to feel responsible for Krista's misery because they were forcing her to attend preschool when she really wanted to stay home. Because of this attitude, they were unable to implement any of the behavioral interventions the counselor suggested. The counselor realized that even if she worked directly with the child, the efforts would be sabotaged by the parents' beliefs about "poor little Krista."

These parents agreed to meet again with the counselor, who explained that their feelings stemmed from their beliefs that Krista should not experience discomfort, that they were responsible for the discomfort, and that it was easier to give in to Krista than to experience more conflict. By working through these beliefs, the parents gradually reduced their guilt and used effective behavioral interventions. Coupled with bibliotherapy and play therapy techniques that the counselor used with Krista, the problems disappeared in a short time and both Krista and her parents were much happier.

Parents and helping professionals concerned about healthy development for young children have identified the following goals:

1. Helping develop a positive self-image.
2. Enhancing social and emotional development.
3. Encouraging independent thinking and developing problem-solving skills.
4. Improving communication skills.
5. Stimulating interest in the natural world.
6. Increasing capability for self-discipline.
7. Advancing the development of fundamental motor skills and abilities.
8. Identifying special individual mental, social, and physical needs.
9. Furthering the development of respect for human dignity and the rights of others.
10. Promoting aesthetic appreciation and expression.
11. Encouraging creativity.
12. Giving and receiving sincere affection. (Hohenshil & Brown, 1991, p. 8)

Despite best efforts, many children "fall between the cracks" for one reason or another, and more directed attention is needed for them to achieve these goals. Oftentimes a child's temperament may interfere with his or her ability to develop in healthy ways. According to Chess and Thomas (1984), children are born with reliable and consistent patterns of behavior, such as activity level, regularity, adaptability, approach or withdrawal, physical sensitivity, intensity of reaction, distractibility, persistence, or positive or negative mood. These individual temperament differences explain why some children are more prone to act in certain ways and why they experience things differently. Their problems may have little bearing on what is developmentally typical. For example, a child whose temperament is not very adaptable may not adjust well to preschool because he or she does not adjust well to any new situation. This is in contrast to the example cited, in which Krista was well adjusted until the transition to preschool when she responded in a way that is not atypical for a 4-year-old starting preschool. Temperament does not preclude the development of appropriate interventions, but it does shed a different light on the problem.

The role parents play in their preschooler's development is critical. By functioning in a consultative role, helping professionals can empower parents, teaching them skills that they can use with themselves as well as with their children for both present and future problems. It is important to convey to parents that counseling facilitates healthy development for both themselves and their children, but it is also critical to be sensitive to cultural factors that may affect parents' responsiveness to consultation.

Problem Assessment and Intervention: Selected Case Studies

The problems selected for this section represent a variety of what practitioners might expect from 4- and 5-year-olds. They range from typical developmental problems, which many children experience with varying degrees of difficulty, to more serious problems some children experience because of family or environmental circumstances or a lack of ability to successfully master developmental tasks to achieve healthy development. With each example, an overview of the problem is outlined, followed by a sample assessment procedure and possible interventions. The intent is to illustrate a variety of problem assessment and intervention strategies appropriate for this age group rather than to present detailed case histories with multiple, complex problems.

Case Study One: 4-Year-Old Mark

Problem overview. Mark, a 4-year-old Caucasian boy, was experiencing a smooth adjustment to preschool, with the exception of swim class. His father informed the teacher that he had given up on lessons during the summer because Mark had become so terrified of the water, unlike his 8-year-old brother. According to the father, there seemed to be no reason for the fear. As a younger child, Mark had played in the wading pool in the backyard, and to his knowledge, Mark had never seen anyone drown or get hurt in the water. The teacher indicated that the school counselor might be of assistance.

Assessment considerations. Preschool children can reason logically about things they know about (Garbarino & Stott, 1992), but when experiencing new or unfamiliar situations, it is not uncommon for children to exhibit some degree of anxiety. Assessment with the parents should include how they responded when Mark expressed his fear, what the relationship with the swim coach had been like, and what role the older brother might have played—had he teased Mark or said things that contributed to the fear? It would also be important to know if a stranger had approached Mark in the locker room or around the pool to rule out the possibility of sexual abuse.

Determining whether Mark had other fears, and if so, how they had been dealt with, would also be a key consideration. Because of this child's level of cognitive development, it is important to be as concrete as possible in the assessment and intervention process.

Assessment procedures. Prior to meeting with Mark, the counselor first met with Mark's parents to learn more about when the problem began and how they and others had reacted. The counselor perceived both parents to be supportive and did not get the impression that they were forcing their child to swim or ridiculing him because he sobbed uncontrollably and was afraid to get in the water. The parents were not aware of any teasing by the older brother, and because both of them had been with Mark every time he had been at the pool, they were certain that he had not been approached by a stranger. Neither Mark nor his brother had ever been afraid of the dark or of monsters and other such fantasy figures. In response to the counselor's question about how frequently Mark had been around other youngsters, they replied that he had several friends in the neighborhood and the parents routinely organized play dates, so he was not uncomfortable around other children. Prior to concluding his visit with Mark's parents, the counselor also verified that there had been no recent extenuating events or previous trauma.

The counselor also met briefly with Mark's teacher, who indicated that although Mark was a little shy and not very verbal, he basically seemed to be adjusting well to preschool except for the swimming lessons. She indicated that he interacted appropriately with other children; it just took him a little while to warm up to them. However, given that it was the 3rd week of school, she did not see this as significant.

The counselor then arranged a time to see Mark. Because the teacher had indicated that he was not a very verbal child, the counselor spent time during the first session just getting to know more about his young client by playing *Button Button* (Vernon, 2002, pp. 21–22), in which they each took turns hiding a button in one of their hands and the other person would guess which hand held the button. If the person guessed correctly, he shared something he liked to do or something about his family. Mark responded well to this simple activity. Then, the counselor got out a cake pan, filled it with water, and set some small plastic figures beside it, inviting Mark to play with them if he wished. As he played with the figures in the water, the counselor casually mentioned that he knew Mark was having some fears about the water. He reassured him that other kids his age were afraid of the water, too, and that he would like to help Mark with this if Mark was willing.

The counselor then pointed to the pan of water and the figures and asked Mark if he could show him what he was afraid of in the water. At first Mark just sat there, but finally he used one figure to push another into the water. As the counselor reflected on what had just occurred, he asked Mark if this had ever happened to him. Mark replied that his brother had pushed him a little, even though he did not fall into the pool, and had called him a baby because he cried. The counselor asked if anything else frightened him, and Mark shoved the figure down into the water and held him, indicating that he was drowning. When asked if there were other worries, Mark shook his head.

Interventions. Prior to meeting with Mark for the second session, the counselor called the parents and shared with them that his fear had come from his brother, which surprised them, but then they recalled that there had been at least one other instance during the summer when they had had to intervene when their older son was a bit rough with Mark. They appreciated the information and said they would keep an eye on things at home. The counselor also shared that he would be reading a book to Mark in which the character learned to deal with his fear by teaching his stuffed animals how to breathe, kick, and float and by practicing this with the animal in the bathtub. The counselor said that he would send the book home so they could reread it to Mark and invite him to practice the procedure.

When he met with Mark, he read *Wiggle-Butts and Up-Faces* (Kolbisen, 1989) to him. Mark enjoyed the story and seemed to identify with the main character, Alex, a 4-year-old who learns to deal with his fear by teaching his stuffed animals how to swim. After discussing the story, the counselor encouraged Mark to try these things at home.

The next time they met was during the class swimming period. The counselor and Mark sat on the side and, as Mark observed, the counselor periodically asked him some directed questions such as "Did you see anyone drown? Did you see anyone get pushed in? Did you see kids having fun? Did you see adults around to help kids if they got in trouble or were scared?" The next week he convinced Mark to put on his swimming suit and sit with him again to observe. The following week he encouraged Mark to sit on the edge of the pool. The counselor also gave him several self-statements to practice: (a) If something bad happens to me there are adults to help; (b) it looks like swimming can be fun and I might have fun, too; and (c) I've never seen anyone drown so it probably will not happen to me.

During the next several weeks, Mark gradually worked his way into the water, first for 3 minutes, then 5 minutes, then 10. He was encouraged to practice the self-statements each time before he went in the water and to continue to practice at home with his stuffed animals. After a few more weeks, Mark was much more comfortable in the pool. His sobbing had stopped completely, and he no longer expressed fear about swimming.

Evaluation/summary. The combination of bibliotherapy, self-statements, and behavior therapy ultimately was effective in helping this youngster overcome his fear of swimming. Involving the parents was also very helpful, because they were able to use the bibliotherapy at home and help him practice in the bathtub. Once they became aware of the older brother's behavior, they addressed that as well. The counselor followed up with this case by conferring with the teacher, observing Mark in the pool, and meeting with him individually. These concrete interventions addressed the problem; Mark did not have any reoccurrence of this fear.

Case Study Two: 5-Year-Old Chang Lee

Problem overview. Chang Lee, a 5-year-old Chinese American boy, was evaluated regarding issues of "identity disorientation or confusion." Like both of his parents, Chang is fluent in both English and Chinese. Despite the fact that he interacts with both Chinese and Euro American kids at school, he refuses to speak Chinese to his parents and relatives, responding to their questions or comments in English. The parents reported that Chang "has become naughty and selfish as most American kids." Since arriving in the United States 2 years ago, Chang's parents have established themselves as successful business people in the community. As a result, both parents are gone for prolonged periods of time on business trips. Despite the fact that Chang is a good student and has above-average scores on intelligence tests, lately he has been more distracted in the classroom and has ignited some physical altercations with other students. Also, on more than one occasion he has been challenging and disrespectful to his teacher. In fact, on one occasion the teacher had to block a punch and physically restrain him when he was having a severe tantrum. After this incident, Chang was unapologetic. Prior to his outbursts of anger and defiance, he had demonstrated age-appropriate behavior.

Assessment considerations. Erikson (1950) described early childhood as a period of "vigorous unfolding" (p. 255). At this developmental stage, children are emerging from toddlerhood with a firm awareness of their separateness from others (Berk, 1999). At the same time, they are still very dependent on the authority and safety figures of the parents. Therefore, their perceived safety is based on the continued presence of the parents. In this case, it would also be important to determine if Chang's behavioral changes were in direct correlation to his parents' absences or if there were other reasons for the problems.

Assessment procedures. A nondevelopmental counselor would have been inclined to render a *DSM–IV–TR* diagnosis of oppositional defiant disorder (American Psychiatric Association, 2000) based on the outbursts of anger displayed in the classroom against his peers and teacher. However, two V codes could be more appropriate: V62.3: Academic Problem and V62.4: Acculturation Problem. These two codes do not imply potential psychopathology; instead these are signs of psychosocial triggers that are affecting Chang's current behavior. For example, the counselor must consider if the focus of the case is Chang's adjustment to a different culture and, most specifically, how Chang has been able to cope with the transition and adaptation patterns involved in the acculturation process as an immigrant. The challenge of assessment is to identify the specific problem or psychosocial stressors that triggered the changes in behavior without overlooking his oppositional behavior.

By interviewing the parents and the teacher, the counselor determined that the negative behaviors started as a result of the increased absence of the parents from home because of multiple business trips. The counselor suspected that Chang's anger was a reaction to the parents' continuous absence, but to verify this, the counselor asked Chang to draw a picture of his family doing something. First, Chang hesitated about who to include as part of the family. It is interesting to note that Chang drew his dog first, then himself and his sister, and in a distant corner of the paper, his parents leaving the house with two big suitcases. Although Chang is a 5-year-old with above-average verbal skills, the counselor did not use traditional methods of assessment that relied on verbal or written feedback because she thought the drawing would present a clearer picture of what Chang was experiencing.

The counselor also suspected that Chang had used the cultural strategy of not speaking Chinese as a way to hurt the parents. Also, Chang's behavior had changed at school because, to his professional parents, schooling was at the forefront of everything. Although he was very young, Chang was also very perceptive, and he no doubt had heard his parents talking about the importance of school. Knowing this, Chang was doing the opposite.

Interventions. It seemed to the counselor that Chang was desperate for attention and that the parents were probably not providing it. To be culturally sensitive, the counselor included the parents in some of the sessions, empathizing with their busy schedules but explaining that they needed to invest quality time in Chang's life because he was longing for love, not only for material possessions.

To deal with Chang's anger, the counselor conducted a Two-Family Contrast exercise. One picture portrayed a family in a park playing with a ball, laughing, and having a great time. The other portrayed a family in which the father was reading a book downstairs, the mother was upstairs working on the computer surrounded by papers, the son was playing by himself in his room, the daughter was talking on the phone, and the dog was looking out the window. The counselor asked Chang to tell a story about each of these families. Although 5-year-olds are imaginative and creative, most of the time their stories reflect their own limited life experiences and the way that they perceive the world and the people around them. As a result, Chang described the parents of the second family in which members were performing activities on their own as "mean and bad." He described the boy and the dog as being "bored and lonely." Of course, Chang made a happy story and presented the parents of the other picture in the park as "good and kind."

The goal of the second intervention was to improve Chang's communication skills by expressing his feelings in the moment to avoid the accumulation of negative feelings and eventually displaying them inappropriately. The counselor drew the figure of a boy in a $7\frac{1}{2} \times 12$ inch paper that had arrows pointing toward the head, abdomen, hands, legs, arms, chest, and face. The counselor proceeded to teach Chang that when he is angry or upset, these parts of his body will "send him a message" that there is something that bothers him. For example, if he saw his parents leaving again for the third time during the week for another business trip, his stomach may feel like it is in a knot, his face might get hot and red, his hands could get sweaty, his heart might start pounding, and his head could get "fuzzy." The counselor taught Chang to identify these signs of anger prior to acting on them. Then, the counselor gave him a "feeling chart" that contained facial expressions and suggested that when Chang felt any of those feelings in his body, he would mark the faces on the feeling chart that showed how he was feeling and share them with his parents or teacher so they could talk things out before he exploded. The main goal was for Chang to communicate his emotions to others in an appropriate manner.

Evaluation/summary. Like many children of professional parents, Chang was desperate to spend time with his parents. His behavior at school and reluctance to speak Chinese to the parents or relatives were a result of his lack of attention. However, unlike monocultural and monolingual children, Chang had a powerful strategy to use to call attention to his unhappiness: He could refuse to speak Chinese to provoke his parents. In the counselor's talk with the parents, they argued that they were trying to do the best for their children and their family, but they did understand that even though they were successful business entrepreneurs they had delegated too much responsibility to the school as far as raising Chang. The parents reached an agreement in which only one parent would travel while the other would stay home. This major change, in addition to the counselor's interventions, resulted in a dramatic improvement in Chang's behaviors at home and school.

Case Study Three: 4-Year-Old Margaret

Problem overview. Margaret, a 4-year-old Caucasian girl, lives with her father, stepmother, and 2-year-old stepbrother. She attends preschool three mornings a week and enjoys going. She sees her mother frequently, and her parents appear to have a good relationship. Margaret is quite verbal and outgoing, relates appropriately with peers, and is doing well academically in this setting. According to both parents, she is usually a happy, carefree child.

Margaret's parents and stepmother are concerned because she recently has developed a terrible fear of the dark, but she cannot explain what specifically bothers her. This results in bedtime problems, which are similar in both households. Thus far, her father has tried giving her a reward for going right to bed (which has not worked), and both parents have tried lying down with her until she goes to sleep. Although she will go to sleep if a parent is in the room, her parents do not want this to continue.

Assessment considerations. Nighttime fears are a common problem for young children and can have a disruptive effect on the child and family (Merritt, 1991). Imagination and vivid fantasies are very characteristic of this stage of development (Bee, 2000; Cobb, 2001). Therefore, it appears as if this problem is a typical developmental problem. However, other assessment considerations should include whether Margaret has been watching scary television shows, if she has been associating with new playmates who may be sharing scary information with her, whether there has been violence in either neighborhood, or if there is a possibility of sexual abuse. Assessment should also include how Margaret has adjusted to her parents' divorce, her father's remarriage, and her relationship with her stepbrother.

Assessment procedures. The counselor first met with the parents and stepmother to discuss the assessment considerations; to learn more about the frequency, intensity, and duration of the problem; and to get a general developmental and family history. Having determined that nothing seemed out of the ordinary, the counselor prepared to meet with Margaret. Because she is normally a self-assured, verbal child, the rapport-building process was accomplished readily by engaging her in a dialogue with puppets to learn more about her and her two families. Once Margaret was comfortable and the purpose of the counseling interview had been explained in simple terms, the counselor was ready to assess the fear of the dark.

"Margaret, I'd like you to show or tell me more about what makes you afraid at night. If you like, you may use these dolls and this play furniture to show what happens when you go to bed and it is dark." As Margaret enacted the bedtime process, the counselor asked directed questions to clarify what occurs. As Margaret continued, it became apparent that she is convinced that there is something in her closet that will come and get her when the lights are out. Through acting out the incident, Margaret revealed that she is afraid to tell her parents about this, because they always tell her to be a "big girl," and she does not think that they will believe her if she lets them know her real fears. The counselor asked her to draw a picture of it, and she drew a large, scary monster. After checking for other fears or traumatic events, it appeared that the monster was the source of the terror, and intervention could be directed accordingly.

Interventions. The counselor explained to Margaret that many 4-year-olds are afraid of the dark and develop fears of animals or imaginary creatures (Merritt, 1991; Newman & Newman, 1991). The counselor emphasized to her parents that this is a common, but not necessarily short-lived problem and commended them for taking it seriously, because it seemed very real to their daughter. The counselor thought that, by empowering Margaret, she could help her deal with the fear. First, the counselor read *Creepy Things Are Scaring Me* (Pumphrey & Pumphrey, 2003), which describes the feelings of a young child who is afraid of the dark and overcomes the fear. Not only did this normalize the fear for Margaret, but it also provided her with some ideas about how to conquer her fear. Next, the counselor suggested that Margaret ask her parents to buy or make a very scary mask to hang on the inside of her closet door to scare the monster from coming out, which Margaret thought was a great idea. Finally, she brainstormed with Margaret and her parents about what else Margaret could do. Margaret suggested moving her bed so that it did not face the closet; her parents suggested buying her a big flashlight to use if she senses that the monster is in the room; and the counselor introduced the idea of a "monster hunt" before bedtime, checking in the closet and using some "monster spray" (a hair spay bottle full of water, with the label replaced by a picture of a monster) that she could spray around her bedroom to get rid of anything scary.

This young client seemed eager to try these suggestions, but at bedtime she still insisted that a parent be in the room with her. The father called the counselor to share this information, and they discussed what else might work in conjunction with the other interventions. After some thought, the counselor suggested that the parents consider having their daughter earn "monster mash" points that she would accumulate to have a special party with some of her friends once the problem was resolved. The parents were willing to try this because their daughter loved parties, and they thought this might be a good motivator.

Evaluation/summary. Both the assessment and interventions were concrete and appropriate for a 4-year-old, which increased the likelihood that they would be effective. At this age, action rather than logic is important (Berger & Thompson, 1991), so checking for the monster, instead of trying to reason with the child that there is no such thing as a monster, is the best approach. Having several different alternatives, as well as good parental involvement, also strengthened the intervention. Because this is a very typical developmental problem that was "nipped early in the bud," the problem was resolved within a few weeks.

Case Study Four: 5-Year-Old Adam

Problem overview. Five-year-old Adam, a Caucasian boy, was referred to the school counselor by his kindergarten teacher. The teacher expressed concern that Adam, a normally outgoing and rather boisterous boy, appeared very frightened about singing on stage with his class during the holiday program. Although he did not verbalize this to his teacher, she noticed that during rehearsal he was shaking and did not open his mouth. As soon as he got to the room, he ran to the bathroom. When she asked him what was wrong, he remained silent. Because the counselor was coming to their classroom later that day, the teacher explained the situation to him and asked if he could visit with Adam afterward. Adam is the youngest child and has three older sisters who are actively involved in music and dance activities. His family is very involved in the community, and the parents are very attentive to their children.

Assessment considerations. New experiences can be overwhelming for young children, and it is not uncommon for them to be somewhat fearful. Their anxiety is heightened, because they worry about pleasing others (Youngs, 1995) or being punished by the teacher (Youngs, 1985). At the same time, their self-esteem is usually quite high (McDevitt & Ormrod, 2002), and they think they are competent in everything (Seiffert & Hoffnung, 1997), so it is important to talk with the teacher about this young child's degree of competence in other areas. Information also needs to be obtained from the parents about whether their child had displayed this fear in preschool or church programs, if he shared anything about this with them at home, if he has others fears or any separation anxiety, how he interacts with his sisters at home, and other significant data about his development and family dynamics. Determining whether this problem is indicative of generalized anxiety also needs to be done.

Assessment procedures. Adam knew the counselor from classroom guidance sessions and willingly went with him. After receiving a negative response when asked if there was anything Adam would like to talk about, the counselor decided to indirectly assess the problem through a mutual storytelling technique (R. Gardner, 1971, 1986), in which the counselor asks the child to tell a story with a beginning, middle, and an end. Then the counselor tells a story using the same characters, setting, and dilemma as the child's story, but incorporating problem-solving techniques and a resolution (Kottman, 2001). Kottman suggested that with children younger than age 7, inviting the child to incorporate toys and other play media into the storytelling process helps make the story more concrete. Knowing that Adam liked animals and spent time with his father at his vet clinic, the counselor put a set of barnyard animals and some animal puppets in a basket next to Adam and asked him if he wanted to pretend that these animals could talk and tell a story. Because Adam was normally quite verbal, he readily engaged in this activity. In essence, the story he told involved a dog being afraid that the other animals in the barn would make fun of him because they wanted him, being a big dog, to be the guard dog when an even bigger dog from down the road wandered into their farm yard. Because his story was very short, the counselor probed a bit to elicit more details, asking Adam how he thought the dog felt when the other animals tried to make him be the guard dog when he did not want to do it. Adam said he probably was scared and mad, because he wanted to stay in the barn and not guard the yard. The counselor asked what the dog did when he was scared, and Adam said that he whined, but he did not let the other animals hear him because he did not want them to know that he was scared or they would make fun of him. The counselor asked him if the dog ever got scared like that in other places or about other things, and he said no.

From these responses, the counselor could see that Adam might be afraid of performing and would have preferred to stay in the classroom and play. However, he did not want his classmates and possibly his sisters to know that he was scared enough to cry. Although this did not appear to be a case of generalized anxiety, it still was not clear why Adam was afraid. To find out more about this, the counselor encouraged Adam to continue his story about why the dog would be scared. Adam replied that the dog got scared when he saw the other dog because the other dog had a very loud bark and when he growled, it sounded like he could eat someone up. He said the dog was so afraid of the bigger dog that he thought he had to pee, and if he did, the other animals would laugh because they thought Adam was such a big, brave dog and only little puppies peed when they were scared.

At the conclusion of the story, the counselor felt he had a sense of the problem, but he checked with the teacher and Adam's mother to see if there were any problems with enuresis. His mother indicated that occasionally when Adam was excited he did have a problem, but she was not aware of anyone making fun of him because of it. She thought he could be somewhat intimidated about performing because he had seen his sisters do that successfully. He had not been in prior performances, had not had problems with separation anxiety or other anxieties, and was a happy, well-adjusted child. Input from the teacher revealed that he approached all other tasks with confidence, which was why she had been surprised by his performance anxiety.

Interventions. When the counselor met with Adam the next day, he told Adam that he really liked his story and the characters and that it reminded him of a story that he wanted to tell Adam. In this story, the counselor had an ending: The dog told the other animals that he would guard the yard, but because it was so big, he would need helpers to make sure that all parts of the yard were covered. In the counselor's ending, the dog picked a cow, a horse, and another dog to help to protect their yard, but they did not want to. The dog told them that if they all did it together it would not be very hard, and they finally agreed to go out of the barn with him. And, because they were all together, the dog was not nearly as scared. As the counselor concluded the story, Adam told him that he really liked it and that he hoped all the animals could scare the big mean dog away.

At a subsequent session, the counselor mentioned that he had seen Adam's class practicing for the holiday program and that he noticed that Adam had looked a little scared. This time Adam admitted that he was, although he did not bring up his fear about wetting his pants or anything about his sisters. To help Adam work through the problem, the counselor brought out several puppets and invited Adam to play with them, suggesting that he could pretend that the puppets were going to be performing in a program. Adam hesitated a moment and then picked up a boy puppet and handed another puppet to the counselor. Because Adam did not seem to know what to do once he had the puppet on his hand, the counselor pretended that he was talking to Adam's puppet, and said, "I'm scared to go up on that stage." Adam's puppet nodded its head but did not say anything. The counselor's puppet then said, "I'm afraid I'll forget the words to the songs or that I might get so scared I'll wet my pants." This time Adam's puppet said that he was afraid of that, too, and that his sisters might make fun of him, because they never forgot their words. As they continued with the puppet play, his other fears came out as well.

To reach some resolution, the counselor picked up a different puppet who said, "I used to be scared like you are, but now I do not get so scared, because I think about something that really makes me happy and that keeps me from being so scared." This puppet also suggested that it helped to put something in his pocket to hold onto when he got scared, and asked Adam's puppet if he thought those ideas might work. The counselor then suggested that he and Adam talk about what the puppet had said and asked Adam to think of the happy thought and what he could put in his pocket. After he had identified these, the counselor read him *Harriet's Recital* (N. Carlson, 1982), a story about a preschooler who overcame her fears about a dance recital. In the following session, he and Adam listened to a tape with soothing music and identified several self-statements ("Even if I forget the words, maybe no one else will even know it"; "Maybe other kids will make mistakes too—I won't be the only one"; and "I just have to remember two songs, so it's not that bad") that they recorded over the music. The counselor suggested that he could listen to this tape before the holiday program to help him relax. As final interventions, the counselor suggested to the teacher that she make sure that Adam had gone to the bathroom prior to leaving for the performance and indicated to the parents that it might be helpful for them to share their memories of being on stage for the first time and any fears they had.

Evaluation/summary. Fear of wetting themselves is one of the major stressors for kindergarten children, according to Youngs (1985). By using the relaxation tape, normalizing the fear, and having Adam select something tangible and comforting to touch during the performance, the counselor succeeded in decreasing Adam's level of anxiety somewhat. Because this appeared to be an isolated situation, the counselor did not feel that it would be effective to continue to work on this problem with a 5-year-old until the anxiety-provoking situation was once again more immediate.

Case Study Five: 5-Year-Old Mariela

Problem overview. Mariela, a 5-year-old girl, was born in Maracaibo, Venezuela, and moved to the United States when she was 3 years old. Her parents have recently become extremely concerned because Mariela said to them: "I hate school and I never want to go back." In fact, the parents maintain that she now is excessively reluctant and fearful of leaving home every morning before going to school, sobbing and clinging to her parents until the bus arrives. On more than one occasion, her mother said that she has found Mariela crying in her room with her face covered with baby powder, but when asked why she was crying and had powder all over her face, Mariela gave no response. According to the parents, Mariela used to be a fairly outgoing, happy, and rambunctious girl prior to her kindergarten experience, and after school she has no problem leaving the house, except that she does not like going to the park if there are other children there. Mariela has a younger sister, her father is a part-time accountant and consultant, and her mother is a full-time physician assistant. Mariela's command of English is excellent and her academic performance is average. She was referred to the school counselor.

Assessment considerations. A child's self-concept, or understanding of who he or she is, changes systematically with age (Cobb, 2001). They have begun to define themselves, know whether they are big or little, male or female. Although they have a good idea of their competencies such as being able to count or solve a puzzle, they do not have a global sense of their self-worth (Bee, 1992). From a cultural standpoint, because they have an awareness of their body size, they are able to understand the differences in skin color and physical features.

Assessment procedures. The school counselor received the referral from the kindergarten teacher regarding Mariela's current situation and had a conversation with the teacher to learn more. She decided to observe Mariela during one of the class activities and also during recess. The school counselor noticed that in fact Mariela seemed to be quiet, reserved, and removed from any activity that required group interaction. However, the relationship between Mariela and the kindergarten teacher was excellent, and the teacher indicated that Mariela was always respectful and attentive.

According to the school counselor's observations, Mariela's mood was sad and flat in the classroom. Also, during recess, Mariela played alone with toys in a corner of the playground. The counselor interviewed Mariela and assessed the following areas: mood, separation anxiety disorder, and culture-bound issues. To assess her client's mood, the counselor used the storytelling technique in which the counselor pretended to "forget" parts of the story and allowed Mariela to "help her complete it." For example, the counselor began with: "Once upon a time there was a litter of six baby rabbits and one of them was left behind by her parents. She was scared and didn't know what to do . . ." The counselor let Mariela complete portions of the story to see whether or not she would portray the left-behind rabbit as one who was willing to be found, fight back if attacked by other animals, and so forth. In Mariela's story, the determination to live and survive by the rabbit was a sign that Mariela did not want to die. However, she did indicate several times that the rabbit was crying and upset.

Using a feeling chart, the counselor assessed Mariela's mood in a contextual and chronological way by asking her to mark the faces that reflected her mood during different times and locations. The first chart was at 7:30 a.m., the time the school bus was going to pick her up; the second chart was at her arrival to school; the third was during recess; and the fourth was her arrival at home after school. The counselor was able to pinpoint a correlation between her negative feelings and the social context in which these occurred.

The counselor wanted to rule out the possibility of separation anxiety disorder and interviewed the parents as to the following criteria from the *DSM–IV–TR* (American Psychiatric Association, 2000, p. 125) because Mariela herself was so young and would most likely not understand the questions:

1. Recurrent excessive distress when separation from home or major attachment figures occurs or is anticipated.

2. Persistent and excessive worry about losing, or about possible harm befalling, major attachment figures.
3. Persistent and excessive worry that an untoward event will lead to separation from a major attachment figure (e.g., getting lost or being kidnapped).
4. Persistent reluctance or refusal to go to school or elsewhere because of fear of separation.
5. Persistently and excessively fearful or reluctant to be alone or without major attachment figures at home or without significant adults in other settings.
6. Persistent reluctance or refusal to go to sleep without being near a major attachment figure or to sleep away from home.
7. Repeated nightmares involving the theme of separation.
8. Repeated complaints of physical symptoms (such as headaches, stomachaches, nausea, or vomiting) when separation from major attachment figures occurs or is anticipated.

From the parents' responses, Mariela did not meet the criteria for a separation anxiety disorder because even though she was attached to the parents and showed persistent worry about leaving home, her anxiety was only related to school or interaction with other children. After ruling out depression and separation anxiety disorder, the counselor wanted to explore cultural issues related to her behavior.

There were two issues related to culture: the strong interdependence among Latino family members and the possibility of cultural and ethnic misunderstanding among the children. The counselor asked Mariela to draw a self-portrait and provided her with markers and paper. Mariela drew a blue-eyed and blond-haired girl. The counselor clarified the instructions again and reminded Mariela that she was supposed to draw a self-portrait and not a picture of one of her classmates. In an almost defiant way, Mariela said to her "This is me!" The counselor was puzzled because Mariela had very dark brown skin, black eyes, and long black hair. After several minutes, Mariela gave the self-portrait the finishing touches and the counselor told her to describe the colors in the picture. Mariela proudly described the blue eyes, the blond hair, and the white skin. When the counselor held up a mirror and asked Mariela to describe the colors in the self-reflection, she became upset and started crying.

In the subsequent session the counselor brought a picture of Mariela from her classroom and put it next to the self-portrait she had previously drawn. Mariela looked at both pictures and said: "How come I am not like the others in my classroom," meaning white skin, blue or green eyes, and light hair color.

The counselor realized that Mariela was seeing herself as different and ultimately inferior because of her ethnic features. She concluded that the incident in which her mother found her crying, with her face covered with white powder, was an attempt to make her skin "lighter." It seemed that

Mariela was feeling rejected, as if she did not belong. This was why, the counselor speculated, Mariela did not want to go to school.

Interventions. The counselor had two goals. The first was to increase Mariela's self-pride in her unique ethnic features, and the second was to normalize her feelings of being different by promoting interaction and integration with other children.

Mariela was placed in an interethnic group comprising children from several different backgrounds. Because there were very few international and multiethnic children in her grade level, the counselor included some of these children from first grade, as well as some of her Euro American peers. A primary purpose of the group was for each one of the members to explain where their parents or grandparents were originally from and to share what they liked about their culture. The next step was for Mariela to understand that being darker than the rest of her peers was not a bad thing and certainly not something to be ashamed of.

The counselor also used a variation of a desensitization technique in which a different picture of a person was brought to every session for Mariela to compare her skin, eye, and hair color against. Intentionally, in an ascendant manner and parallel with every session, the individuals in the pictures became darker. The counselor's plan was for Mariela to increase her level of self-image. Technically, the counselor wanted to bring her back to reality.

Similarly, the counselor introduced her to pictures of ethnically diverse families and Mariela was asked to describe the feelings of the family members. There was one picture of a multiracial family, and Mariela was asked to devise a story about them.

Finally, the counselor brought some stuffed animals that were diametrically different in size, form, and color. Mariela had the option of selecting the one that she liked the most and the counselor picked another one. Mariela picked a red bear and the counselor a green turtle. The counselor started the play therapy by saying to Mariela: "Hello, I am the green turtle, would you like to be my friend? I feel very lonely because nobody looks like me." Immediately, Mariela (red bear) empathized with the green turtle and told her that she wanted to be her friend. The green turtle (counselor) replied: "Oh, but you are bigger and darker than me, I am afraid that you will not like me!" Similar scenarios were used to increase Mariela's level of confidence and self-image.

Evaluation/summary. Developing a sound self-image based on ethnic pride is a process that takes years. It is especially difficult for young children to value the idea of being bicultural when they are desperately eager to be like the rest of the children. Mariela demonstrated considerable progress over a period of time. Gradually the morning crying episodes ceased, she was not as reluctant to go to school, and she felt comfortable playing in the park with other children after school and during the weekends. The parents reported that Mariela seemed to be more relaxed and happy at home, and the teachers reported the same at school.

Case Study Six: 5-Year-Old Leia

Problem overview. Five-year-old Leia, a Caucasian girl, entered counseling during the summer just before first grade, 2 months after the birth of her sister, when she began to complain about stomachaches and headaches. Normally very cheerful and social, Leia was whiny, tearful, and did not want to play with her friends. Her parents were eager to address the problem before school started. Prior to the onset of these symptoms, they had been considering counseling, because their daughter did not have a particularly good year in kindergarten. Her teacher was overcritical and, although she was very bright, Leia was nervous about doing well in school, was demonstrating some perfectionistic behaviors, and was overly concerned about pleasing others.

Assessment considerations. Five-year-olds work extremely hard to "do the right thing," according to Youngs (1995, p. 125). Because they center on their own perceptions and one aspect of a situation rather than a broader view (Berk, 2003), it is not unusual for youngsters to assume that if they do something once that is displeasing to a parent or teacher, they will always be upset with them. Because they conceptualize things in either–or terms, it may be difficult to deal with temporary displacement with the birth of a sibling and understand that their parents can love two children equally, but in different ways. Developmentally, "children want to be first in the affection of their parents . . . and the firstborn, who knows what it is like to receive all the attention and affection of parents, wants very much to retain the spotlight" (Orton, 1997, p. 74). Because their ability to recall past events is limited, it is understandable that they do not remember having the same degree of attention when they were young, just as their sibling requires now.

Assessment should address how this young child dealt with the overly critical kindergarten teacher, how the family dynamics have changed since the birth of the baby, how the parents were addressing the needs of both children, the nature and extent of the perfectionistic behavior and how that affected Leia, the parents' expectations for their daughter's performance, and any other pertinent developmental milestones or environmental stressors. In all likelihood, this youngster's problems were anything but developmental and related to adjusting to new circumstances, both at home and at school, but further assessment could reveal something more significant.

Assessment procedures. The counselor first decided to direct assessment toward the family unit, asking Leia to draw a picture of her whole family. In her drawing, baby Susan was as large as Leia, positioned between her two parents, with Leia standing behind her mother some distance away. This confirmed the counselor's hypothesis that she was feeling somewhat displaced after the birth of her sister. In describing her picture, Leia indicated that she felt left out and sometimes felt sick, because then her mommy would pay more attention to her than to her sister.

Second, because Leia was very intelligent as well as verbal, the counselor served as secretary and used a series of unfinished sentences, such as the following, to assess the school situation.

1. The best thing about kindergarten was_____
2. The worst thing about kindergarten was _____
3. My kindergarten teacher was_____
4. When I did my work at school I_____
5. When I was at school I worried that _____
6. If I made a mistake I_____
7. When I think about first grade I_____
8. If I could change something about school, I would change_____

From Leia's responses to this assessment activity, it was apparent that she had a lot of anxiety about doing well and was very perfectionistic. Although many perfectionistic behaviors are academically adaptive, they can also be self-defeating (Kottman & Ashby, 2000). Therefore, it would be important to address the degree to which the perfectionistic behaviors were problematic and intervene before extreme self-criticism and high anxiety resulted. Leia verbalized that she sometimes got stomachaches when she thought about first grade, because she was afraid her teacher would not like her or would be mean like the kindergarten teacher. She also said that she was afraid that she would make mistakes and that now that she was a "big girl in first grade," she should not make mistakes. As children mature, their worries shift from early fears of monsters to more realistic worries about school (Orton, 1997), so this concern about her teacher seemed rather normal.

Although the counselor now assumed that Leia's reluctance to play with friends had more to do with not wanting to be away from her mother, she again used several open-ended sentences.

1. I like to play with _____
2. If someone asks me to play, I might not want to go because_____
3. Kids in my neighborhood are _____
4. My favorite place to play in my neighborhood is _____
5. Sometimes I'd rather stay home because _____

Prior to designing interventions, the counselor met with the parents to share and verify impressions. They concurred that Leia was ordinarily quite social and that the withdrawal began after the baby was born. They also saw evidence of perfectionism at school and in her violin lessons, stating that Leia often was very demanding of herself. They maintained that they did not intentionally reinforce her perfectionism and did not think that she would be modeling after them, although they both admitted to some perfectionism themselves. After discussing the other assessment considerations with them, they concluded that the targeted areas for intervention were dealing with the birth of the baby, the perfectionism, and anxiety about first grade.

Interventions. The counselor first read *Darcy and Gran Don't Like Babies* (Cutler, 1993), a story about a young girl who does not like her baby brother because he smells, looks funny, and demands too much attention. Everyone except her grandma tries to tell her that the baby is just like she was and that she will like him better when he can do more things, but her grandma listens to her doubts and, through modeling, helps Darcy realize that ultimately she will probably like the baby more than she does now. The counselor and Leia discussed her similar feelings, and the counselor helped her prepare a list of her worries about her "place" in the family to discuss with her parents at the next session. At that meeting, Leia was reassured that she was not less important, and she and her parents made plans to spend special time together and involve her more in helping with the baby, as appropriate. Leia was also invited to make a book about her family, which she illustrated and dictated to her mother what she wanted to say about each picture.

To deal with the school and perfectionism issues, the counselor first read *Oops!* (Vernon, 1989b, pp. 19–20), a story about a first grader making a mistake. She and Leia talked about the fact that no one is perfect, and that while it is important to try your best, no one expects people to always do things perfectly. The counselor pointed out that headaches and stomachaches develop when she starts to think that she always has to do everything exactly right. As a second intervention to address the perfectionism, she engaged Leia in an activity called I'm Not Perfect (Vernon, 2002, p. 97), in which Leia had to pick the "perfect" pencil from several others. Discussion centered on how people are like pencils—some of them perform better than others, but all function well in different areas. Then the counselor gave the pencil to Leia and a copy of a rational rhyme to help her remember that she did not always have to be perfect.

In addressing the anxiety about the upcoming school year, the counselor read *What If It Never Stops Raining* (N. Carlson, 1992), a story that describes how a young boy worries about many things that never happen, and the things that he worries about that do happen are not as bad as he thinks they will be. After reading the story, the counselor and Leia discussed the fact that even though it is possible that she could have a mean teacher in first grade, it is also possible that she could have a very nice teacher, or one that was nice sometimes and not nice at other times. Because children at this age are so concrete in their thinking, the counselor made a chart and had Leia draw faces to illustrate each category: very mean all the time, mean a lot of the time, sort of mean and sort of nice, nice most of the time, and nice all of the time. She encouraged Leia, with help from her parents if needed, to complete the chart based on discussions with older children in the neighborhood.

After several sessions, Leia's mother indicated that while she seemed more accepting of the baby and less worried about school and having to be perfect, she kept bringing up other minor problems that she said she had to "talk to the counselor about." After some discussion, the counselor and the mother seemed to think that because her mother took her out to lunch before the sessions and gave her a lot of attention, that perhaps Leia assumed that she had to continue to have problems to get attention.

At the next session, the counselor said that she would like to teach Leia to be her own counselor so that when she left on vacation, Leia would know how to take care of her problems. She asked Leia to sit in one chair and pretend that she was herself, speaking into the tape recorder about one of her problems. When she had finished describing how she was worried about her teacher in first grade being mean, the counselor asked her to switch chairs and pretend to be the counselor helping her with the problem. Leia said into the tape recorder, "Now Leia, just because your teacher was mean in kindergarten doesn't mean you will have a mean teacher in first grade. The teacher could be nice or sort of nice."

Leia practiced this procedure with other problems and was encouraged to use it at home. Frequency of the visits was reduced.

Evaluation/summary. Because of the parental involvement, Leia quickly began to feel better about her place in the family. Her parents began paying more attention to her, and the frequency of the headaches and stomachaches declined. She was more willing to spend time with friends. Because the anxiety about school was in the future, the counselor continued to work with her over the course of the summer and had her make her own version of *What If It Never Stops Raining* to help her remember that often times, things are not as bad as she imagines them to be. Although there was still some anxiety when school started, Leia was able to go into the situation knowing that her teacher would not necessarily be like her previous one, and that she did not always have to be perfect. Over time, there was improvement on this dimension as well.

Other Typical Developmental Problems

Young children take things quite literally. Therefore, it is not uncommon for them to become easily frightened because of their interpretation of an event. Elkind (1991) shared the example of the young child who was told that when he returned home after preschool he could see his new "half brother." Because he was frightened by the thought of seeing half of a brother, he refused to go home. I (Ann Vernon) can recall my son suddenly refusing to walk to day care after preschool with the high school student who had accompanied him every day for 3 weeks. When asked why he was frightened, he explained a police officer visiting school the previous day warned them not to go with strangers. In Eric's words, "I really don't know AnnaBeth too well; she's still a stranger."

Four- and 5-year-olds face uncertainty as they begin to experience new situations. They may be hesitant to leave the house to play in the yard, to visit a friend, or to be left at preschool, because they are afraid of separation from a parent. They also have numerous other fears, such as dark rooms, noise at night, large or wild animals, snakes, bodily injury, and bad people (Robinson, Rotter, Fey, & Robinson, 1991). As they try out new things, they may develop new behaviors, such as lying or stealing, which results in stress because concerned parents will pressure them to stop the behaviors (Youngs, 1995). Five-year-olds also worry about abandonment and the safety of their parents, according to Youngs. It is important to remember that cultural traditions and experiences must be considered within the context of typical developmental concerns.

Summary

All too often, parents and professionals have to be reminded that childhood is not an easy time, and that although a young child's problems may seem minor in comparison with those faced by adults, they are extremely significant to 4- or 5-year-olds who do not have the repertoire of coping mechanisms nor the verbal or cognitive skills to "put it all together" and make sense of what they are experiencing. For this reason, the developmental assessment and intervention processes are critical.

The goal of developmental assessment is to look at where children are in relation to what is normal for a particular stage of development. In many cases, the problems are indicative of normal developmental issues, as illustrated by Adam's anxiety about wetting his pants, Margaret's fear of the dark, Leia's jealousy over a new sibling and anxiety about first grade, and Mark's swimming terror. The goal of the assessment then becomes twofold: to determine the severity of the symptoms (do they go beyond what would be considered typical for a problem of this nature?) and to design assessment procedures appropriate for the child at this age. If the problem is something many children commonly experience but not reflective of a normal developmental issue, the goal of the assessment is to determine if the child's conceptualization of the problem and response to it correspond to what is characteristic of this developmental period or if the child has regressed significantly.

Effective assessment and intervention must also be culturally responsive, based on the unique experience of the multicultural client (Ridley, Espelage, & Rubinstein, 1997). The two case studies of Chang and Mariela in this chapter illustrated key assessment considerations and effective interventions that addressed the specific needs of ethnically diverse children.

Examples of age and culturally appropriate interventions described in this chapter included bibliotherapy, visual arts, storytelling, drawing, behavioral techniques, therapeutic games, and role play. By utilizing a wide variety of developmentally based interventions, parents and professionals can collaborate on the most effective way to address problems.

Chapter 6

Middle Childhood:
Assessment and Intervention

✳

Many people have vivid memories, both positive and negative, about what it was like to be an elementary school student: sharing secrets with a "best friend," being selected as the teacher's "helper," being picked last for a team, or being teased or bullied by classmates. People may recall not being able to read or do math as well as some of their classmates, or being commended for outstanding verbal abilities. Throughout the grade-school journey, people continued to master various developmental tasks, some of which were more challenging and required more effort than others. Although many readily mastered these tasks, others struggled or suffered developmental delays in some areas.

✳

"Rich years, filled with growth and change" is how Cobb (2001, p. 448) characterized middle childhood. Berger and Thompson (1991) contended that these are the best years of the life span because children master new tasks at a rapid rate and are physically and intellectually stronger than when they were younger. Most children are able to think more logically and differentiate between right and wrong. They also become more self-reflective. Berger and Thompson described this period as one in which children see their parents as helpful, their teachers as fair, and their futures as promising. They noted two clouds on the horizon, however: school failure and peer rejection.

Others have a different view of these early school years, citing increasing evidence of childhood stress (Porter, 2003), the pressure to grow up "too fast, too soon" (Elkind, 1988), and the high percentage of children who suffer from emotional or other problems and need mental health services (Thompson & Rudolph, 2000). Orton (1997) discussed the staggering impact of poverty on more than 14 million children in the United States, and Brazelton and Greenspan (2000) expressed concern about the effects of complex and often unstable family constellations on children. In addition, children are growing up in a world filled with tension, in which their basic safety is increasingly being threatened (Thompson et al., 2004). It seems that the number of children who enjoy secure childhoods is diminishing.

Although middle childhood is a more stable growth period than those preceding or following it, helping professionals who routinely work with middle-age children (ages 6–10) are aware that while many children breeze through this period of development, others get hung up because of a combination of personal, environmental, or cultural factors. Because they are limited somewhat by their ability to conceptualize and verbalize what they are experiencing, this age group of children needs support as they forge new territory.

In this chapter, descriptions of developmental characteristics are identified for the middle-age child, ages 6–10. This information is followed by several examples of problems this age group experiences, accompanied by specific developmental assessment strategies and interventions.

Characteristics of Children in Middle Childhood

Cobb (2001) noted that in the middle years, children develop skills that they will use throughout their lives. In some ways, it is like having "a foot in two worlds" (p. 408); they are quite grown up in many ways but still do not have it all figured out. According to Cobb, school has a significant impact on children's lives and contributes to their changing world. Perhaps more important is the shift in cognitive processing that occurs between the ages of 5 and 7, which has major implications for other areas of development (Rathus, 2004).

As described in the following paragraphs, there are transitions and consolidations that occur during this period that contribute to the growth of children ages 6–10.

Self-Development

As their cognitive abilities mature, children's self-understanding expands and becomes more complex (Harter, 1999; Siegler et al., 2003). They develop a multidimensional view of themselves (K. B. Owens, 2002), describing themselves in terms of several competencies at once: "I am tall, athletic, and get good grades." Their self-descriptions reflect general traits such as "I am good at sports" as opposed to specific behaviors, such as "I good at throwing a ball" (Cobb, 2001). Cobb noted that they are also more likely to describe themselves in terms of their relationships with others rather than in terms of their possessions. As they mature during this period of development, they are also able to form higher order self-concepts so that they are able to construct more global views of themselves (Siegler et al., 2003). Their internal locus of control is beginning to evolve (Vernon & Al-Mabuk, 1995), and they are less likely to blame someone else or bad luck on their failures or weaknesses (Berger, 2003). They can progress from explaining their actions by referring to events in the immediate situation ("I hit her because she hit me") to relating actions to personality traits or feelings ("I was upset about something else and just hit her").

Throughout middle childhood, children's self-concepts are increasingly based on how others, especially peers, evaluate them (Siegler et al., 2003). As they begin to compare their skills and achievements with others, they become self-critical, feel inferior, or may experience a decrease in self-esteem (Berger, 2003; Cole & Cole, 1996). They are very sensitive to feedback from peers and may become more inhibited about trying new things (Bee, 2000). According to Bee, they become more aware of their specific areas of competence, and they may approach the process of self-evaluation with self-confidence or self-doubt. Because they are more readily able to differentiate the areas in which they are more or less successful, they start to take failure more seriously, which in turn negatively affects self-esteem. Harter (1983) posited that self-esteem reaches a low at age 12 before it starts to rise gradually in the teenage years.

Social Development

Socialization in the context of a peer group becomes a central issue for the middle-age child. Acceptance in a group and a "best friend" contribute significantly to a child's sense of competence (Berger, 2003; Berger & Thompson, 1991). Friendships serve important functions: Children learn to cooperate and compromise, negotiate, and assume roles as leaders and followers (Berger, 2003; Vernon & Al-Mabuk, 1995). Dealing with peer group pressure, rejection, peer approval, conformity, and intimate friendships help children begin to formulate values, behaviors, and beliefs that facilitate their social development (Pruitt, 1998).

Throughout this period, friendships become increasingly more intense and intimate, particularly for girls, and they generally choose friends who are of the same age, gender, and ethnicity and who have similar interests (Cobb, 2001; Siegler et al., 2003). As they grow older, their friendship patterns become more rigid, making it difficult for an outsider to join an established group. The size of their friendship network also decreases with age, although boys tend to have larger and less intimate networks (Berger & Thompson, 1991).

As opposed to early childhood, when children were more egocentric and did not need friends as much, children in middle childhood are becoming more dependent on friends for help in academic and social situations, as well as for companionship and self-validation (Berger, 2003; Siegler et al., 2003). Social skills, cooperative behavior, and self-esteem can be developed through participation in clubs such as scouts and 4-H. Team play is a new dimension of social development, helping children learn to give and receive feedback, to value their role as part of a larger system, to experience personal satisfaction from victories and frustration from defeat, and to contribute to team goals (Newman & Newman, 1991).

By age 7, children begin to outgrow their egocentrism, and the universe no longer revolves around them (Crenshaw, 1990). They develop more prosocial behaviors, such as sharing a lunch or showing concern for others (Berger & Thompson, 1991). They are better able to interpret social cues (facial expressions, vocal intonation) and communicate information to listeners (Hartup, 1984). Selman and Schultz (1998) noted that between the ages of 5 and 9, children gradually become better able to differentiate "between physical actions (behaviors) and psychological characteristics (thoughts, feelings, and intentions) of others" (p. 12), which means that they can distinguish between intentional and unintentional actions of others. However, these authors pointed out that the children's thinking is still quite simplistic, so if they see someone smiling, they assume the person is happy. In other words, "this unilateral way of thinking lacks a sense of reciprocal perspectives" (Selman & Schultz, 1998, p. 12). As the reciprocal understanding of friendship develops, children are able to understand feelings and intentions of themselves as well as others and become more aware of jealousy, trust, and rejection among friends (Selman & Schultz, 1998). As they move toward early adolescence, children begin to develop the ability to look at things from another person's perspective: to put themselves in someone else's shoes and understand that others are able to do this as well.

By and large, children in middle childhood are much more adept at social problem solving and can master a variety of alternatives for resolving conflict. However, despite their more advanced social abilities, children of both sexes can engage in either overt aggression, which involves physical acts such as kicking or hitting, or relational aggression such as spreading lies or sharing secrets (Cobb, 2001). Crick and Grotpeter (1995) indicated that overt aggression is more characteristic of boys and relational aggression is more typical for girls, although children of either sex can participate in both forms. Overtly aggressive children may bully others who tend to have poorer social skills, but according to Hodges, Boivin, Vitaro, and Bukowski (1999), children are less likely to be victimized if they have a friend, and friends can buffer the effects of bullying if it does occur.

Although parents remain an important source of support, some psychologists maintain that peers have much more influence in determining self-concept and personality (Harris, 1998). Although this may be an extreme opinion, Rubin, Bukowski, and Parker (1998) suggested that there is evidence to support the fact that difficulties with peers put children at risk for developing psychological problems. Suffice it to say that peers are very influential in children's lives.

Emotional Development

School-age children's understanding of emotions is more complex, and generally, they are more sensitive, empathic, and better able to recognize and communicate their feelings to others (McDevitt & Ormrod, 2002). They now understand that a person can have two conflicting emotions simultaneously (happy that she got to go to her grandparents' house, but sad because she only got to stay for a short time). These children have learned that feelings can change and that they are not the cause of another person's emotional discomfort (Kaplan, 2000). They also recognize that their thoughts and interpretations determine how they feel, and as a result, they understand that because others may think differently about a situation, they may have different feelings (McDevitt & Ormrod, 2002). According to Berk (1999), they are also more adept at hiding their emotions when they do not want to hurt someone else's feelings.

During middle childhood, fears and anxieties are related to real life, as opposed to imaginary issues. For example, they are no longer afraid of ghosts but are worried about tests and grades, their parents' health, and being harmed by someone. Happiness is often related to peer acceptance and achieving goals (Siegler et al., 2003).

Physical Development

This is a period of relatively stable growth for most children (Bee, 2000; McDevitt & Ormrod, 2002), although they grow taller, their body proportions change, and their muscles become stronger (Schickedanz, Schickedanz, Forsyth, & Forsyth, 1998). Children continue to gain a little over 2 inches in height each year and gain an average of 5 to 7 pounds each year during middle childhood (Rathus, 2004). In fact, because of the high amount of energy they expend, they need to eat more, which causes the average body weight to double. Gender differences in weight and height are insignificant in middle childhood (Cobb, 2001).

Maturation varies from child to child, and it is normal to find various rates of development. Rathus (2004) reported that by age 10, children's weights may vary by 30–35 pounds and their heights by as much as 6 inches. Some children begin puberty by age 10 or 11. This variation sometimes can be a source of distress for children who think they "look different" or who are noticeably lacking in physical skills as they compare themselves with others (Vernon & Al-Mabuk, 1995).

Because of the slow growth rate during this period of development, children have a high degree of self-control over their bodies and are not as clumsy as when they enter puberty, for example. Their gross motor skills improve steadily (Rathus, 2004) to the point at which they can master almost any motor skill (Berger, 2003). Some motor skills rely on reaction time, which gradually improves as the brain matures. Fine motor skills also improve during this period. Children have much better manual dexterity, holding a pencil or scissors with much more control, for example.

At this age, boys and girls are about equal in most physical abilities. However, girls have better limb coordination and overall flexibility and boys have greater overall strength (Berger & Thompson, 1991; Rathus, 2004).

Cognitive Development

During this school-age period, vast differences occur in cognitive development. According to Piaget (1967), a transitional period between preoperational and concrete operational thought occurs between the ages of 5 and 7, but by age 7 or 8, children are definitely concrete operational thinkers. As such, children in middle childhood are able to understand logical operations, such as identity (the content of an object remains the same even if the appearance changes), reversibility (a process can be reversed into the original form), reciprocity (a change in one dimension affects a change in another), and classification (categorizing objects by classes). These principles can be applied in many contexts, such as friendships, rules in games, or team play.

School-age children's thinking is characterized by a broader grasp of underlying assumptions, rational thought, and more comprehensive logic (Santrock & Yussen, 1992). They acquire new ways to organize facts and learn best by questioning, exploring, and doing (Gauvain, 2001). Their problem-solving abilities are enhanced, and, as a result, they begin to view social and personal situations with more confidence.

Although language development is more subtle, children continually understand more about how language can be used, which results in more control of comprehension and use of language. They are able to use vocabulary in more sophisticated ways, tailoring words, sentence length, content, and nonverbal cues to the situation (Berger & Thompson, 1991; Berk, 1999).

Newman and Newman (1991) maintained that the most impressive area of growth during these middle years is in the acquisition of skills, particularly reading. They emphasized that the energy that middle-age children apply to learning new skills is similar to that of a toddler who strives for competence and mastery.

It is important to note that despite the growth in cognitive development, there are limitations. Although children in middle childhood can reason more logically, they have difficulty with abstract concepts; they do not readily think about things they cannot see (Cobb, 2001). And, because they focus on what they can see, their problem-solving abilities are limited because they do not consider other possible solutions. They also struggle with how to systematically combine information (Siegler et al., 2003). Elkind (1978, as cited in Cobb, 2001) pointed out that children operate from assumptions that they make based on limited information. They mistake their assumptions for facts and jump to conclusions. All of these factors have a considerable impact on how children respond to events in their lives.

Moral Development

Most elementary school children reason at Kohlberg's preconventional level of moral judgment, reflecting the lowest level of development, because they do not consider social norms when making a decision. These children assume that adults define what is right and wrong, and their judgments about whether behavior is moral or not is based on the consequences of those behaviors (McDevitt & Ormrod, 2002). As they move from the primary to the intermediate grades, some children begin to exhibit conventional morality, in which they understand that it is necessary to conform to laws and rules. They are rather rigid in their adherence to rules and obey even if there is no reward for good behavior or negative consequence for disobedience (Berk, 2003; McDevitt & Ormrod, 2002). Peer interaction, which facilitates opportunities to take another perspective and generate new rules and standards, promotes moral development at this age, as do parent–child interactions and discussions about value-laden topics, according to Walker and Taylor (1991).

Colangelo and Dettmann (1985) found that children in Grades 3–5 were most concerned about moral issues relating to peer and family relationship issues; conflicts regarding honesty, cheating, stealing, and lying; and decisions about whether to intervene or report. Boys at this age also reported dilemmas about alcohol and tobacco. These practical, everyday experiences become sources of conflict for children as they strive to develop these moral skills.

Parental Involvement With Children in Middle Childhood

As children grow up and begin to experience new things, so do their parents. I (Ann Vernon) vividly remember "our" first experience with grades in elementary school. When my son brought home a spelling test with a less-than-average grade, I immediately assumed he would be a poor speller forever and wondered what I should have done as a parent to prevent this from occurring. Luckily, my 8-year-old was more rational than I was, putting it in perspective by saying, "Just because I got one bad grade doesn't mean that I'll flunk spelling. I just have to work harder." It became obvious to me that although the teacher helped my child deal with the ramifications of this new set of circumstances, no one prepared me for this.

During this period of development when peers gradually become more important and families less important, at least in some cultures, significant changes begin to occur in the way parents and children interact. Parent–child communication becomes increasingly important. Helping children learn to accept responsibility, deal with success and failure, and develop social skills are critical tasks.

Fortunately, the role of the counselor as consultant has expanded to provide parents with information about normal development and what to do when their children deviate from the norm (Dustin & Ehly, 1992; Mathias, 1992; Vernon, 2004). Parent education and support groups exist in many schools and communities to help parents deal with developmental issues and parenting skills, and with the special needs of the single parent, stepparent, parents with terminally ill children, or parents of children with physical or mental disabilities, for example. Counselors must be sensitive to cultural differences when working with parents and be careful not to judge or impose values. Remembering that all parents want what is best for their children builds a common bond.

During middle childhood, children gain access to new settings and circumstances, which present them with developmental challenges. The role of parents, although somewhat diminished because teachers, coaches, peers, and other adults also exercise varying degrees of influence, is still critical.

Problem Assessment and Intervention:
Selected Case Studies

It is interesting to speculate why some children negotiate developmental milestones with seemingly little difficulty, whereas others struggle with them. Even more perplexing is how some children experience incredibly negative circumstances and still achieve healthy development. Because middle childhood spans a number of years, children live through numerous "firsts," some stressful and some exhilarating, as their horizons broaden.

In this chapter, problems experienced by 6- to 10-year-olds are described. Problems selected represent typical developmental issues as well as situational problems. The intent is to provide the reader with a brief description of the problem, followed by examples of developmentally and culturally appropriate assessment and intervention strategies.

Case Study One: 6-Year-Old Steven

Problem overview. Steven, a 6-year-old Caucasian boy, and his father had lived with Steven's grandmother for the past 5 years. Last month, after a brief illness, the grandmother died of heart failure. Since then, Steven has said very little about the incident, which is not unusual, because young children "often fail to exhibit the normal signs of bereavement observed in adults" (Wagner, 2003, p. 192). However, the school recommended counseling because they noticed that he had become very withdrawn and was exhibiting some regressive behaviors such as thumb sucking and enuresis. According to the father, Steven and his grandmother had been very close, and, because his mother left them when Steven was a baby, the grandmother had been his primary caretaker and had been like a mother to him. Prior to her illness and death, Steven was a well-adjusted little boy.

Assessment considerations. The death of a grandparent can be extremely painful for young children and is often their first personal experience with death (Crenshaw, 1990; Kroen, 1996). Charkow (1998) and Crenshaw (1990) noted that the degree of attachment to the deceased is an important factor in the way the child experiences grief, and it is sometimes quite profound, particularly if the grandparent played a special role in the child's life, as was the case with Steven. Typically children ages 3–9 may experience adjustment disorders, psychosomatic disorders, depression, regression, or disruption of habits (Cunningham & Hare, 1989); anxiety, guilt, anger, and sadness (Worden, 1996); behavioral problems and increased aggression (Kroen, 1996; McGlauflin, 1998); and lack of concentration and inability to complete tasks that can result in poor academic performance (Pennells & Smith, 1995; Worden, 1996). Counselors working with grieving children must understand that children's understanding of death is based on their awareness of irreversibility (finality of death), causality (understanding the actual cause for the death), inevitability (awareness that all living things ultimately die), and cessation (understanding that all biological functions stop with death), according to Lazar and Torney-Purta (1991). These authors noted that between the ages of 6 and 8 years, children are becoming more aware of the irreversibility of death but still may think that the deceased person is asleep or away on a trip. According to Crenshaw, children under age 9 tend to have scary ideas about death.

Assessment should focus not only on the relationship this young boy had with his grandmother but also on his level of understanding about her illness and death and what he had been told about it, who has assumed the role as his primary caretaker and how he relates to this individual, what routines or rituals have changed since the death, and how the father and significant others have dealt with the regressive behaviors. Verifying that all of these behaviors are a result of the illness and death is also important.

Assessment procedures. Given that Steven was very shy, the counselor decided to use play media to assess how he was feeling and what he was thinking. Before Steven entered the room, the counselor placed a basket of puppets and toys beside a small chair. After introducing himself to Steven, the counselor informed his client that he knew something sad had recently happened when his grandmother had died and that he would like to help Steven deal with his feelings. He invited Steven to play with the puppets or toys in the basket.

During the first session, Steven held one of the stuffed animals but did not talk at all until the end of the session. The counselor respected his silence but occasionally made comments, such as "I bet that raccoon loves to have you touch him" and "It looks like you like to hold things close to you." Finally, Steven shared with the counselor that his grandma had given him a really big stuffed animal for his birthday. The counselor asked him to tell him more about what kind it was and what it looked like, and Steven did elaborate some in response to these questions. When the time was up, the counselor asked if Steven would be willing to come back again, and he nodded affirmatively.

In the next two sessions, with some prompting, Steven used puppets actively to act out what it was like when his grandmother was very sick and when she died. From this, the counselor learned that Steven thought it was his fault that she died, because he had had a cold and his dad had said not to get too close to her so she would not catch it. It was apparent that he felt very guilty because one of his puppets kept saying "bad boy, bad boy" to the other puppet.

The counselor also asked his young client to draw a picture of what it was like for him now that his grandmother was gone. From this assessment, the counselor noted fear. His picture revealed three coffins—one for his grandma, one for his dad, and one for him. When the counselor asked him about this, Steven said that if his grandma's heart stopped beating, maybe that would happen to him and his dad too. His second picture revealed him standing beside his bed at night with a frightened expression on his face. When asked, he told the counselor that he was afraid to go to sleep at night, because someone had told him that his grandmother was just sleeping, but then she never woke up again.

As a 6-year-old, it is likely that Steven still has many preoperational thought processes that would explain why he personally feels responsible for his grandmother's illness (egocentric thinking) and why he is generalizing about this situation to his own life, and why he is having difficulty distinguishing between death and sleep. Although these are fairly typical concerns for a 6-year-old, intervention is essential to help him deal effectively with this loss to stop the progression of the regressed behaviors.

In conjunction with the sessions with his young client, the counselor also met with Steven's father to learn more about what Steven had been told about the illness and death, who was assuming the role as primary caretaker and how his son was relating to that individual, changes in routines and rituals, and any concerns or questions he had about how this 6-year-old was reacting to this loss.

Interventions. Play therapy in the form of sand play was used to help Steven work through the sadness and guilt. Using a sand tray and a collection of figurines, Steven was invited to create sand pictures. His first picture depicted his grandmother sick in bed, with his father scolding him to stay away. His next picture showed his grandmother in a box beside a big hole. His third picture showed him standing by himself, with his father off in the distance. As he created his pictures, Steven began talking more about his grandma's death and how he missed her, and initiated a dialogue with the father figurine, telling him how he did not mean to make his grandmother sick. In subsequent sessions, Steven worked through more of his guilt and sadness using sand play.

Because Steven was so convinced that his father blamed him for his grandmother's illness and subsequent death, the counselor invited the father in to the session, having first explained to him that it is not at all uncommon for 6-year-olds to take things very literally, and that when he had told his son not to get close to his grandmother because he did not want her to catch Steven's cold, Steven assumed the blame. During the session, Steven's father reassured him that he was not at fault and together the father and the counselor explained as simplistically as possible what had happened to his grandma's heart, using the book *I Miss You—A First Look at Death* (Thomas, 2000) to help answer some of Steven's questions.

Bibliotherapy also was used in the next session with this young client. Through reading *The Saddest Time* (Simon, 1986) to Steven, the counselor and Steven were able to discuss how this story related to his situation, clarifying misconceptions and helping him deal with his feelings through catharsis. The counselor also invited him to collect some things that reminded him of his grandma and together they could make a memory box. At the following session, the counselor invited Steven to draw some pictures on the outside of the box that reminded him of things he liked best about his grandma, and on the inside they put his artifacts. In a subsequent session they made a memory book, which Steven illustrated and dictated to the counselor what he wanted him to write underneath each picture. Finally, the counselor suggested to the father that they plant a tree or a bush in her memory.

Eventually the teacher and parent reported that this young boy was acting more like himself. There was less evidence of regressive behavior, and he appeared happier much of the time.

Evaluation/summary. Parents of young children need to understand how their children are experiencing death and how to talk to them about what has occurred. In Steven's case, the variety of concrete interventions helped him work through the loss. The behaviors he was exhibiting were thought to be normal reactions, but had the thumb-sucking and enuretic behavior continued, further intervention would have been necessary. Evaluation involved consultation with his teacher and his father, as well as observation in the classroom to determine if he was less withdrawn and more cheerful.

Case Study Two: 8-Year-Old Keg

Problem overview. Keg, an 8-year-old boy from Thailand who has been living with his immigrant parents in the United States for 3 years, was sent to the school nurse because of self-reported health problems. The teacher also reported a steady decline in his academic performance and indicated that he continuously complained of headaches and frequently asked to leave the classroom. According to the teacher, Keg lacked energy, seldom ate much lunch, and demonstrated little interest in games or fun activities. During a routine check, the nurse noticed that his skin was extremely dry and hot, with a series of bruises and marks following a regular pattern.

Suspecting child abuse, but concerned about cultural issues, the school nurse and the counselor contacted the parents immediately prior to making an official report. During the initial interview conducted by the counselor and nurse, the parents were very upset and in disbelief that their son could potentially be removed from the home if they could not explain the origin of Keg's abrasions. The parents reported that the bruises and marks came as a result of rubbing a coin against the skin and extinguishing the light of a candle with a glass. They indicated that this healing method has been a long and proven tradition practiced by their ancestors for many years.

Assessment considerations. As children integrate social standards and cultural expectations into their self-definitions, the self-conscious emotions of pride and guilt become clearly governed by personal responsibility (Berk, 1999). Shame is often felt when violating a standard that is not under their control. Sometimes feelings of frustration and confusion are manifested through psychosomatic symptoms. There are multiple variables in this case that the counselor has to consider prior to rendering a tentative assessment. Most importantly, on the basis of the symptoms, the counselor would need to rule out the possibility of a medical condition associated with Keg's changes in behavior at school, as well as child abuse.

Assessment procedures. After meeting with the parents, the counselor and the school nurse had researched indigenous Thai medical interventions and consulted a local individual who was familiar with Southeast Asian cultures. They learned that in order to calm the symptoms associated with fever, colds, and other related illnesses, Southeast Asian folk healing practices include rubbing a warm coin on the body of the individual. Therefore, they concluded that the bruises did occur as a result of a cultural practice.

In conjunction with the school nurse, the counselor contacted the parents and recommended a medical checkup because, occasionally, diabetes and heart conditions mimic mental health disorders such as depression and anxiety. Because the parents had signed a release, the counselor was able to confer with the physician, who indicated that Keg had the presence of a bacterial infection that needed to be treated with antibiotics for 10 days. The physician shared that Keg appeared to be dehydrated and underweight. However, Keg's condition was stable and with the combination of rest, fluids, and antibiotics, the doctor predicted that they would see considerable progress within 2 weeks.

Interventions. In a long conversation with Keg's parents, the counselor normalized and acknowledged the folk healing interventions and explained the situation in light of the U.S. legal and educational systems. First, the parents were reluctant to stop their practices but eventually realized that Keg could possibly be removed from their home if these practices continued. They agreed to cooperate with the counselor and nurse but wanted to be involved in the process.

Second, in light of the medical recommendations, Keg stayed at home a few days and returned to school refreshed and noticeably energized. The counselor talked to the teachers and recommended that they provide Keg with additional breaks between tasks and the privilege of eating snacks frequently. After 3 weeks, Keg's demeanor had changed completely, and his school performance was back to normal. His parents were scheduled to talk to the counselor biweekly for 2 months to keep the situation under control.

Third, the counselor met with Keg twice a week to reestablish Keg's self-confidence. The counselor devised a small puppet stage and both Keg and the counselor performed various scenes titled "Trusting My Family," "The Weak and the Strong," "Proud of My Two Little Worlds," and so forth. The counselor's plan was to reestablish Keg's self-image after being physically ill; help him regain his trust in the family in spite of the stressful moments among the doctor, school staff, and family; and help him appreciate his bicultural status.

Evaluation/summary. The initial concern was Keg's physical and psychological safety. The counselor continued to obtain feedback from the homeroom teacher for suspicious marks on his body or for sudden changes in health and academic performance. Apparently, the parents understood the diametrical approaches to health in both cultures and agreed to maintain an equilibrium between the two cultures. They agreed to sign a follow-up contract with the school nurse and counselor indicating their willingness to contact them at any time if they needed clarification and direction.

Case Study Three: 8-Year-Old Jennifer

Problem overview. Jennifer, an 8-year old Caucasian girl, was brought to counseling by her mother because of Jennifer's anxiety about bad things happening to the family. This began last year when they were staying in a hotel where the fire alarm went off during the night. Although the fire was minor and no one was injured, this is when the problem began. Later in the summer, Jennifer was staying with her elderly grandmother and a tornado touched down nearby. According to Jennifer, she and her grandmother had gone to a storm cellar, but when they tried to get out they were not strong enough to push the door open and were trapped there for a short while until a neighbor happened to come by. In addition to these two concerns, she worried about being in a car accident. Other than this anxiety, Jennifer is a well-adjusted child with lots of friends. She does well in school and presents no problem at home except typical sibling conflict.

Assessment considerations. Anxiety is one of the most commonly occurring but least commonly treated internalizing disorder among children (Doll & Doll, 1997), perhaps because children may not communicate how anxious they are. Doll and Doll reported that children who are anxious often dwell on thoughts about being out of control and worry about disasters, and it is not uncommon for children this age to overgeneralize about situations and imagine the worst (Vernon, 2002). At the same time, if the anxiety is high, some children will work diligently to avoid experiences, to the point that they do not have a normal life. Therefore, it is important to take their worries seriously and devise concrete ways to help them come to their own conclusions and reduce the level of intensity of the anxiety.

During assessment, it will be important to identify any physical symptoms: nausea, shortness of breath, sweating or chills, racing pulse, physical weakness, or uncontrollable shaking. Looking at the frequency, intensity, and duration of the anxiety and the circumstances in which it occurred will help rule out generalized anxiety disorder. Assessing for panic attacks, when the onset of the anxiety is sudden and unexpected and intense, is also important.

Assessment procedures. Jennifer was a very verbal child, thus it was not difficult for her to describe her fears. To get a specific assessment of the intensity of the anxiety and the frequency with which it occurred, the counselor gave her three charts (fire, storm/tornado, accident) marked with the days of the week. For each worrisome situation, Jennifer was to mark a 1–10 (from *low* to *high*) each day to represent how much she worried about the particular situation. During the next visit, they discussed the degree of worry, which was higher for the accidents because they were in a car daily, and for the storms because the weather had been changeable. To determine the specific thoughts about each of these fears, the counselor asked this young client to make a list of all the things she thought about in relation to each. For storms, Jennifer listed the following: A tornado would destroy their home, bad lightening would set their house on fire, or high winds would knock trees into their house. For the car accident, Jennifer listed herself and family members being seriously hurt and one or more of them dying in a crash. For the fire, she listed that they would have flames all over their bodies or that the fire would make the hotel blow up and they would all die.

In discussions with both Jennifer and her parents, it appeared that her anxiety was confined to these issues involving natural disasters or accidents, so generalized anxiety was ruled out. She had not had panic attacks.

Interventions. In this case, the counselor gave Jennifer a chart and asked her to watch the weather portion of the news each night. She was supposed to note the following from her observations: Was the following day going to be (a) sunny and pleasant; (b) cloudy, but no rain; (c) rainy, but no storms; (d) windy and rainy; (e) high winds, rain, lightening, and thunder; or (f) tornado? When she and the counselor discussed the information, Jennifer was able to see that there had been no bad storms all week. To see if this was more of an exception than a rule, Jennifer charted the weather for several weeks to help her see that there only had been severe weather very occasionally. She and the counselor also researched tornadoes in the encyclopedia, discussing the rare combination of circumstances needed to produce them. She learned to use self-talk and wrote the following on index cards that she could quickly refer to in case of a storm: "The weather is not horribly bad very often," "Instead of being upset all the time, I can learn what to do in case of a tornado," and "I can keep reminding myself that a bad storm does not mean there will be a tornado." This helped reinforce the idea that although bad things can happen, it is not necessary to worry every day. To deal with the other two worries, the counselor used a similar strategy. She had Jennifer interview her father, who sold car insurance, about the number of serious accidents compared with more minor ones; read the newspaper to chart occurrences of fires in her town; and interview the fire chief about causes of fires and fire prevention tips. Empowerment strategies also were used: Jennifer and her family purchased additional smoke alarms and bought fire extinguishers for the house.

All of this information seemed helpful to Jennifer, and she announced that she was no longer as fearful of bad storms and fires. However, she was still very anxious about riding in the car, so further intervention was needed. Because Jennifer was bright, the counselor discussed with her the concept of probability versus possibility, explaining that anything was possible, but how likely would the things she worried about occur? She used a continuum with Jennifer, in which she drew a line across a sheet of paper and labeled one end "the worst that could happen" and the other end "the best that could happen." Then she worked with Jennifer to identify the worst ("We would be in a car accident and everybody would die") and best ("We would not be in an accident") and several points in between: "We could be in a very bad accident and all of us would get hurt badly but not die," "We could be in an accident and only one of us would get hurt badly," "We could get in an accident and someone would only be hurt a little bit," and "We could be in an accident and the car would get hurt but we wouldn't." This strategy is very effective for concrete thinkers who often only imagine the best and worst case scenarios but fail to see that there are also other things that could happen. Jennifer's assignment was to put this continuum in the glove compartment of the car and get it out each time she was in the car to help her see the situation from a broader perspective.

Although Jennifer reported only mild nausea and some shaking when she was very anxious, it appeared that some relaxation techniques would be beneficial. The counselor used several activities from *Ready, Set, Release* (Allen & Klein, 1996), which targeted deep breathing and muscle relaxation.

Evaluation/summary. Although this was not a problem that disappeared overnight, the charting, interviews, and relaxation techniques helped. The continuum strategy was also very effective because it helped this young concrete thinker, who only imagined the best and worst case scenarios, see that there were also other things that could possibly happen, all of which would be better than the worst case scenario. This combination of interventions helped this 8-year-old learn how to put her worries in perspective and reduce the anxiety with self-talk and fact-finding.

Case Study Four: 9-Year-Old Carrie

Problem overview. Carrie, a 9-year-old Caucasian girl, asked to see the school counselor, because, in her words, she was "scared to death to take tests." The counselor learned from the teacher that Carrie was a good student but became extremely anxious prior to and during a test, to the point at which she sometimes missed school on the day of the test or felt sick to her stomach at school as test time approached. Although she normally did quite well, Carrie was very self-critical about all her work. She was particularly hard on herself if she did not perform up to her standards on an exam.

Carrie and her 10-year-old brother have been living with their mother since their parents' divorce 5 years ago. They have very little contact with their father but seem to have adjusted to the situation, according to the mother, who indicated that Carrie does not experience anxiety about anything else as far as she knows. The children are sometimes alone after school for about an hour, but Carrie seems to handle that situation without feeling anxious.

Assessment considerations. Many children in this stage of development are very self-critical as they become more aware of their abilities and compare them with others' (Berger, 2003; Newman & Newman, 1991). Because they can differentiate the areas in which they are more or less successful, they take failure more seriously, so it is not uncommon for some children to experience test anxiety, particularly in subjects that are more difficult for them. Furthermore, because they have a more internal locus of control, they blame themselves, not bad luck or others, for their failure, which contributes to self-downing as well as anxiety (Vernon & Al-Mabuk, 1995).

Although input from the teacher and parent seemed to indicate that the test anxiety was the only issue, it would be important to determine if there was anxiety in other areas of performance as well. Perfectionism might also be contributing to the problem. A general assessment of the "health" dimension on the HELPING model (see chapter 2) would help determine if she was getting adequate sleep the night before an exam.

Assessment procedures. Because Carrie referred herself and wanted help with the problem, she had no difficulty verbalizing what she was experiencing. The problem began this year, because she received letter grades for the first time as a fourth grader. According to Carrie, she gets nervous about doing her homework well, but, because she has plenty of time to do it and check it over, it is not the same as taking a test under time pressure. To get a more comprehensive picture, the counselor drew five columns on a sheet of paper and asked Carrie to respond in writing to the following: (a) what she is thinking prior to taking the test, (b) what she is feeling physically prior to taking the test, (c) what she imagines will happen, (d) how she feels emotionally prior to taking the test and during the test, and (e) what she thinks and feels when the test is over. The counselor also used the following unfinished sentences with Carrie to determine if she gets anxious about other things, asking her to identify a feeling and the intensity of it on a 1 (*low*) to 5 (*high*) scale:

When I perform at school music concerts, I feel_____ 1 2 3 4 5
When I stay overnight with friends I feel _____ 1 2 3 4 5
When I am home alone I feel _____ 1 2 3 4 5
When I get called on in class I feel _____ 1 2 3 4 5
When I have lots of homework to do I feel _____ 1 2 3 4 5
When I have to figure out math problems
on the board I feel _____ 1 2 3 4 5
When I have to spell words out loud in front of
the class I feel _____ 1 2 3 4 5
When I don't do something right I feel _____ 1 2 3 4 5

From the completed assessments, it appeared that Carrie had some anxiety about doing well academically, but it was not significant; she sometimes felt overwhelmed when she had a lot to do and felt a little nervous about being called on in class, which is normal. The counselor also probed to see if Carrie was too perfectionistic, using the game *P Is for Perfect* (Vernon, 2002, pp. 98–99) as an assessment. This game involves moving a token along a game board and responding to questions about perfectionism and making mistakes. From her responses, it did not appear that Carrie was overly perfectionistic.

Interventions. On the basis of the assessment, the counselor determined that the test anxiety was the primary problem. To help Carrie, the counselor first introduced several relaxation exercises from *The Anxiety and Phobia Workbook* (Bourne, 1995), teaching this young client to practice abdominal breathing and a progressive muscle relaxation technique to help her relax before the test. She also gave her eight test-taking tips written on index cards that could be taped inside her desk (Sycamore, Corey, & Coker, 1990). In addition, she taught Carrie to use rational coping self-statements by explaining the concept of self-talk (Bourne, 1995; Vernon, 2002). This involves Carrie mentally asking herself questions such as, "If you try your hardest, how badly do you think you will do? Even if you don't do well, does that mean you are dumb? If you get a bad grade, what does that mean?" The counselor and Carrie practiced this technique by pretending the counselor was Carrie's friend and verbalizing fears about taking a test. Carrie responded as she would if a friend talked to her about this. An example of this procedure follows:

> *Counselor playing the friend:* "I know I'll fail this test."
> *Carrie's response:* "You don't know that; you could do well."
> *Counselor:* "If I get a bad grade on this test, people will think I'm dumb."
> *Carrie:* "You're not dumb even if you get a bad grade."
> *Counselor:* "If I don't get a good grade on the test I won't pass fourth grade."
> *Carrie:* "Tests are only part of your grade, so if you do okay on other stuff, you'll pass."

Following this activity, they discussed the likelihood of Carrie getting horrible grades on the tests, what her past performance had been, and what it said about her if she did not do as well as she expected. This helped her develop a more realistic view of the situation.

Prior to taking her next test, Carrie met with the counselor and they practiced the relaxation techniques and coupled this with the Globe of Light visualization (Bourne, 1995, pp. 248–249), in which Carrie imagined that she can see a globe of light suspended above the top of her head and that as it turns, it picks up tension and anxiety-producing thoughts, allowing her to be calmer and more focused. They also identified rational coping self-statements, such as she had in the role play, and wrote these on index cards so that she could review them just before the test.

Evaluation/summary. Using a combination of intervention techniques to address different dimensions of the problem was helpful in this case, but test anxiety is somewhat difficult to deal with at this age, because it is coupled with the self-critical nature of the child who is just beginning to assess strengths and weaknesses. For these interventions to be effective, the relaxation, visualization, and coping self-statement techniques needed to be implemented just prior to each test-taking situation, with discussion afterward about how Carrie had done, how she felt, what she did to help herself feel less anxious, and what she could do in the future if she continued to feel nervous about taking tests.

✳

Case Study Five: 10-Year-Old Pedrito

Problem overview. Pedrito, a 10-year-old boy born in Puerto Rico, moved to the South Bronx with his aunt and uncle a year and a half ago. Pedrito was referred to the school counselor by his homeroom teacher for his inability to participate in most of the mainstream classroom activities. Pedrito has been in the English as a Second Language (ESL) program since he arrived in the United States and was originally expected to be in the mainstream program at the end of the first year. His homeroom teacher believes that he may have a learning disorder or may be mildly retarded because Pedrito is highly disinterested in schoolwork, makes no effort to participate in class, does not concentrate on his tasks, and does not do well academically. During recess, he seems to have strong social skills, but these are only displayed with his Puerto Rican peers. At home, his aunt and uncle are not involved with the supervision of homework because of their own busy work schedule. Only the Spanish TV channel is viewed, and Spanish is spoken at home. The family has instilled a degree of distrust against the "gringos" and has encouraged their nephew to "hang out only with Puerto Rican kids."

Assessment considerations. As a 10-year-old boy, Pedrito may be experiencing difficulties with selective attention. Although it is expected that a fifth grader should work independently for sustained periods of time, it is not unusual that some 10-year-olds become easily distracted, fidgety, and impatient during class activities (Berger, 1998). The counselor must be aware of the challenges encountered by immigrants who have to face a new culture with a different set of values and beliefs (Clemente, 2004). Language is the primary instrument of communication and understanding that allows individuals to interact with the host culture (Lynch, 1992). In this case, the counselor must consider the interactions between culture and language. Also, limited English-proficient clients in counseling sessions must be assessed carefully because of the counselors' own multilinguistic limitations and awareness (Clemente & Collison, 2000; Clemente, Collison, & Clark-Hanify, 2001).

Assessment procedures. Because the counselor wanted to have a comprehensive perspective of the situation, he gathered reports from teachers and observed Pedrito in various classes, as well as during recess. Also, he asked for a report from the ESL teacher regarding language acquisition progress, which confirmed that Pedrito's language acquisition was below average. To rule out mental retardation or a learning disorder, the counselor researched Pedrito's academic records from Puerto Rico and found out that he had been a B student. In conjunction with the special education teacher, the counselor suggested a psychometric evaluation in his native Spanish language (i.e., Wechsler Intelligence Test). The results reflected that Pedrito had the intelligence of an average 10-year-old and was capable of performing at grade level.

The counselor also determined that because Pedrito was not living with his biological parents, it might be important to interview the aunt and uncle to learn more about the family situation and if there was anything about his living arrangements that might be contributing to his problems at school. However, they were unwilling to go to the school, so the counselor arranged for a home visit and took an interpreter with him. What they found was that the apartment was very small, with no good place for Pedrito to study. It also appeared that there was minimal family support; the relatives seemed to resent that because the parents had serious financial problems, they sent Pedrito to live with them. This attitude was apparent in their rather harsh interactions with Pedrito. From many of the comments made by the uncle in particular, it seemed like the family was instilling in Pedrito a distrust in North Americans, therefore resulting in ethnic encapsulation.

Interventions. Although the counselor was Caucasian and not very fluent in Spanish, he was fairly knowledgeable of the Puerto Rican culture owing to the large Puerto Rican presence in the South Bronx. To help Pedrito perform at the level at which he was capable, the counselor devised a progressive plan that included the following:

1. Because the counselor was aware of the importance of including family members in the counseling process, he included the uncle and aunt as part of the intervention plan. Understanding the influence that they had over Pedrito's perception, the counselor's plan was to "win them as allies" and reverse the negative influences.

2. The counselor assigned an older peer helper to be a role model to Pedrito. He selected a Puerto Rican immigrant who had adapted to the U.S. system and was successful academically. They were to meet once a week during the lunch hour.

3. The counselor met with the ESL teacher and classroom teachers to explain the current situation. He suggested more individual attention in the classroom and encouraged them to find ways to increase Pedrito's participation during group activities by placing him with students who were either bilingual or non-judgmental. The counselor predicted that this would slowly increase Pedrito's self-confidence in a group setting.

4. The counselor met twice a week with Pedrito, first with an interpreter, and later without, as Pedrito's conversational skills improved. He used Esmeralda Santiago's story *When I Was Puerto Rican* as a source of inspiration. In every session he read portions of Santiago's story and put them in perspective with Pedrito's situation. Santiago's story revolves around the struggles experienced by a Puerto Rican immigrant to New York and her dilemma of maintaining her identity and integrating to the U.S. culture.

5. The counselor put Pedrito in a friendship small group composed of ethnically diverse members. The intent of these weekly group sessions was to promote Pedrito's interactional skills, normalize his fears toward the English language, and encourage the idea that he could make new friends regardless of their ethnic origin.

Evaluation/summary. Some of the indicators of success were Pedrito's ability to socialize across ethnic groups, to verbalize situations that provoked discomfort, and to trust teachers and staff of non–Puerto Rican descent. The counselor maintained constant communication with the homeroom and ESL teachers.

Case Study Six: 10-Year-Old Anthony

Problem overview. This 10-year-old Caucasian boy was referred to the counselor because, 6 months ago, he had been in a serious car accident, which resulted in the amputation of his right arm. His parents indicated that initially he adjusted quite well, but suddenly he was displaying a lot of anger and would explode at the slightest provocation. As an only child, Anthony was encouraged to participate in activities such as scouting and team sports and had done very well, but he had withdrawn from those activities and even had declined his annual visit to his grandmother's cabin, which was something he used to looked forward to each year because he also spent time with cousins close to his age. Teachers at school also had concerns that he was much less social, appeared sad, and was not performing well academically, which was a drastic change in behavior.

Assessment considerations. Ten-year-olds are more aware of their bodies (McDevitt & Ormrod, 2002), and their self-concepts are increasingly based on how others, especially peers, evaluate them (Siegler et al., 2003). A child with a disability that makes him or her feel different often feels very self-conscious (Tarver-Behring & Spagna, 2004); anxiety, fear, shame, or other negative feelings are often prevalent (Thompson et al., 2004). A child with a disability has a high risk of being depressed.

Assessment should address depression, self-concept, and self in relation to peers. Also, it would be important to know whether Anthony's withdrawal from sports activities and lower academic performance has resulted from his belief that he cannot do things that he used to excel in. Given that he has experienced a major loss, understanding which stages of grief he is experiencing would also be helpful. Assessment should also include how the parents are handling this: They may feel guilty, depressed, or confused and may inadvertently overfunction for him, thus contributing to learned helplessness.

Assessment procedures. When they initially contacted the counselor, Anthony's parents warned her that he was normally rather quiet and they sensed that he would be reluctant to be in counseling. On the basis of this information, the counselor asked to meet with them first to assess for depression and to learn more about how they were reacting to their son's disability. At this meeting, she explained that depression would be common after such a significant loss and administered a short questionnaire based on the *DSM–IV–TR* criteria for depression: Were there significant behavioral changes in Anthony including withdrawal from peers and activities? Had there been changes in eating and sleeping? Did he appear lethargic and disinterested? Did he appear sad or tearful? Did they note increased irritability? Had there been a drop in his grades and was he having difficulty concentrating? Had he made disparaging remarks about himself that would indicate feelings of worthlessness? In reviewing their responses to the questionnaire, it was very evident that Anthony was depressed, and the counselor told the parents that if the depression did not improve following intervention, medication might be needed as well. Another concern that was addressed at this initial meeting was how the parents were responding to this loss. Naturally, they felt very helpless as they watched their son struggle with this major adjustment at such a young age, but based on advice from the doctors, they were trying not to do things for him that he should learn to do for himself, despite the fact that at times this was very difficult. The counselor reinforced the importance of letting Anthony learn to do things for himself and suggested that she could help him work on managing the frustration and anger.

When she met with Anthony for the first time, the counselor thought it best to not deal directly with the disability issues but rather to get to know him by playing a simple game called People, Places, and Things (Vernon, 2002, p. 22), which he responded to quite well. During that first assessment session she also got out a box containing lots of pictures of animals and asked Anthony to select three that he thought were most like him. The purpose of this was primarily to put him at ease, but the counselor also thought she might learn something about him from this projective technique.

Having learned from the parents that he liked to draw and could do this quite well with his left hand, in the next assessment session, the counselor addressed the issue of his loss and explained through concrete examples the feelings associated with loss: anger, loneliness, anxiety, sadness, denial, helplessness (Glass, 1991; Worden, 1996). She gave him sheets of paper labeled with each of these words and invited him to draw how he felt or what he was thinking or worrying about in response to any of them. This assessment activity was enlightening. Anthony very graphically portrayed himself sitting on the sidelines while his friends played ball, getting bad grades in school because he could not write well with his left hand, being teased by peers for having one arm, and looking different from others.

As is often the case, the counselor sensed this young client's anger was masking vulnerable feelings, such as fear about the implications of the loss and depression, but she wanted to determine the extent of the anger, so at the next session she administered an adaptation of an anger survey (Wilde, 2000, pp. 9–10) with 10 questions that Anthony responded to on a Likert scale. From his responses, it appeared that his anger had to do with not being able to do things he used to be able to do, as well as being angry when others treated him differently.

Interventions. Taking the lead from his drawings, the counselor asked Anthony if he could talk more about having to sit on the sidelines while his friends played ball. He told her that kids with one arm cannot play baseball or other sports. The counselor suggested to him that they do some research on this, and they spent time looking through sports magazines to find baseball players with one arm. When they did, Anthony and the counselor made a list of questions he had about how to get along with this disability and they sent it to the player, who eventually responded. The counselor also gave him the book *Good Answers to Tough Questions About Physical Disabilities* (Berry, 1990), which explains how to function with a physical disability.

An adaptation of the activities *Just Different* (Vernon, 1989b, p. 87) and Performance Wheel (Vernon, 1989b, p. 179) were used to help Anthony learn that just because he had this disability did not mean he could not do anything; and that even though he was different in some ways, this did not mean he was worthless. To help him deal with the anger, the counselor suggested that he dictate a letter to his disability into a tape recorder, expressing how this disability made him feel and to make a "mad pillow" that he could pound or kick when he felt angry and frustrated. They also played the *Anger Solution* card game (Childswork, Childsplay, 2003) to help him learn to deal more effectively with his anger.

A final intervention involved the counselor inviting Anthony to be a peer helper for a first grader who was in a wheelchair. Each week Anthony met with this child and read him books about adjusting to disabilities or they played games. Using Anthony as a role model helped him work on his own adjustment by helping another child work on his.

Evaluation/summary. Adjusting to a disability can be a long-term process. In Anthony's case, a combination of supportive counseling and direct intervention to help him accept the disability was essential. Anthony eventually let the counselor listen to his taped letter to his disability, and at the end of the counseling sessions, she asked him to tape another letter to determine whether the interventions had made a difference. His second tape, while still revealing themes of loss, also indicated more acceptance and better adjustment.

Other Typical Developmental Problems

In addition to the problems previously identified, this section lists a sampling of typical concerns children experience during middle childhood (Youngs, 1985, 1995). Some of them are so common that it might not even occur to adults that children worry about them. Unfortunately, adults often take for granted that children easily can handle some of these seemingly minor things that trouble them, forgetting that they may not always think logically enough to pull the pieces together, despite the fact that their cognitive skills are more fully developed with each passing year. Knowledge of these issues increases the sensitivity of parents and professionals, helping them anticipate problems to help children deal with them before they become full-blown concerns. According to Youngs, specific problems can be sources of childhood stress at different ages.

Age 6

Children at this age fear riding the bus and may try to persuade parents to drive them to school. They are also afraid of wetting in class because others might make fun of them. They fear teacher disapproval, exhibiting dependent behavior and constantly seeking approval. Ridicule by classmates and older students in the school, fear of receiving the first report card, and not passing to second grade are also concerns.

Ages 7 and 8

Fear of being rejected if the teacher calls on another child to be a helper often results in trying to be the teacher's pet without being obvious about it. Children also fear not being able to do well in class and worry about having time to finish their tasks, wanting to be independent, but then getting frustrated and not being able to manage time wisely. Because they want to please the teacher, they are afraid of being disciplined; and because they feel self-conscious, they are afraid of being different from others in dress or appearance.

Ages 9 and 10

Being chosen last on any team is a fear that is verbally expressed by stating that the game is stupid or that they do not want to play, or by being absent on physical education days. Children at this age also are afraid of losing a best friend's affection, approval, and respect. They also worry about not being liked by the teacher, as well as taking a test and not having time to complete their work. Concerns about appearance are also common at this age because cliques are formed on the basis of appearance, particularly for girls.

Summary

In this chapter, typical problems for the child in middle childhood were described: anxiety about performance and anxiety about disaster affecting the family. Helping professionals not only need to know these are commonly experienced issues but also must be able to adjust assessment procedures to determine the exact nature of the problem. Problems exemplified by Steven and Anthony are not characteristic of normal developmental problems but may be experienced by children at some point in their childhood. It is equally important for the practitioner to apply knowledge of developmental theory in problem conceptualization, the assessment procedure, and the intervention strategies with these types of issues. Finally, counselors have to be sensitive to the cultural factors, as in the cases of Keg and Pedrito, because their symptoms could have been easily misconstrued, resulting in inappropriate intervention.

Although these middle childhood years are a time of relatively stable growth, there are important developmental tasks to be mastered. In addition, an increasing number of children are faced with stressors resulting from family and environmental issues over which they have little control. Growing up is a challenge, but sensitive professionals can make a difference for children by assisting them in preventing and resolving problems.

Chapter 7

Early Adolescence:
Assessment and Intervention

❋

"Struggling toward maturity" is an appropriate way to describe adolescents as they move from childhood to adulthood (Bireley & Genshaft, 1991, p. 1), but it certainly does not convey all that is involved in the transition. I (Ann Vernon) have vivid memories of the dichotomies characteristic of this period: receiving a teddy bear and a transistor radio for my 14th birthday, painstakingly packing away my dolls with some regret, and being kissed on the cheek in the back row of the movie theater. In The Diary of a Young Girl *(Frank, 1963), Anne Frank so aptly captured the essence of early adolescence as she wrote,*

> Yesterday I read an article . . . it might have been addressed to me personally . . . about a girl in the years of puberty who becomes quiet within and begins to think about the wonders that are happening to her body. I experience that, too, and that is why I get the feeling lately of being embarrassed about Margot, Mummy, and Daddy . . . I think what is happening to me is so wonderful, and not only what can be seen on my body, but all that is taking place inside. (p. 115)

❋

The purpose of this chapter is to identify specific characteristics of the early adolescent in the areas of self, social, emotional, physical, cognitive, and moral development, followed by six case studies that illustrate assessment and intervention procedures for a variety of problems.

According to Jaffe (1998), "adolescence is a unique and important stage of physical, cognitive, emotional, and social change" (p. 18). Steinberg (1996) characterized adolescence as a "series of passages from immaturity into maturity" (p. 5), noting that some of the passages are smooth and others rough. As Atwater (1996) stressed, the traditional definition of adolescence has become synonymous with puberty, but he pointed out that in fact, "adolescence also includes psychological and social changes that may begin earlier and last longer than the biological changes of puberty" (p. 5). Meece (2002) concurred, noting that changes in self-confidence, self-image, and family relationships, as well as other changes, occur during puberty.

In a basic sense, early adolescence refers to the period of rapid growth between childhood and adolescence, and it is important to note that the needs and dynamics of early adolescence are different from middle and late adolescence (Martin, 2003). According to Atwater (1996) and Steinberg (1996), it has become increasingly common to distinguish between early adolescence, which is closely associated but not synonymous with the onset of puberty (from about age 11 through age 14), mid-adolescence (from about age 15 through age 18), and late adolescence (from age 18 through about age 21).

Schave and Schave (1989) described early adolescence as "a distinct and qualitatively different developmental phase" (p. xi). These authors indicated that the dramatic changes in cognition and the intensification of affect contribute to a fluctuating sense of self, and it is not until adolescence proper that self-integration actually occurs. Head (1997) reported that while adolescence is often considered to be a unique phase that distinguishes it from other parts of the life span, there is some disagreement about the exact nature of this uniqueness. For example, there is often a negative image of adolescence; that it is a period of extreme "storm and stress," a term used by G. Stanley Hall to describe the moody, rebellious nature of adolescence (Jaffe, 1998). In contrast to this typical view of early adolescence as turbulent, the Schaves and others (Dusek, 1996; Head, 1997; Jaffe, 1998; Kaplan, 2000) do not view this as a uniquely stressful period; rather, they see it as part of a normal, healthy developmental process. Martin (2003) concurred, noting that most adolescents mature in a gradual, continuous manner without major disturbance. Furthermore, although there are stressors, they do not occur simultaneously. That is not to say that young adolescents do not struggle during this developmental period, but the current psychological opinion is that this is not an extraordinarily stressful phase of development.

Steinberg (1996) stressed that although all adolescents go though the social, biological, and cognitive changes, the effects of these changes vary significantly from adolescent to adolescent. For example, he noted that puberty makes some adolescents feel self-conscious and ugly, whereas others feel attractive and self-confident. Dusek (1996) noted that adolescence is "an experience" (p. 3) that takes place within a specific time frame, cultural context, and subculture defined by ethnicity and gender. Although there are commonalities, there are also unique experiences, influenced by one's own special circumstances. Dusek stressed that adolescence differs between cultures and that as the culture changes, so does the nature of adolescence. It is critical for practitioners to "pay close attention to how diversity tempers the nature of the adolescent experience" (Dusek, 1996, p. 4).

According to several researchers (Berk, 2003; Jaffe, 1998; LeFrancois, 1992), most teenagers negotiate this phase without extreme difficulty and do not resort to delinquency, acting out, drug dependence, school failure, sexual promiscuity, and other self-destructive behaviors. Berk (2003) noted that boys tend to react more with anger and irritability, and girls with anger and depression, which supports Klimek and Anderson's (1989) contention that that boys tend to "act out" and girls tend to "act in," experiencing more powerful mood swings, depression, and low self-esteem.

Characteristics of the Early Adolescent

Early adolescence can be a frustrating developmental stage for teenagers, as well as for their parents and teachers. The hormonal, pubertal, social, and physical changes contribute to their emotional upheaval and often result in defensive, ultrasensitive, and temperamental behavior (Schave & Schave, 1989). As they shift to formal operational thinking, adolescents are psychologically vulnerable (Schave & Schave, 1989) and more emotionally volatile than younger children (Arnett, 1999), becoming self-absorbed and feeling alienated from their own bodies. Teachers and parents may compare this period to riding on a roller coaster with a great deal of unpredictability in moods and behaviors, often misinterpreting the defensiveness and temperamental behavior and failing to see how this masks vulnerability, in part because the teenagers send mixed messages. As a result, they may overreact to these overt behaviors and symptoms, which results in conflict and misguided attempts to deal effectively with youths at this age.

Following are general descriptions of early adolescence in terms of self, social, emotional, physical, cognitive, and moral development. These developmental characteristics can assist professionals in appropriate assessment and intervention.

Self-Development

Self-definition and integration are the critical developmental tasks of early adolescence (Dusek, 1996; Head, 1997; Jaffe, 1998, Martin, 2003; Moshman, 1999). As Meece (2002) noted, "young people need to achieve a positive, coherent identity" (p. 402), which also includes developing an ethnic identity. Gender is also a key component of self-development, and Meece reported that gender differences in interests and activities are evident in early adolescence. According to Farber (2003), a psychological shift occurs as girls move from childhood to adolescence. Their self-confidence and sense of mastery decline, and as they enter adolescence, "girls experience sudden and dramatic declines in self-esteem" (p. 14). Meece attributed lower self-esteem for girls to the fact that they enter puberty earlier than boys and have fewer coping skills to help them deal with their physical changes as well as social expectations.

During this period of development, it is not unusual for young adolescents to be very egocentric: They see themselves as more important than they really are, or feel that no one else experiences things the way they do (Berger & Thompson, 1991; Bjorklund, 2000; Jaffe, 1998). Closely linked to this egocentrism is the "time warp" concept, adolescents' inability to link events, situation, and feelings together to form a comprehensive sense of their own "history." For example, they are unwilling to accept that their behavior influences whether they will be able to go out with friends on Saturday night or the idea that they got a bad grade because they did not study (Schave & Schave, 1989). Schave and Schave maintained that if young adolescents connected these events, they would feel guilt, shame, or anger. Because they become overwhelmed by these feelings, they tend to dissociate feelings from events and place responsibility for problems away from themselves.

As they become more capable of self-reflection, early adolescents are also very self-conscious (McDevitt & Ormrod, 2002; Meece, 2002). They assume that everyone is looking at them or thinking about them. Elkind (1984, 1988) attributed this to the concept of the *imaginary audience*, the belief that others are as concerned with them as they are and that they are the focus of everyone else's concern and attention. As a result of the imaginary audience, early adolescents fantasize about how others will react to them. Thus, they become supersensitive and overly concerned with their performance and appearance, or they become vain and conceited. According to McDevitt and Ormrod, girls are more concerned with the imaginary audience than are boys, becoming very obsessed with their physical appearance and being very critical of themselves. Accompanying the self-consciousness and extreme sensitivity to embarrassment is a decrease in self-esteem, which is especially pronounced for girls (Sadker & Sadker, 1994).

Elkind (1974) described the *invincibility fable*, a belief in one's invulnerability. In essence, this fable contributes to the notion that, because of "my" uniqueness, bad things may happen to others but not to "me": For example, teenagers' friends may get pregnant, but they will not; they can take risks, because they will not get caught; they can take drugs, but they will not become addicted. Closely tied to this is the *personal fable* (Elkind, 1984), in which adolescents imagine their lives as heroic or special; they may see themselves becoming world-famous rock stars or destined for fame and fortune. They may also believe they are unlike anyone else (Lapsley, 1993); their experiences are unique and no one experiences things the way they do (Steinberg, 1996). Accordingly, they think no one else could ever understand what it is like to break up with someone, despite the fact that this is a relatively common occurrence.

Generally by age 13, egocentrism peaks, but it is not until several years later that it declines enough for adolescents to feel more at ease with themselves and in social situations. Although the "search for self" begins during early adolescence, it is not until late adolescence that full integration is achieved.

Although early adolescents in many cultures need to feel empowered and push for autonomy (Cobb, 2001; Martin, 2003; Meece, 2002), they are still immature and lack life experiences (Weisfeld, 1999). These contrasts, coupled with teenagers' cognitive, physical, pubertal, and social changes, leave them very vulnerable. As a result, they show increased dependency, which confuses them as well as the adults in their lives.

Social Development

As early adolescents move away from their families, peers play a dominant role and are a vital part of the growing-up process, although in some cultures, this is not as pronounced (Head, 1997; McDevitt & Ormrod, 2002; Wolman, 1998). Cobb (2001) aptly described the importance of peers by stating that "in larger numbers, they are socialization agents, guiding adolescents into new, more adult roles. And one on one, they are mirrors into whom adolescents look to glimpse the future within" (p. 591). Jaffe (1998) noted that peers also provide a "safe haven for trying out new beliefs and behaviors" (p. 281). While they become significantly more involved with peers and see them as a source of support, adolescents are extremely sensitive and vulnerable to peer humiliation and often fear rejection and ridicule (Johnson & Kottman, 1992; Vernon & Al-Mabuk, 1995). The imaginary audience contributes to this sensitivity, because adolescents see themselves as the center of attention but fear disapproval, judgment, or putdowns. To protect against this, they tend to conform to peer norms and expectations (Meece, 2002), often dressing alike, using the same idiosyncrasies in their speech, and developing "rules" about what topics to discuss or which activities to pursue (Klimek & Anderson, 1989).

As children get older, their friendships become increasingly more intimate (Meece, 2002), and adolescents confide in their peers more than in their parents (Fisher, Munsch, & Greene, 1996). By early adolescence, a friend is described as "someone who understands your feelings, makes you feel better when you're 'down,' and who knows almost everything there is to know about you" (Berndt, 1992, p. 495). Adolescents distinguish between friends and acquaintances, using the term *best friend* only for someone with whom they have a very close relationship (Berndt, 1992). Adolescent friendships are more emotionally bonding and stable than they were in childhood; adolescents want psychological closeness, loyalty, and mutual understanding (Berk, 2003). In general, adolescents have fewer friends than younger children—four to six best friends is typical (Hartup & Stevens, 1999). Intimate friendships are more prevalent for girls than for boys; girls demand more closeness (Parker & Asher, 1993) and prefer more same-sex friendships. Boys' friendships are less intimate, and they have more friends of both sexes (Sippola, Bukowski, & Noll, 1997). Typically adolescents choose friends who are like themselves, although as they expand their school and community networks, they may choose some friends who differ from themselves (Berk, 2003).

During this developmental period, young adolescents have a strong need to belong and to be accepted, which is why conformity to peer norms and expectations is so prevalent (Martin, 2003). At this time, more complex social relationships develop due primarily to two factors: (a) norms and standards of conduct and (b) association by reputation. For example, adolescents may be a "jock," a "dirthead," or a "preppie," assuming the behavior, styles, and image that are associated with a particular group. They also may be part of a clique or gang and adopt the norms and standards of this group. In either situation, peer pressure becomes a salient issue, accompanied by both positive and negative aspects. Ethnic similarity also becomes more important as peer groups and friendships are formed. Unfortunately, young adolescents tend to be ethnocentric and lack a multicultural perspective, which makes social relationships even more complicated (Quintana, 1999). Wolman (1998) noted that while the importance of belonging to a peer group is relatively universal, the nature of these groups varies across cultures.

Although adolescent egocentrism can negatively affect the teenager's ability to learn about others' feelings and motives, social experience helps reduce this (Jaffe, 1998). However, because they often have difficulty stepping outside of themselves and looking at their behavior objectively, they may behave obnoxiously, which influences how others respond to them. According to Jaffe, only as they mature cognitively are they better able to consider others' viewpoints.

Between the ages of 11 and 13, early adolescents tend to have more negative than positive feelings about the opposite gender, depending on when pubertal changes occur, which affect when sexual interest begins (Berger & Thompson, 1991). They typically enter dating relationships gradually as a group of young female associates with a group of young males, although some adolescents date infrequently at this age.

Emotional Development

Heightened emotionality and rapid mood fluctuations characterize this period, with the adolescent shifting from intense sadness to anger to excitement to depression in a brief time (Larson & Richards, 1994). It commonly is assumed that the increase in negative emotions can be attributed to the hormonal changes associated with puberty, but several authors have found a minimal relationship between negative affect and hormonal status (Brooks-Gunn & Warren, 1989; Jaffe, 1998). Steinberg (1996) cautioned that the direct connection between hormonal changes associated with puberty and moodiness should be looked at carefully, and that it is not so much the increases in hormones during puberty but the rapid fluctuations early in puberty that affect young adolescents' moods. Others have posited that stressful events contribute to negative emotion, or that it is more of an ecological issue, because adolescents spend more time away from the family than do preadolescents, and being alone often is associated with a lower mood (Colten & Gore, 1991). It may be that each of these is a contributing factor. Nevertheless, this emotional disequilibrium is accompanied by egocentrism, pubertal changes, and an increased need for independence. Ambivalent feelings accompany this struggle for autonomy.

Early adolescence includes unpredictable moodiness, often accompanied by emotional outbursts (Larson & Richards, 1994; Newman & Newman, 1991). Negative and painful emotional states are experienced more frequently (Cobb, 2001; Siegler et al., 2003), along with troublesome emotions: anxiety, shame, depression, embarrassment, guilt, shyness, and loneliness (Arnett, 1999; Vernon, 2004). As they struggle to gain autonomy, conflicts with parents may increase, resulting in frustration and anger (Meece, 2002).

As they shift from concrete to more abstract and hypothetical thinking, early adolescents are better able to see discrepancies between the real and the ideal, the expected and the actual. However, these insights frequently result in disappointment (Larsen & Asmussen, 1991). Early adolescents also are more aware of others' feelings and thoughts. Consequently, they are more sensitive to the ups and downs associated with social interactions, often overreacting to who said what about whom. As Meece (2002) stated, although their more advanced cognitive abilities help them interpret unpleasant emotional experiences, this often results in an increase in self-consciousness and self-criticism.

There are cultural as well as gender differences related to emotional expression. Cultures vary in terms of what feelings are acceptable and how they can be expressed; in some cultures, emotional openness is not valued (Saarni, Mumme, & Campos, 1998). Respect for these cultural differences is essential, as well as an understanding of gender differences in emotional expression. For example, boys and girls respond differently to their heightened awareness of negative feelings: Boys are more activity based and external, experiencing more anger and contempt (Larsen & Asmussen, 1991), whereas girls are more emotionally expressive and more sensitive to the emotional states of others (Bukatko & Daehler, 1992). Girls also experience more anxiety, shame, guilt, and depression (Garber, Kelley, & Martin, 2002; Larsen & Asmussen, 1991; Meece, 2002). Girls, more so than boys, are depressed by problems in their peer relationships, according to Nolen-Hoeksema (2001). Garber et al. reported that in addition to peer relationships, another contributing factor to the higher rate of depression for girls is that girls are more concerned about their bodies and their appearance and express more dissatisfaction with their body image than boys do.

Because they experience a wider range of emotions, a major task for young adolescents is developing tolerance for their emotionality rather than feeling ashamed of their feelings or being afraid they are "going crazy" (Newman & Newman, 1991). The increased intensity of emotions permeates all aspects of early adolescents' lives; they feel confused and anxious about the roller coaster of emotions they may experience (Vernon, 2004). Their negative emotions can be overwhelming, resulting in increased vulnerability and making this a challenging time for early adolescents and their families.

Physical Development

Except during infancy, physical changes occur more rapidly during early adolescence than at any other point in the life span (Dusek, 1996; Meece, 2002). As Steinberg (1996) noted, "Puberty encompasses all the physical changes that occur in the growing girl or boy as the individual passes from childhood into adulthood" (p. 23). The onset of puberty varies considerably, according to Meece (2002). For girls, it begins at about age 10 or 11 and typically lasts 2½ years, although it may begin as early as age 8 (McDevitt & Ormrod, 2002; Meece, 2002) and last up to 4 years (Cobb,

2001). The average age of onset of menstruation is 12.8 years for Caucasian girls and slightly earlier for African American girls, according to Meece. For boys, puberty begins anywhere from age 9 to 14 (McDevitt & Ormrod, 2002), and they usually reach their peak in growth 2 years later than girls (Cobb, 2001).

With the onset of puberty, increased production of sex hormones occurs, as well as maturation of the reproductive system (ovaries in girls and testes in boys) and the appearance of secondary sex characteristics (pubic hair, breast development, and hip widening in girls and the development of facial and pubic hair and voice change in boys). A growth spurt also occurs, with increases in weight and height and a redistribution of body tissue and proportions. This growth spurt lasts for about 3 years but begins approximately 2 years earlier in girls than in boys (Cobb, 2001; Malina, 1991).

Girls first develop breast buds and pubic and underarm hair, followed by changes in the vagina, clitoris, and uterus. Girls generally experience their first menstruation between ages 9 and 15, depending on their weight and amount of body fat (Frisch, 1991; McDevitt & Ormrod, 2002). The average age for Caucasian girls is age 12.8 and is 6 months earlier for African American girls, according to Meece (2002).

In boys, the beginning of sexual maturity occurs when the testes and scrotum enlarge. About a year later pubic hair develops and the penis begins to grow and continues to enlarge for at least 2 more years. Underarm and facial hair appear at about age 14. Internal sex organ changes also begin to develop, and by age 13 to 14 boys are capable of ejaculating (McDevitt & Ormrod, 2002). During this period, boys experience nocturnal emissions (Newman & Newman, 1991).

Because the rate of development for both boys and girls varies considerably, young adolescents are affected in several ways (Newman & Newman, 1991). First, physical growth affects their ability to perform certain tasks. For example, teenagers may be uncoordinated, because the size of their hands or feet is disproportionate to other body parts. Second, physical development influences the way others perceive them. Adults may comment on how they have grown and how different they look, which may embarrass or please them. Third, it affects the way they see themselves. Early adolescents are painfully aware of being awkward or different, or being more or less mature than peers (K. B. Owens, 2002). They may develop "locker room phobia," because they do not want peers to see their bodies (Jaffe, 1998). Just as there is considerable discontinuity in the rate of pubertal change, there is also great variability in the significance young adolescents attribute to puberty (Cobb, 2001).

Gender differences exist between early-maturing boys and girls (Meece, 2002). Early-maturing girls are more self-conscious and have a more negative body image than late maturers, but at the same time are often more popular, according to Cobb (2001). Early-maturing girls are more dissatisfied with their bodies and are at greater risk to develop eating disorders

(Smolak, Levine, & Gralen, 1993), as well as more prone to depression and anxiety (Ge, Conger, & Elder, 1996; Weinshenker, 2002). Irwin and Millstein (1992) also found that early-maturing girls are more prone to risky behaviors such as sexual promiscuity, substance abuse, and reckless driving.

According to Cobb's (2001) research, early-maturing boys tended to be more socially attractive, be more popular, and receive more recognition in activities. Meece (2002) also noted that early maturity in boys has many positive consequences; they are more likely to be chosen as leaders, have fewer psychological problems, have more positive self-images, and are more self-confident and less dependent than late maturers. At the same time, this may put pressure on them to commit themselves to goals and live up to others' expectations.

In contrast, late-maturing adolescents often feel socially inadequate and frustrated by their rate of development. Like their early-maturing counterparts, they also feel self-conscious. In addition, they worry about being teased or disliked. It appears that the rate of maturation is a "mixed bag" that creates anxiety for both boys and girls (Newman & Newman, 1991), but overall, boys have a more positive body image than girls (Benedikt, Wertheim, & Lave, 1998).

Because adolescents vary so tremendously in their rate of physical maturity, this can be one of the most difficult periods of development; the physical changes occurring during this period have psychological meaning as well, affecting the way young adolescents think and feel about themselves (Meece, 2002). Cobb (2001) used the term *asynchrony* to describe how all changes do not occur at once, either within an adolescent or from one to another.

Keep in mind that adjustment to puberty is determined in part by social and cultural contexts (Meece, 2002). For example, some cultures celebrate the onset of puberty by formal celebrations (McDevitt & Ormrod, 2002). It is important, therefore, to take these factors into account when assessing the impact that pubertal changes and the dramatic shift in cognitive development have on young adolescents.

Cognitive Development

The cognitive changes that gradually occur during adolescence "have far-reaching implications for the young person's psychological development and social relations" (Steinberg, 1996, p. 64). Schave and Schave (1989) considered the shift from concrete to formal operational thinking as "the most drastic and dramatic change in cognition that occurs in anyone's life" (p. 7). Kaplan (2000) noted that formal operational thinking begins at about age 11 but is not attained until at least age 15–20. As early adolescents move into this realm, they begin to think more abstractly and hypothetically (Cobb, 2001), often engaging in idealization and then comparing themselves and others to these ideal standards (Berger & Thompson, 1991). In addition, they begin to make predictions about hypothetical events and develop the ability to think about things they have never experienced, such as what it would have been like to be held hostage during a war (Meece, 2002).

Steinberg (1996) emphasized that the changes in cognition allow adolescents to think about possibilities, which has a positive impact on their problem-solving abilities. In addition, they also become better arguers: They do not accept others' viewpoints without questioning them. They also are more likely to understand more subtle humor and abstract logic inherent in puns and analogies.

With an increased ability to use abstract thinking comes an ability to think more logically, although, as Cobb (2001) noted, adolescents do not always think logically nor apply this logic to themselves. Newman and Newman (1991) identified the following new conceptual skills that accompany formal operational thought:

1. Adolescents are able to mentally manipulate more than two categories of variables simultaneously. They can consider how much they would have to save per month and for how long to buy a compact disc player.
2. They have the ability to think about future changes. For example, they are able to see how their relationship with their parents will be different in 10 years.
3. They can hypothesize about the logical sequence of events, thus being able to see that their behavior on the job influences their ability to keep that job.
4. They can predict consequences of actions, understanding that if they skip school repeatedly they could be expelled.
5. They can detect logical consistency or inconsistency in statements. For instance, they can see that although there are laws against discrimination, it still occurs in practice.
6. They understand that they are expected to act in certain ways because of the norms of their family, culture, or community, but they realize that the norms may be different in other cultures, communities, or families.

In comparing this list with early adolescents you know, you may see discrepancies between what is and what is supposed to occur conceptually at this period of development. It is important to note that considerable variability exists in the way early adolescents think. According to Cobb (2001), "thinking, like every other aspect of development, is highly individual" (p. 536). Variation also occurs in the degree to which young adolescents use formal operational thinking consistently. For example, it is not uncommon to find an early adolescent who uses formal operational thinking to solve math problems but does not use it when reasoning about interpersonal relationships (Santrock & Yussen, 1992). And although thinking continues to improve throughout adolescence, even by the end of middle school, most young adolescents have not attained formal operational thinking

(Meece, 2002). Cultural expectations and experiences also influence the development of formal operational thinking, so as Rogoff (1990) stressed, it is very important to consider the cultural context with regard to how thinking skills develop.

Moral Development

As early adolescents begin to achieve formal operational thinking, they gradually enter into what Kohlberg termed *conventional morality* (Atwater, 1996), which focuses on social relationships and compliance with social norms and laws (Siegler et al., 2003). As such, they look to parents, teachers, and popular classmates for guidance about what is right or wrong (Meece, 2002), and they are concerned about sharing, trust, and loyalty in interpersonal relationships. Keeping promises and commitments is also very important to them (McDevitt & Ormrod, 2002), and the affection and approval of friends and relatives motivate good behavior (Berk, 2003). Adolescents at this stage believe that people should act like others expect them to act; for example, a friend should be loyal or a teacher should be fair.

Not all early adolescents have reached the conventional morality level, however. Many are still at the preconventional level, in which their judgments about the morality of behavior are determined by rewards and consequences, as opposed to what society defines as the correct way to behave (Meece, 2002). At this level, they will obey people who have control of punishments and rewards, but according to McDevitt and Ormrod (2002), they will also disobey rules if they think they can get by with it. Early adolescents at the preconventional stage will make moral decisions based on what is best for them without considering the needs of others.

During early adolescence, some minor differences in moral reasoning emerge but disappear by late adolescence (Eisenberg, Martin, & Fabes, 1996). For the most part, there are more similarities than differences in the way both sexes reason (Atwater, 1996). Cultural differences can affect moral decision making in that different cultural groups sometimes have different standards for what is considered right and wrong. For example, lying is considered wrong in U.S. culture but is a legitimate way of saving face in other cultures, according to Triandis (1995).

Between the ages of 10 and 18, young people progress more in moral reasoning than at any other stage of life (Colby, Kohlberg, Gibbs, & Lieberman, 1983). However, because their moral reasoning develops in varying degrees along with their ability to think abstractly, it is important to give young adolescents the opportunity to discuss moral issues and make choices that facilitate development of more complex moral decision making.

Parental Involvement With Early Adolescents

Although conflict with parents typically increases, making it appear as if early adolescents no longer need their parents (Arnett, 1999; Laursen, Coy,

& Collins, 1998), they still continue to require their support in setting limits, providing structure, and being emotionally available (Colten & Gore, 1991; Vernon, 2004). This can be very confusing to parents: The adolescent may be loving one minute and hostile the next, with tantrumlike behavior similar to that of a toddler.

As young adolescents strive for autonomy, parent–child interactions are often more tense (Atwater, 1996), and there is greater distance between them (Steinberg, 1996). It is during this period of development that the frequency of adolescent–parent conflict is the highest (Laursen et al., 1998) and that parents' and adolescents' feelings about each other are more intense (Jaffe, 1998). It is important to remember that the adolescent's attainment of independence is predominately a value reflective of the dominant culture in the United States and is not shared by all ethnic groups (J. Carlson & Lewis, 2002). Independence is considered more dysfunctional and unhealthy in a collectivist culture such as Chinese or Hindu (Pedersen, 2000), and Inclan and Hernandez (1992) emphasized that individuation and separation are not culturally universal.

In cultures such as the United States where independence is valued, questioning parental authority is common (Barrish & Barrish, 1989; Vernon & Al-Mabuk, 1995). According to Meece (2002), conflicts are typically about choices of music and clothing, as well as privileges and responsibilities. Generally after the adolescent growth spurt, the tension and distance gradually diminish and the conflicts decrease.

However, despite their attempts to scare parents away with their assertive or, at times, aggressive attempts to be independent, adolescents still need their parents' support (Meece, 2002), and parents play a vital role in the young adolescents' development (Vernon, 2004). In many respects, early adolescents are like 2-year-olds who say "No, me!" But unlike toddlers, early adolescents may be more successful in getting parents to abdicate their role, leaving the 12- to 14-year-olds struggling to grow up without a parental support system. Although they are reluctant to admit it, adolescents need a gradual relaxation of rules and limits so they can "try their wings" with a safety net.

Because an important developmental task in many, but not all, cultures is for adolescents to become more independent, parents have to determine how much autonomy to allow. Balancing dependence and independence often necessitates a shift in parenting style as parents attempt to maintain some closeness while at the same time accommodating the significant developmental changes in their young teens. Helping professionals play an important role in educating parents about early adolescent development and encouraging parents to continue to facilitate their youngsters' growing-up process without interpreting their teen's desire to spend less time with them as a sign that they will never again have a close relationship. As they mature, relationships with parents generally become more positive.

Problem Assessment and Intervention:
Selected Case Studies

Early adolescents are frequently in a state of flux, on "cloud nine" one minute and "down in the dumps" the next. Although these moods are unpredictable and not easily controlled, they often are related to developmental processes rather than circumstances in their lives (Johnson & Kottman, 1992). Of equal consideration is the fact that adolescents move through the developmental sequence at different rates, resulting in a great deal of variation in maturity levels, which affects adolescents, their parents, and their peers in numerous ways.

In the following sections, problems of the early adolescent, ages 11–14, are described. Examples of typical developmental problems and more circumstantial problems are identified, along with assessment and intervention strategies.

Case Study One: 12-Year-Old Jeff

Problem overview. Jeff, a 12-year-old Caucasian boy, was referred to the school counselor by his parents because he had refused to go to school for the last 10 days, shortly after entering junior high school. According to the parents, this had not been a problem during elementary school. Jeff had a few friends and did well academically. However, this year he began complaining that he did not feel well and needed to stay home. At first they allowed this, but after several days they realized that he did not seem sick and insisted that he go to school. Because Jeff did not like to ride the bus, his father dropped him off but later in the day received a call from the school saying that Jeff had skipped his fourth-hour class and had left the building. Jeff's explanation to his parents was that he felt sick again. However, after school he seemed to feel better and wanted to skate board with his friend, which confused his parents and also indicated to them that it must be something at school that he wanted to avoid.

Assessment considerations. Young adolescents often feel very self-conscious, fantasizing about how others will react to their appearance and behavior (Steinberg, 1996). Therefore, some adolescents are reluctant to go to school, because they create the imaginary audience, overgeneralizing about how "awful" they look or that "everyone" is looking at them (Berger & Thompson, 1991). In addition, the transition from elementary school, in terms of structure and academic expectations, can be a source of anxiety. Steinberg pointed out that many middle-level teachers have not had specialized training in working with this age group. Consequently, many enter the classroom with negative images about adolescents, which may interfere with their ability to relate effectively to students. Steinberg also noted that while this transition is not uniformly stressful, it is more difficult for vulnerable adolescents who may have fewer sources of social support.

Because the prevalent problem appears to be school avoidance, assessment should include how Jeff perceives the transition to junior high, his relationship with the teachers, and his social support system. In addition, it would be important to assess how his parents are dealing with this: Are they consistent in the way they were handling it? Are there consequences at home if he does not attend school? Are there any other situational changes or stressors in the family? Finally, it would be important to rule out any physical illnesses and to determine the degree of anxiety Jeff experiences when he is at school.

Assessment procedures. When he called the school counselor for help, Jeff's father agreed to take his son to school the next day and the counselor agreed to see Jeff first period before he had a chance to leave school. Because Jeff was quite shy and the counselor sensed that he might be resistant to talking about the school attendance problem, during the first session he explained that he typically met with all new students to get a sense of how they were adjusting to junior high and engaged him in a non-threatening activity in which he and Jeff wrote their first and last names on an index card and identified something about themselves beginning with each of the letters. Rapport was established in this way, and the counselor invited Jeff back for a second session to learn more about how he felt about junior high.

In this second session, the counselor shared that his teachers had expressed concern that he was missing a lot of school. The counselor indicated that he wanted to know more about what was bothering Jeff and asked him to write his responses to these unfinished sentences.

1. When I go to school, I feel _____.
2. The part of the school day I like best is _____.
3. The part of the school day I like least is _____.
4. The subject that is easiest for me is _____.
5. The subject that is hardest for me is _____.
6. I am afraid of _____.
7. Other kids in this school_____.
8. Teachers in this school _____.
9. This year at school is different from last year, because _____.
10. If I could change something about this school, it would be _____.
11. When I don't go to school, my parents _____.
12. When I think about being in junior high, I feel_____.

In analyzing the responses to this informal assessment, the counselor noted that Jeff seemed more concerned about being made fun of in the locker room than he was about academics, although this was also a factor. The counselor knew that the first-year students had to dress for physical education. Because Jeff was slight and appeared much less physically mature than many others in his class, the counselor hypothesized that Jeff was not as fully developed as his peers and that this could result in self-consciousness and in the teasing that Jeff had expressed concern about on his assessment exercise. Furthermore, Jeff's responses indicated he was afraid of getting bad grades in school, because junior high seemed a lot harder than elementary school, the routine was confusing, and Jeff was worried about getting to the right class on time. When the counselor asked him more about the classes that were most difficult for him, he shared that he hated to get up in front of his classmates to give a speech. Because of Jeff's shyness, the counselor was not surprised by this response, but he also asked Jeff more about what specifically bothered him. According to Jeff, he did not have many friends in this class and he was afraid that if he made mistakes, others would laugh at him. He also thought the teacher was "pretty mean" because she had already "yelled" at him for not speaking up or making eye contact.

To understand how anxious Jeff was about these school-related experiences, the counselor gave Jeff a sheet of paper with five continuums, each labeled at one end, *very anxious or nervous,* and at the other end, *not very anxious or nervous.* He asked Jeff to put a mark on each line relative to his degree of anxiety about the following: giving a speech, dressing for physical education, getting to the right class on time, pleasing the teachers, making mistakes. Jeff's responses indicated that he had moderate anxiety to high anxiety overall, and the counselor speculated that his way of dealing with this was to avoid the situations.

From his responses to the sentence completion assessment, it did not appear that there were any consequences at home when Jeff missed school. When the counselor interviewed the parents to find out more about the situation and their reaction to it, he learned that while Dad got angry and insisted that he go to school, Mom was more lenient and seemed to believe that her son really was ill. There appeared to be considerable disagreement between the parents about whether he could do something with his friend after school if he had been absent that day, but they usually allowed this because he did not have many friends and they were concerned about his socialization. At this same meeting the counselor suggested to the parents that they schedule him for a physical to rule out the possibility of any illness.

As a final part of the assessment, the counselor spoke with the speech teacher and was invited to observe the class. Although this first-year teacher did not seem as strict as Jeff had portrayed her to be, she did seem somewhat insensitive to the fact that standing in front of an entire class might be difficult for students this age because they are so self-conscious.

Interventions. To address these problems, the counselor first assured Jeff that his concerns were quite typical for his age and that some of his classmates might be experiencing similar feelings of anxiety. Second, he explained to Jeff the concept of the imaginary audience, followed by some reality-check techniques that he thought might help Jeff deal with the situation more effectively.

He adapted an activity called *Magnify* (Pincus, 1990, p. 25), in which several events were listed and Jeff was instructed to magnify their importance by turning them into a catastrophe. For example:

1. You walk into class late, because you could not get your locker open.
   Catastrophic thoughts: _____.
2. You go into the locker room to change for physical education.
   Catastrophic thoughts: _____.
3. You do not understand how to do an assignment.
   Catastrophic thoughts: _____.
4. You get a bad grade on your first test.
   Catastrophic thoughts: _____.
5. You stand up in front of the class to give a speech.
   Catastrophic thoughts: _____.

After Jeff identified the worst case scenario, the counselor taught him to look at the probable situation by adapting *Getting Straight Our Magnifications* (Pincus, 1990, p. 26). Examples:

1. You walk into class late because you could not get your locker open:
   Best case scenario: _____.
   Worst case scenario (previous activity): _____.
   Probable scenario: _____.
2. You go into the locker room to change for physical education:
   Best case scenario: _____.
   Worst case scenario: _____.
   Probable scenario: _____.
3. You stand up in class to give your speech:
   Best case scenario: _____.
   Worst case scenario: _____.
   Probable scenario: _____.

By identifying best, worst, and probable outcomes for each question, Jeff began to dispute some of his anxieties about various middle school issues. The counselor helped him look at best and worst case and probable scenarios for not going to school and then helped him develop self-statements to deal with his anxiety about going to school: (a) "Even though it seems like everyone is looking at me, in reality I know they are not"; (b) "If I do not understand how to do an assignment, I can ask the teacher and it does not mean I'm dumb"; and (c) "It is scary now to be in a bigger school, but elementary school seemed big too when I started, and I adjusted."

The counselor also invited Jeff to keep a "worry box," writing down the things he was worried about for that day and putting them in a box, then checking the box at the end of the day to see if what he had worried about actually had been a problem for him.

The counselor also met with the parents, who confirmed that there were no physical problems. He also helped them understand that this appeared to be a mild case of school phobia and that it was important that they establish consequences at home for not going to school. He suggested that they read *Parents, Teens, and Boundaries* (Bluestein, 1993). Together they met with Jeff and established a contract that he signed, agreeing that if he felt sick enough to stay home from school he would have to stay in bed all day without Nintendo or television and that he would not have after-school privileges with friends.

Evaluation/summary. If Jeff's parents had not been concerned about this problem, it easily could have become more serious. In this case, Jeff agreed to the contract, and the intervention strategies gradually helped him control the problem. Although it is not uncommon for seventh graders to have school avoidance issues, it is sometimes difficult for them to identify specifically what they are avoiding. By being aware of developmental concerns, the counselor can design assessment instruments that help pinpoint the specific concerns so the anxiety can be resolved. In some cases, behavior modification techniques or desensitization also may need to be considered.

Case Study Two: 12-Year-Old Ronnie

Problem overview. Ronnie, a 12-year-old African American boy, was referred to a counselor by the minister after he had received a call from Ronnie's mother, who tearfully told him that Ronnie had told her that he wanted to shoot himself, because in his words, "Life ain't worth it." When the minister asked the mother for more details, she told him that according to Ronnie, nothing was right at school or at home. He had told her that the other kids had made fun of him during basketball tryouts because he was too slow, and he did not make the basketball team because he was too fat; the coach had recommended that he "cut out the Twinkies." During the last month she had noticed that he had become more withdrawn and sullen and indicated that he had put on more weight. She also told the minister that she was probably putting Ronnie under a lot of pressure because she wants him to do well in school and not be a "gangsta" like his brother. After talking to the minister at length, she requested a prayer session with the family. At this prayer session, Ronnie told the minister that he did not mean to say that he wanted to shoot himself because he realized that "people who commit suicide go to hell." After the intense prayer session, Ronnie reportedly felt better. His mother wanted to believe that he did not mean to do anything bad to himself and others and that everything was under control because God has the control of his life. The minister, however, felt that it was better to err on the side of caution and convinced Ronnie's mother to get professional help for her son.

Assessment considerations. As a 12-year-old, Ronnie's self-concept is largely based on peer standards and acceptance (Dusek, 1996; Jaffe, 1998), and Ronnie has become more self-critical as he evaluates himself through social comparison, comparing his skills and achievements with those of others. Furthermore, at this age, young adolescents are very self-conscious about their appearance (K. B. Owens, 2002), so being teased and rejected because of his weight is very discouraging because he so desperately wants peer acceptance. Along with his developing self-understanding comes greater self-regulation, as he is trying to control his reactions for strategic purposes. It is possible that, because he has failed to gain recognition and acceptance in sports, he is calling attention to himself by threatening to shoot himself.

However, given that he has been more withdrawn and sullen lately, it is important to assess for depression. According to Garbarino and Kostelny (1992), "many children from low-income homes—especially those in dangerous neighborhoods—come to think of themselves as worthless and their futures as hopeless, and this makes them unmotivated, depressed, and angry" (p. 146).

In Ronnie's case, and not with the intention to overnormalize or oversimplify his behavior, racial discrimination does not seem to be associated with his current depressive symptoms or negative behaviors. On the other hand, it is instrumental to indicate the complex long-term effects of racism on African Americans and all the potential behavioral issues associated with it. Ronnie has clearly been a victim of discrimination with regard to weight. From a cultural standpoint, religion seems to be at the center of many African American households and Ronnie's situation exemplifies this. It is not unusual to see the involvement of the church minister in the family affairs.

Assessment procedures. The counselor administered a self-esteem and suicidal assessment to explore Ronnie's current emotional state. Initially, she tried to assess Ronnie's depression by asking questions such as the following: (a) Are you feeling hopeless? (b) Do you feel worthless or guilty? (c) How is your level of energy? (d) Tell me about your sleeping and eating habits—have there been any changes? (e) Do you feel lonely or anxious? (f) Are you able to concentrate at school? (g) Do you want to live? (h) How often have you thought about hurting yourself? (i) Do you have a plan? The answers were somewhat inconclusive, so the counselor proceeded to use a nontraditional method of assessment by exploring Ronnie's emotions through drawing. She used a variation of Draw-a-Story (Silver, 1988, 1993), a technique to assess Ronnie's depression. First, she drew a set of random lines of different sizes on a large piece of paper. Second, she told Ronnie to "complete" a drawing using the segments on the paper and during the creative process tell a story of what was happening in the drawing. Initially, Ronnie was reluctant to draw anything until the counselor took the initiative, although he appeared somewhat thoughtful and reflective prior to fully engaging in the activity. Like most children who are experiencing some type of depressive symptoms, Ronnie's creativity expressions were limited. He drew a very stereotypical house, a car, and a house. Also, he did not venture to use multiple colors and used a very small section of the paper instead of the whole drawing area. Although somewhat limited and showing some emotional numbness, Ronnie had a positive attitude at the completion of the activity.

In a second session, the counselor supplied her client with a large piece of paper, tempera paint, and brushes of all sizes, instructing Ronnie to draw the story of his most difficult moments using the format of a comic book. The counselor's goal was not to look for hidden symbols or obscure interpretations in the drawings. Her intent was to help Ronnie illustrate his pain through the creative process. After this assessment, the suicide assessment questions, the variation of the Draw-a-Story technique, and the comic book story, the counselor determined that while Ronnie had shown some signs of mild depressive symptoms, he had no suicidal ideation. Rather, the counselor suspected that like many young adolescents, a combination of factors had left him feeling rather hopeless and he made an overgeneralized statement about not wanting to live.

Interventions. The counselor decided to target self-esteem and suicidal ideation/depression in the intervention process. To improve Ronnie's self-esteem, the counselor devised an exercise called *Who Am I?* The counselor asked Ronnie to bring a recent picture of himself and glued it to the center of a poster board. Multiple arrows that had a question at the end of each one connected the picture. The following were some of the projective questions:

1. When I look in the mirror I see . . .
2. My mother and brother think that I am . . .
3. My friends in schools see me as . . .
4. I am upset when . . .
5. I am tired of . . .
6. I am . . .

On the opposite side of the poster board the counselor put a copy of the same picture with a different set of questions based on how he would like to see himself. Some of the questions were as follows:

1. I would like to be like . . .
2. I want to change . . .
3. I am proud of . . .
4. I like . . .
5. I feel loved by . . .
6. I can . . .

After completing these activities, the counselor and Ronnie discussed the fact that all people have strengths and weaknesses but also that if there were some things he wanted to change about himself, they could work on a plan to do that. After talking about his responses in more depth, Ronnie concluded that maybe working on his weight would be the most important way for him to feel better about himself. Therefore, he and the counselor briefly discussed his eating and exercise habits, and he set some healthy goals. The counselor also scheduled an appointment for Ronnie with the school nurse so they could talk more in depth about healthy eating habits and exercise routines.

Also, to improve his awareness of what depression "looks like," the counselor showed Ronnie a video called *Hills and Valleys: Teen Depression* (1998). Then, the counselor and Ronnie talked about the similarities of his ups and downs with those cases in the video and followed this discussion with things Ronnie could do when he felt depressed: find someone to talk with, go shoot baskets, listen to music, or draw. Also, to be culturally sensitive, the counselor scheduled an appointment with the minister to establish a working plan in which both could communicate their progress and challenges to better serve Ronnie. The minister agreed and subsequently kept the counselor updated with youth activities that Ronnie had been participating in since his last depressive episode.

Evaluation/summary. The key factor regarding Ronnie's success was to monitor the depressive symptoms to avoid an episode that could bring back the suicidal thoughts. Once the counselor observed considerable progress, she reduced the frequency of the counseling sessions, but she met periodically with both Ronnie and his mother to ascertain that in fact Ronnie was getting along better. The counselor was pleased that Ronnie had taken the initiative to become involved in a neighborhood basketball team and was eating healthier. His attitude was noticeably improved, according to his mother.

Case Study Three: 13-Year-Old Kara

Problem overview. Kara, a Caucasian girl in eighth grade, was sent to counseling because her mother was concerned that she had recently begun to restrict her eating, make disparaging remarks about her body, and was increasing her exercise beyond her normal participation in track, volleyball, cheerleading, and ballet. Although it did not appear to her mother that Kara had lost much weight, she was aware that if Kara continued her present behaviors, an eating disorder could easily develop. Her mother could not identify any particular event that precipitated this change in eating and exercise. There had been no recent loss or change in Kara's life, except that her older sister, who was slightly heavy and carefully monitored what she ate, had been home from college over the summer. She and Kara were very close, and the mother speculated that maybe this had something to do with Kara's sudden preoccupation with food. Other than this presenting symptom, Kara was very popular and performed exceptionally well in school and in extracurricular activities.

Assessment considerations. Adolescents are very conscious of their appearance, and for girls, weight is of most concern. Young women in particular become so concerned about gaining weight that they may take "drastic—and dangerous—measures to remain thin" (Steinberg, 1996, p. 519). Berg

(1997) speculated that dancers and female athletes may be at greater risk of developing an eating disorder because they need to stay thin, which would apply in Kara's case. According to Lask (2000), personality traits play a role: Children with anorexia nervosa are typically well behaved, popular, successful, conscientious, compliant, and high achieving. They are often characterized as perfect children (Christie, 2000). Difficulty expressing negative feelings such as anger, anxiety, or sadness is common, as is low self-esteem (Button, Sonuga, Barke, Davies, & Thompson, 1996).

Given the factors that can contribute to the development of this disorder, it is important to do a family assessment to determine whether there are aspects of family functioning that may be contributing to or perpetuating the problem. Christie, Watkins, and Lask (2000) recommended looking at the quality of the parental relationship, boundaries (are one or more of the parents overly close to the adolescent), and the family atmosphere and communication patterns. Individual assessment should include a physical examination. Because depression plays a role in eating disorders, it would be important to assess this, as well as eating and exercise patterns, the client's perception of the problem, and her feelings about it. Self-esteem and expression of negative feelings should also be considered.

Assessment procedures. Some unhealthy eating is inevitable in adolescence, but it is important to be alert to changes, in terms of either restricting or binging. To assess the extent of Kara's problem, the counselor asked her to complete the Questionnaire for Eating Disorder Diagnoses (Mintz, O'Halloran, Mulholland, & Schneider, 1997), a self-report form that is linked to the *DSM–IV* criterion, and a 30-item scale adapted from an eating disorder questionnaire used by a local hospital to measure attitudes, feelings, and behaviors about food, exercise, and body image. Kara was to rate each question as *always, usually, often, sometimes, rarely,* or *never.* Sample items included:

1. I feel satisfied with the shape of my body.
2. I think about dieting.
3. I think that I am too fat.
4. If I gain a pound, I worry that I will keep gaining.
5. I think that my stomach is too big.
6. I like the way my thighs are shaped.
7. I think about being thinner.
8. I feel guilty about eating.
9. I want to exercise a lot.
10. I feel comfortable eating in front of others.

Because people with eating disorders often do not experience a full range of feelings, distort them, or are unable to express negative feelings, Kara was asked to respond in the same manner to questions relating to feelings:

1. I have trouble expressing how I feel to others.
2. I get confused about how I really feel.

3. I feel angry.
4. I get easily upset over little things.
5. I feel inadequate.
6. I feel depressed or very sad.
7. I feel anxious.
8. I feel that no one understands what I feel.

Body image is also an issue for clients with eating disorders, as they frequently have very distorted views of themselves (Wright, 2000). To assess this, the counselor invited Kara to draw a picture of herself as she presently saw herself and a picture of her ideal self. The counselor also asked her to respond to open-ended sentences such as the following to determine if Kara felt she had to be perfect to please herself or others, how she felt about growing up, and how she perceived relationships within her family.

1. Now that I am an adolescent, I feel_____.
2. The person(s) who expect(s) the most from me is (are)_____.
3. If I were younger, I would feel _____.
4. If I disappoint my parents or teachers, I feel_____.
5. If I do not do well in school, athletics, or music activities, I feel _____.
6. I would describe my family as _____.
7. I wish my family would _____.
8. Communication in my family is _____.

The counselor obtained further information about Kara's eating patterns and exercise by having Kara keep a food and exercise chart.

The counselor then analyzed all the data, including input from the physician, and determined that although the problem was not severe at this point, Kara was beginning to develop some unhealthy patterns based on her desire not to "be fat" like her sister. Perfectionism did not seem to be a major issue, but there definitely were distorted ideas about body image that affected her self-esteem. Some depression was evident, as she had checked "often" on the feelings assessment scale. After an interview with the family, it did not appear that there were problems with the family dynamics, although the counselor cautioned the parents about becoming overly involved because this could turn into a power and control issue and make matters worse.

Interventions. The first intervention consisted of Kara looking through magazines and the counselor's collection of photographs to identify people who were skinny, heavy, huge, and just right. After grouping these pictures, the counselor asked Kara to bring in a recent picture of herself and asked her to put her picture in one of the piles. As the counselor anticipated, Kara put hers in the "heavy" pile. To make the comparisons more relevant, the counselor asked Kara to bring snapshots of her friends. Once again she categorized these, and although it was apparent to the counselor that Kara was among the thinnest of her peers, Kara saw herself as heavier than most. The counselor then asked direct questions such as the following to help Kara develop a more realistic perspective: Are you approximately the same height as this friend? Are your legs fatter than hers? Is your waist bigger? Does your stomach stick out? Because these were specific questions and not a global assessment of the entire body, Kara was more realistic in her responses. The counselor helped her see that she had answered "no" to several of the questions, and that although it might seem that she was bigger, in reality she was not.

Because Kara did not seem to realize the serious ramifications of restricting her eating and increasing her exercise, the counselor shared a true story with her that was written by a young woman who had a serious eating disorder for several years. *I Hate My Weight* (Vernon, 1998c, pp. 89–93) emphasized the distorted thinking and the serious consequences, including hospitalization, associated with this disorder. Reading this story seemed to have a significant impact on Kara.

Other interventions included having Kara watch the video *Dying to Be Thin* (McPhee, 2000), making a list of the advantages and disadvantages of restricting her eating, rational self-statements such as, "If I keep on restricting my eating I could end up in the hospital" or "The doctor says my weight is normal for my age and height, so if I eat sensibly I should be okay." The counselor also asked her to create a collage by cutting out pictures of healthy versus unhealthy food choices, and make a "Stop, Go, and Caution" chart of what she would not consider eating ("stop"), foods she would eat ("go"), and foods she felt somewhat comfortable eating ("caution"). She was encouraged to set goals to eat healthy meals and to add foods from her caution list to expand her eating options. She also read *So You Think You're Fat?* (Silverstein & Silverstein, 1991), a book about weight and body image, and they discussed how the concepts related to her situation.

Evaluation/summary. Adolescence is a high-risk period for the development of eating disorders (Weinshenker, 2002; Wright, 2000), so it is critical to intervene at the first sign of problems. Although Berger and Thompson (1991) noted that treatment for eating disorders usually is successful in stopping destructive eating patterns, it can be a very long and difficult process, and hospitalization is often necessary (Jaffe, 1998). Even though Kara was just beginning to restrict her eating and develop distorted images about her body, it still was difficult to dispute her sense of being too heavy and combat her fear about getting fat. Although some of the accompanying issues such as perfectionism, excessive compulsive behavior, and other physiological issues had not developed yet, the fact that she was very conscious of her weight was a signal that early intervention was necessary. Through a variety of cognitive–behavioral methods, bibliotherapy, and work on self-image and acceptance of her body, Kara gradually stopped restricting. As she began to develop more rational thinking, healthier eating patterns, and a more sensible exercise program, she became less depressed. A follow-up of the self-portrait exercise indicated a more realistic self-image.

Case Study Four: 13-Year-Old Trisha

Problem overview. Trisha, a 13-year-old Caucasian girl, asked to see the school counselor, because she frequently felt unhappy and did not really know why. Her grades were fine, and things were all right at home, but as she tearfully explained to the counselor, "Sometimes I feel like the only one who understands me is my dog."

Trisha has an older brother, her father is a minister, and her mother is a teacher. The entire family is very involved in community outreach. Trisha has been active in church and school activities, although recently she expressed to her parents that she wanted to drop choir and track.

Assessment considerations. Early adolescence can be a confusing time, and it is not unusual for youngsters to have vague feelings of discontent or to feel "all alone." Early intervention usually is successful in preventing problems from developing into more serious concerns.

Because this young client could not pinpoint exactly what bothered her, assessment should first be global, then more specific as concerns emerge. Because she was tearful and expressed that she frequently felt unhappy, depression needs to be ruled out. McWhirter, McWhirter, Hart, and Gat (2000) noted that depression is increasing significantly among children and adolescents. Depression is usually accompanied by discouraging thoughts about oneself, and this may contribute to self-esteem problems. Furthermore, depression can affect interpersonal relationships that are very important during early adolescence, so assessment may need to address this area as well.

Assessment procedures. Because Trisha could not point to any one thing that was disturbing her, the counselor used a needs assessment form, Concerns I Have (Strub, 1990/1991). This 50-item checklist assesses a wide variety of concerns pertaining to the early adolescent. The youngster responds to each item by identifying it as *a big concern, a small concern, sometimes a concern,* or *not at all a concern.* Sample items include:

1. I wish I could talk more in a group.
2. Other boys and girls are better than me.
3. I often feel lonesome.
4. I wish my parents understood me better.
5. I wish I had more friends.
6. I would like to change many things about myself.
7. My feelings are too easily hurt.
8. I am not doing as well in school as I can.
9. I would like to be more important to my family.
10. I wish I felt better about myself.

From the results of this checklist, items of most concern seemed to fall in the category of wanting to feel better about herself, being too emotionally sensitive, and feeling insecure with regard to friendships.

To learn more about this client's sadness, the counselor used a 16-item checklist, How to Tell If You're Depressed (Cobain, 1998, pp. 16–17). Trisha's responses indicated that she was often sad and lonely, sometimes felt worthless, and did not enjoy things as she used to. However, her eating and sleeping patterns had not changed and she did not appear to be having difficulty concentrating or remembering things. The counselor asked Trisha to keep a feelings chart (Vernon, 2002, p. 133) that required her to rate her depression or sadness on a scale of 1–5 throughout the day and evening for a week in order for the counselor to learn more about the frequency and intensity of the negative feelings.

The counselor asked Trisha to write a story about a day in her life with her friends to help him understand the specific issues regarding friendship. Themes that emerged included being left out, being jealous if her best friend ignored her, and being confused about the "off and on again" nature of her relationships. The counselor also used a series of open-ended sentences such as the following to gain further information:

1. If my best friend does not sit by me every day, it means that _____.
2. If my best friend does something with another friend, I feel _____ and think_____.
3. If my best friend says something mean to me, I feel _____ and think_____.
4. If others leave me out, it means_____.

The combination of the story and the unfinished sentences helped the counselor understand that Trisha felt helpless and more like a victim when things did not go well with her friends. She felt inadequate rather than angry, which is an important distinction in designing an appropriate intervention.

Interventions. To address this client's desire to feel better about herself, the counselor asked Trisha to make an adjective wardrobe (Canfield & Wells, 1976), writing words that described herself on individual pieces of paper and rank ordering them from most to least pleasing. Trisha then decided which ones she wanted to expand on and which she wanted to eliminate so she could establish goals for change. The counselor also encouraged Trisha to read *Why Can't Anyone Hear Me? A Guide for Surviving Adolescence* (Eichoness, 1989), which focuses on improving self-esteem.

To deal with Trisha's sense of emotional vulnerability, the counselor adapted two activities from the book *Feeling Good About Yourself* (Pincus, 1990). In the first activity, Trisha identified situations in which she felt guilty, angry, embarrassed, sad, and hurt. Next, she examined what she was thinking about herself or the situation when she had a particular feeling. In the second activity, Trisha learned that how she thinks affects the way she feels about a situation and was taught how to change her feelings by changing her thoughts.

To help Trisha deal with the friendship issues, the counselor used the book *Friendship Is Forever, Isn't It?* (Youngs, 1990) to help her realize friendships change. He also engaged her in an adaptation of Fights With Friends (Vernon, 2002, pp. 225–227), a game that helped her identify assumptions, how they cause problems in friendships, and how to combat the negative effects caused by assumptions by adopting more effective behavioral coping strategies.

Although the above-mentioned interventions might also alleviate some of the depressed feelings, the counselor suggested that Trisha draw an outline of her hand and on each finger write something that she could think or do to help her feel better, hanging it in her room or taping it inside her desk as a visual reminder of how to combat bad feelings. He also encouraged her to write a journal, exercise, and read joke books or watch funny movies when she felt sad.

Evaluation/summary. Trisha was a very eager client. The combination of interventions was helpful, although she continued to need reinforcement to help her deal with the ups and downs of friendships. Consequently, the counselor put her in a friendship group. Evaluation consisted of a posttest of the depression quiz and an analysis of the weekly feeling charts, both of which noted a decrease in the depressive symptoms and ratings.

Case Study Five: 14-Year-Old Shenika

Problem overview. Shenika, a 14-year-old Black girl of African descent, was referred to counseling because of anger outbursts at home. Her parents came from Zimbabwe when she was 10 years old. The parents reported that Shenika has become too Americanized and that she does not want to spend time with the family anymore. On Sundays, the family has a picnic at the public park and play games together. Shenika said that "picnics are stupid" and that she is "not a kid who likes to play family games anymore." At home, she does not speak the native tribal language anymore and is ashamed of her parents when they use the language in public places. She does not spend time with the native Africans from Zimbabwe, preferring to listen to hip-hop music with her new African American friends. Shenika is constantly arguing with her parents and little brother and has offended them many times by saying things like "If you like Zimbabwe so much, why don't you go there and leave me here by myself?" Her school performance is below average.

Assessment considerations. During this stage of development, friends are often more influential than parents (Jaffe, 1998). Socially and cognitively, adolescents see themselves as part of the whole and not as independent individuals. Because they want to be like their peers, it is not unusual that they reject their families. In Shenika's case, culture also plays a role.

The counselor suspected that there were three important aspects related to Shenika's sudden change in behavior. First, she is undergoing a critical transition from preadolescence to adolescence. Second, she is trying to find her own self-identity separate from the family, which is a typical adolescent task (Dusek, 1996). Third, Shenika is going through a cultural identity crisis as an immigrant.

Assessment procedures. The counselor proceeded to use the Acculturation Scale (Clemente, 2004) to explore Shenika's level of cultural identity. Typical questions on this scale included:

1. My generation is: (e.g., If my grandparents were the first to come to the United States, I am a third generation)
   a) First
   b) Second
   c) Third
   d) Fourth
   e) Fifth
2. The language that I prefer to use most of the time is: (e.g., at home, with my friends, etc.)
   a) Mine only
   b) Mostly mine
   c) Both mine and English
   d) Mostly English
   e) Only English
3. When not attending school, I like to spend my time: (e.g., in the neighborhood, YMCA, sport and social activities, etc.)
   a) Only with friends of my own ethnic group
   b) Mostly with friends of my own ethnic group
   c) Within and between different ethnic groups
   d) Mostly with a different ethnic group
   e) Only with a different ethnic group

From the results of this, it appeared that Shenika was in complete negation of her cultural background. She did not want to "feel or look different from the others" and as a result of this attitude, she turned away from her culture and embraced the U.S. culture. Consequently, she adopted a hostile attitude toward her immediate family because they represented the African culture.

To assess the level of emotional and psychological stress associated with the self-identity issues, the counselor developed a self-identity chart:

Self-Identity Chart

Family	Me (Shenika)
My family told me that I can . . .	I can . . .
My family believes that I am aware of . . .	I am aware of . . .
My family says that I don't need . . .	I don't need . . .
My family thinks that I have to . . .	I think that I have to . . .
My family believes that occasionally I . . .	I belief that I . . .

Through the use of the chart, the counselor wanted to explore Shenika's perceptions about her life versus those she thought her family held. Shenika's responses indicated that she was experiencing an internal dichotomy in which every statement or action by the family was perceived as a form of confrontation against her. Consequently, she developed some defense mechanisms to protect herself from what she perceived as attacks from the family. At that point, Shenika was unable to believe that the family had good intentions.

Interventions. To explore and monitor Shenika's perceptions and feelings, the counselor recommended that she keep a journal and invited her to bring it to the counseling sessions and discuss its content as much as she felt comfortable doing. Also, because Shenika liked hip-hop music, the counselor encouraged her to write a song depicting her current struggles. She had the option to tape-record it and bring it to the session or write it. In addition, the counselor wanted to promote a healthy bicultural identity and showed her, in two different sessions, the following documentaries: *Zimbabwe: The Lost City of Africa* (2000) and *Kwanzaa: An African American Celebration* (1995). The first video depicts a historical perspective of Zimbabwe and the pride of its people, and the second video deals with religious practices among African Americans. The intent of these videos was to underscore the genuine interest of some African Americans to rediscover their hidden past by rescuing African American practices.

The counselor's goal was to emphasize the importance of knowing and valuing cultural roots without being ashamed. After showing her the videos, they discussed the content. Shenika seemed genuinely interested in some of the information and the counselor emphasized that she was fortunate to know the history of her ancestors and their cultural practices. He asked her if she would be interested in doing some research into her own family background by drawing a family tree and gathering information from her parents about various ancestors. She seemed interested in doing this, and the counselor thought this might be a good way for her to see that her parents play a vital role in keeping the cultural links alive.

To encourage empathy and foster a healthy relationship with her parents, the counselor used the Adlerian "What If" technique. The counselor provided more context to this technique by dedicating various separate counseling sessions to different family members. Following this example, the counselor extended the number of questions and developed similar tables for each family member (i.e., mother, father, etc.):

Session 1
What if you were your father?
1. What would you think about Shenika?
2. What would you think about Shenika every time that she came late home?
3. How would you feel about Shenika's shameful attitudes regarding her native Zimbabwean language?
4. How would you discipline Shenika?
5. How can you help Shenika?

Evaluation/summary. The counselor monitored Shenika's progress by checking on her academic progress and the quality of the relationship with her parents as reported by her or occasionally by interviewing them. Promoting a healthy acculturation cannot be imposed; rather, it is a process in which the individual has to take ownership to find it meaningful. Over the course of time, this young client became less hostile and rejecting, participating more in family functions and inviting friends into the family home.

Case Study Six: 14-Year-Old Jamie

Problem overview. Jamie, an eighth-grade Caucasian boy, was caught smoking in the school restroom twice during the same week. The principal requested a conference with Jamie's parents and recommended counseling, because in addition, his grades were slipping and he had been truant from school on several occasions. At home he was becoming more defiant, challenging rules, and ignoring his curfew. His parents had tried a number of things, including grounding (which had not worked because he just snuck out the basement window) and taking away his computer (which he then used as an excuse for not doing his homework).

The parents had noticed more defiance during the summer when he began associating with a different peer group. On several occasions they expressed concern that he never invited friends to his house anymore and always seemed so secretive. Jamie dismissed this by saying that his friends were his business and he would rather be at someone else's house. They had confronted him about smelling like smoke, but he said it was because he had been in a room where parents had been smoking. They said no more because they wanted to believe him.

Assessment considerations. As Larsen and Asmussen (1991) noted, boys at this age experience anger and contempt. Their increased need for independence prompts them to decide what they can do without being ordered and directed (Nelsen & Lott, 2000), and this sense of entitlement often results in rebelliousness. Early adolescents also are influenced easily by peer pressure (Head, 1997; Newman & Newman, 1991), so knowing more about this client's peer group would be helpful.

Because Jamie's grades are declining, it is important to look for other indicators of depression, such as the increased anger, that could be masking depression. Because he was caught smoking cigarettes, he might be using other drugs or alcohol, which could account for his behavioral and academic changes. Newton (1995) noted that when kids start experimenting with adult substances, it usually starts with cigarettes, followed by alcohol and marijuana as the entry drugs. Rebellion against parental structure and limit setting can affect how parents discipline, so assessment needs to include input from the parents about their parenting style and their knowledge of early adolescent development.

Assessment procedures. Jamie refused to attend the first session, so his parents met with the counselor. The fact that they were not able to get him to counseling indicated that there also might be some parenting issues that needed to be addressed. The counselor decided to start at this point, requesting each parent to respond to questions such as the following by circling *always*, *sometimes*, or *never* on each item:

1. We agree on rules for our adolescent.
2. If our adolescent breaks a rule, there are consequences.
3. We are consistent about enforcing consequences.
4. If our adolescent has problems, it must mean we are bad parents.
5. It is easier to let our adolescent do as he or she pleases than to enforce rules.
6. Getting angry is an effective way to get our adolescent to obey.
7. If we get too firm, our adolescent will reject us.
8. It's impossible to be kind and firm at the same time.

From the responses to these types of questions, the counselor verified that working with the parents on effective discipline was part of the intervention. However, she also felt that it was important to work with Jamie, but because he refused to come, she suggested that the parents pick him up at school the following week and bring him to the appointment without informing him ahead of time. Although this was not her preferred way of operating, she thought that once Jamie was there she could deal with his resistance and eventually develop a counseling relationship.

Jamie was indeed resistant, informing the counselor that he did not have a problem and did not intend to talk. The counselor assured him that she understood that counseling would not be his activity of choice but indicated that the school was concerned and that if he did not want them or his parents on his back all the time, it might be a good idea to let the counselor help him.

Because this young client was not willing to talk, the counselor asked if she could share some advice for parents, written by other teens (Vernon & Al-Mabuk, 1995). As she read examples such as the following, Jamie nodded his head and admitted that he felt that way too: "Don't assume that I'll do bad things or screw up," "Don't keep bringing up all the bad things I do," "Don't blow it all out of proportion and think that I'll never change" (Vernon & Al-Mabuk, 1995, p. 98). This broke the ice somewhat, and he was willing to share some examples of how these pieces of advice applied to him and his parents. Although he seemed more receptive but was still not very talkative, the counselor asked him if he would be willing to complete a short checklist that would help her understand his point of view. He agreed and completed a checklist (*strongly agree, agree, disagree, strongly disagree*) with questions such as the following

1. I should get to choose my friends.
2. I should have some responsibilities/chores to do as a member of the household.
3. I should be allowed to set my own curfew.

4. It's my right to decide if I want to do my homework.
5. If I break rules, there should be consequences.
6. Parents and teachers should let me do things my way.
7. Before I make decisions, I think about the consequences.

It is clear from his responses that challenging authority and wanting power was a predominant theme that would have to be addressed tactfully in the intervention phase.

The counselor learned from his parents that Jamie had been an above-average student prior to this year. When asked about his declining grades, Jamie said he did not like most of his subjects and he had better things to do with his time.

To assess for depression, the counselor asked Jamie to complete a short checklist titled How to Tell If You're Depressed (Cobain, 1998) that consisted of statements with a yes–no answer format such as:

1. I often feel sad and anxious.
2. I'm easily irritated.
3. I have little or no energy.
4. I use alcohol or other drugs to help me feel better.
5. I skip school or have dropped school activities.

Jaime answered no to 14 of the 16 problems. He denied using alcohol or drugs, denied being sad, but admitted that he skipped school and felt irritated. He described himself as being happy as long as adults "keep off my case." Parents indicated that his eating and sleeping patterns were normal, and they were going to monitor his activities more closely and check out his peer group to determine if drugs or alcohol might be a factor, although they did not think so at this time.

Interventions. After assessing the situation, the counselor thought this was a rather typical case of adolescent rebellion that could get worse without intervention, for both Jamie and his parents. She first worked with the parents to dispute their belief that it is easier to give in than to follow through with discipline by having them read *Surviving and Enjoying Your Adolescent* (Barrish & Barrish, 1989). This book normalizes the adolescent quest for independence and helps parents understand that they can tolerate their own discomfort if their child is upset with them for imposing rules. The counselor explained the importance of parental consistency and adolescents' need for limits, instructing them on the use of logical consequences. She recommended *Kids, Parents, and Power Struggles* (Kurcinka, 2000) to help them learn more about these points.

The counselor engaged Jamie in a chain reaction activity to help him identify the consequences of his decisions (adapted from Vernon, 1998a, pp. 313–315). She gave him several strips of paper that listed the problematic behaviors identified by parents and teachers: school truancy, mouthy behavior, breaking curfew, being disrespectful to parents, declining grades, and smoking. She then asked Jamie to take one of the problem strips and write on a blank strip a positive or negative consequence, and then on another blank strip, a positive or negative consequence for that consequence, and so forth. When he was finished with one problem, she stapled these together into a paper chain. She had him do this for each of the problems. By looking at it in this manner, Jamie saw that there were more negatives than positives. The counselor also adapted What's the Impact? from *The Passport Program* (Vernon, 1998b, pp. 81–84), which helped this client look at short- and long-term consequences and the effects of the decision on self and others.

The counselor also worked with Jamie to give up his demand that he always should get to do what he wanted by asking how his actions were helping him, and focused on Jamie's anger. To do this, the counselor used an activity, Where Feelings Come From (Knaus, 1974, pp. 21–24), to show this young client the connection of events, thoughts, feelings, and behavior/reactions. The counselor asked Jaime to identify several situations that angered him and used the HTFR (happening, thought, feeling, behavior/reaction) format to show Jamie how his anger developed and how to change his thinking to decrease the intensity of the anger. Because Jamie's parents had some concerns about his peers, the counselor worked with the school counselor to establish a small group with some positive role models and work on the issue of rules and consequences.

Evaluation/summary. As can be expected, once the parents agreed on rules and started to enforce consequences, the rebellion temporarily escalated. They continued in counseling to strengthen their parenting skills, at the same time stressing to Jamie that he was choosing his consequences as a result of his behavior. They monitored his activities more and were not as intimidated by his angry outbursts and threat because they had learned not to take Jamie's verbal abuse so personally. By being firm and consistent with their follow-through, keeping him accountable for completing his homework, and lecturing less but listening more, things gradually improved. The bibliotherapy helped them understand more about early adolescence and effective parenting for this age. The interventions with Jamie helped him look more carefully at decisions and consequences. A follow-up with school officials indicated that his attendance was also better. The parents continued to monitor this so further problems did not develop.

Other Typical Early Adolescent Concerns

As previously stated, the transition from childhood to adolescence, generally labeled *early adolescence*, is characterized by tremendous change and significant challenges (Jaffe, 1998; Kaplan, 2000; Vernon, 2004). During this period, the adolescent knows that most things will be changing but has no idea how things will turn out, accounting for the prevalent anxiety during this phase of development. Although a good deal of stress is associated with this period that some adolescents find overwhelming and difficult, others see this as a stimulating period that presents challenges and opportunities for growth (Petersen, Kennedy, & Sullivan, 1991).

Part of the difficulty during this period is that there are simultaneous changes occurring. For example, as they experience puberty, early adolescents also confront other developmental changes, such as changing school structure and format, experiencing more pressure from peers to try new things, and dealing with parents' responses to their pubertal changes, which often have implications for the parents' aging and their own thoughts of impending separation from their child (Petersen, 1987). Additional problems typically experienced are described subsequently in order of intensity with accompanying behaviors that may help identify the problem (Youngs, 1985, 1995). The degree to which adolescents experience these problems depends on many factors, including cultural considerations.

Age 11

At this age, a common worry for adolescents is whether or not they are popular. They may also feel anxious about sex, not knowing much about it, perhaps feeling pressure to experiment, and not knowing what members of the opposite sex expect. Young adolescents are very conscious of their bodies, worry about being over- or underdeveloped, and worry about gym class and having to undress in front of others. They also are concerned about their moods, "fretting for hours over their own emotional states" (Youngs, 1995, p. 131). Fear of not being able to complete schoolwork and fear of the school calling home are overshadowed at school by their insecurity about their appearance and fears that they will be mocked by friends for the way they look.

Age 12 and 13

At this age, adolescents are afraid of being selected first and having to lead, and they also fear being selected last and feeling unpopular and disliked. They fear dealing with their own sexuality and often refuse to participate in activities that require them to expose their body. They are confused about the sexual changes they are experiencing and feel stressed as a result of the onset of menstruation, erections and nocturnal emissions, and masturbation. They worry about emotional happiness and unhappiness, often avoiding dealing with specific issues and rejecting feelings associated with being unhappy.

Age 14

Fourteen-year-olds may begin to experiment with sexual desires with the onset of sexual maturity. They may feel guilty and confused. Their raging hormones result in erratic behavior that leaves them feeling inferior, anxious, and fearful. They continue to feel insecure about their bodies and often feel that they are "going crazy" because their hormones are creating mood swings (Youngs, 1995, p. 134). Both sexes fear a confrontation over a boyfriend or a girlfriend, and they continue to worry about being unpopular. Jealousy is also very prevalent, as they worry about anyone or anything that gets in the way of their friendships.

Summary

Although in some cultures there is no rite of passage that marks the transition from childhood to adulthood, early adolescence initiates this process. The changes in self, physical, intellectual, social, emotional, and moral processes are dramatic and are negotiated with varying degrees of success depending on the individual and on cultural and societal influences. Contemporary theorists dispute the belief that adolescence is normally pathological; rather, they see it as a phase in which challenging developmental tasks need to be mastered (Head, 1997; Martin, 2003).

As discussed in this chapter, the needs and dynamics of early adolescents, ages 11–14, are qualitatively different from those of middle or late adolescence. Healthy adolescent development is fostered by providing a prolonged supportive environment during early adolescence, with gradual steps toward autonomy (Vernon & Al-Mabuk, 1995). Successful completion of developmental tasks at this level positively influences the 15- to 18-year-old.

Chapter 8

Mid-Adolescence:
Assessment and Intervention

✳

A parent remarked recently that she thought they had achieved another milestone with their 15-year-old son. Instead of insisting that his parents let him out of the car a block from the movie theater so he would not have to be seen with them, they actually had spent an hour together in the shopping center and their son had not even walked several feet behind them. Another parent commented how relieved she was that her teenage daughter reacted calmly when the mother scorched her daughter's dress for a formal dance. This calmness is what parents hope mid-adolescence brings. Yet, although the turbulence of early adolescence is past, mid-adolescence arrives with new challenges and developmental tasks. The exact nature of these tasks and how they are experienced and resolved are mediated or influenced by culture and subculture, various social factors such as parenting styles and peer influence, as well as by psychological factors (Atwater, 1996; Dusek 1996).

✳

In this chapter, specific developmental characteristics in the areas of self, social, emotional, physical, cognitive, and moral development are described, followed by case studies that provide detailed descriptions of effective assessment and intervention processes.

Characteristics of Mid-Adolescence

"In all societies, adolescence is a time of growing up, of moving from the immaturity of childhood into the maturity of adulthood" (Steinberg, 1996, p. 4). As noted in the previous chapter, it is a time of biological, psychological, and social transitions. Steinberg described adolescence as an exciting time of life in which individuals "become wiser, more sophisticated, and better able to make their own decisions" (p. 4). Because adolescence may not only begin earlier but may also last longer than puberty or the teenage years, it is difficult to put an exact chronological age on mid-adolescence; it depends on which criteria of development are used. Generally speaking, it corresponds to ages 15–18 (Steinberg, 1996), with late adolescence beginning in the late teens and extending through the early 20s (Atwater, 1996) when more adult roles are assumed (Dusek, 1996).

During mid-adolescence, the yo-yo nature of early adolescence is replaced by greater stability for the most part (Schave & Schave, 1989). Parents, teachers, and adolescents welcome this change, although, depending on the rate at which they reach formal operational thinking, some adolescents still appear much like early adolescents. Mid-adolescents achieve new freedoms and responsibilities, signified in part by a rite of passage. In some societies, the rite of passage that marks the end of childhood and the beginning of adulthood defines adolescence, making it virtually the time from the beginning to the end of the rite of passage (Dusek, 1996). In other cultures such as the United States, the rite of passage is not formal but is often associated with obtaining a driver's license. As a soon-to-be 16-year-old recently said, "Everything's going to change when I get my license!"

Mid-adolescence frequently is described as a period when teenagers try out adult roles (Dusek, 1991, 1996), discover who they are and are not (Cobb, 2001), establish new beliefs and behaviors (Kaplan, 2000), and achieve autonomy from parents and teachers (Head, 1997). Havighurst (1972, as cited in Atwater, 1996, p. 44) described eight major stages of adolescence:

Stage 1: Accepting one's body and using it effectively.
Stage 2: Achieving a masculine or feminine social role.
Stage 3: Achieving new and more mature relations with peers of both sexes.
Stage 4: Attaining emotional independence of parents and other adults.
Stage 5: Preparing for an economic career.
Stage 6: Preparing for marriage and family life.
Stage 7: Desiring and achieving socially responsible behavior.
Stage 8: Acquiring a set of values as a guide to behavior.

Jaffe (1998) pointed out that adolescents' lives change as society changes, resulting in new challenges and potential problems. Dusek (1996) speculated that some of the tasks associated with adolescence are more difficult to master in a contemporary society. For example, it is more challenging to prepare for and enter the job market because there are fewer lower skills jobs but more jobs that require advanced training, which adolescents might not have access to. In addition, Dusek (1991) stressed that adolescents may have more trouble becoming adults than their parents did, which may contribute to other problems. Dusek's concerns were expressed years ago by Elkind (1988), who posited that it is harder to grow up, attributing this to the fact that children are forced to grow up too soon. By the time they reach adolescence, Elkind said, they are ready to experiment with many things that are "off limits" until they reach a certain age, such as drinking and smoking. Elkind noted in particular the rush for sexual experimentation, which results in high teenage pregnancy rates and an increase in sexually transmitted diseases and AIDS among teenagers. According to Elkind, other negative ramifications result from this pressure to grow up fast: greater stress, more youth crime and violence, and teenage suicide. Perhaps the most significant implication is that some young people are trying out new behaviors and experiencing things without the necessary level of developmental maturity. It is clear that Elkind's concerns are still very relevant for today's adolescents, who have multiple choices to make in an increasingly stressful, highly technological society.

Thus, although some maintain that mid-adolescence is a calmer, more predictable stage of development, social, cultural, and environmental factors impinge on the developmental process and may affect the smooth-sailing scenario one way or another. Although it is difficult to describe universal patterns of adolescence, because personal circumstances, cultural factors, and rates of maturation have a strong impact, the following descriptions provide general trends.

Self-Development

"Who am I?" and "What will I become?" are central to the gradual process of identity development that begins at birth and solidifies during adolescence or early adulthood as adolescents integrate childhood identities with their own desires as well as cultural and societal expectations (Meece, 2002). According to Cobb (2001), "adolescents who achieve a personal identity appreciate their uniqueness even while realizing all they have in common with others" (p. 580). As they develop a stronger sense of self, they are less dependent on others' opinions and are generally better able to maintain personal boundaries in intimate relationships.

Berk (2003) described the process of constructing an identity as defining who you are, what you value, and what directions you pursue in life. Adolescents do this by trying on various roles and responsibilities, engaging in discussions, observing adults as well as peers, speculating about the future, and doing a lot of self-questioning and experimenting (Vernon, 2004). Developing an identity affects vocational choices, interpersonal relationships, community involvement, moral and political beliefs, and religious affiliation. As Yoder (2000) noted, the family, peers, school and community, the larger society, and one's personality all influence identity development, as do cultural values (Cobb, 2001).

The process of forming an identity may be more complicated and painful for ethnic minority adolescents who may be caught between the values of the larger society and those of their own culture (Meece, 2002). It is not uncommon for these youth to hold negative attitudes toward their own cultural group in their desire to fit in, but identifying closely with the majority culture may result in rejection by their own ethnic group (Phinney, 1990). Some adolescents even develop a negative identity, rejecting their own values as well as those of the majority culture, according to Meece. It is very important to be sensitive to these issues in helping these youth resolve their identity conflicts.

Developing a sexual identity can also be very difficult and traumatic. Meece (2002) reported that same-sex attractions can occur before age 15, and acknowledging this attraction can be very anxiety provoking because of widespread antigay attitudes that can result in harassment and physical abuse for those who choose to "come out" (McFarland & Dupuis, 2001). Once again, sensitivity to the difficulties these youth face as they come to terms with their sexual identity/orientation is critical.

In his classic work *Identity: Youth and Crisis* (1968), Erikson described adolescence as a turning point in life, during which young people expend a tremendous amount of energy on issues related to self-definition and self-esteem. According to Erikson, young people attempt to establish themselves as separate individuals and at the same time preserve some connection with meaningful aspects of the past, including family. The process of "finding themselves" involves establishing a moral, sexual, vocational, political, and religious identity. Erikson maintained that identity is achieved through a crisis of emotional stress that requires an alteration in one's viewpoint. The crisis precipitates a change, either forward toward adulthood or backward toward earlier developmental levels. Although researchers now use the term *exploration* as opposed to *crisis* (Atwater, 1996), the essential concept is the same: that adolescents are actively exploring their identity and making a decision about their direction in life. Although most adolescents are able to deal successfully with the stress and anxiety associated with this exploration, some remain confused and have few commitments to goals or values.

Marcia (1980) identified four major identity statuses: diffusion, foreclosure, moratorium, and achievement. Identity diffusion occurs when adolescents are not actively exploring options and have difficulty meeting the typical demands of adolescence. They cannot make firm commitments about their beliefs, relationships, or vocational choices and consequently struggle to make friends, complete schoolwork, or make decisions about the future. These youth often have low self-esteem, are dependent, and are frequently isolated. High anxiety and high apathy are common (Waterman, 1999), and these youth are at high risk for developing psychological problems (Meeus, Iedema, Helsen, & Vollebergh, 1999).

Identity foreclosure occurs when young people have committed themselves to certain choices but have not explored all possibilities. This often happens because they are strongly attached to their parents, adopting their values without thorough exploration. According to Meeus et al. (1999), this stage is associated with high levels of psychological well-being. Marcia (1980), however, noted that these youth are easily influenced by others and can be very dependent.

During identity moratorium, adolescents are actively exploring relationships and occupational plans, but they are not ready to make commitments (Meece, 2002); it is like they are taking a timeout to experiment with different identities. Waterman (1999) suggested that these youth may experience more anxiety as well as conflict with parents, but they are less rigid. Moratorium is a necessary part of identity development but is considered a transitional period, according to Meece.

Identity achievement is the desired goal and occurs when adolescents develop their own goals, accepting some values from parents and society and rejecting others. High self-esteem, self-control, and self-directedness characterize this status.

Much of what happens in terms of self-development in mid-adolescence depends on the degree to which formal operational thinking is attained and the level of self-esteem of the early adolescent as he or she enters this next developmental level. Typically mid-adolescents become more self-reflective and are beginning to take all aspects of their personalities and consolidate them into a consistent personality (Jaffe, 1998). Jaffe noted that by the late teenage years, "they are better able to come to terms with their personal inconsistencies and contradictions . . . and they feel comfortable revealing different sides of themselves on different occasions to different people when playing different roles" (p. 194).

Social Development

The importance of peer relationships continues into mid-adolescence, and the increased time spent with peers serves a variety of functions for the teenager: to try out various roles, to learn to tolerate individual differences as they come in contact with people who have different values and lifestyles, and to prepare themselves for adult interactions as they begin to form more intimate relationships (Dusek, 1996). In addition, because peers are also searching for autonomy and dealing with emerging sexuality, it is comforting to be with others who share the same anxieties and concerns (Head, 1997).

For the adolescent who has attained formal operational thinking, relationships take on a new dimension. Because they are more self-confident, they are not as dependent on peers for identity and emotional support (Jaffe, 1998), although peers continue to play a very important role in adolescents' psychological development (Steinberg, 1996). The decline of egocentrism also leads to less need to conform to peers; they have begun to develop personal values and identity and are more willing to express their uniqueness. They select friends on the basis of compatibility, shared experiences, and their contribution to the relationship as well as on their personality (Dusek, 1996; Jaffe, 1998). Their friendships are more stable and less exclusive, according to Steinberg, and their increased interpersonal sensitivity makes it more likely that they will appreciate people with differing characteristics.

At this stage of development, adolescents expect more from relationships, seeking friends who will be loyal, intimate, and sympathetic. Trust and honesty are also important qualities, in addition to dependability. Adolescent friendships are more intense and adultlike, according to Steinberg (1996).

Intimate friendships with both the same gender and opposite gender increase during mid-adolescence, with girls seeking these intimate relationships sooner than boys. Dusek (1996) noted other gender differences:

Female friendships fluctuate more than male friendships and are also more intense. These kinds of friendships have several positive outcomes for adolescents: They develop more social sensitivity, they become more adept at affective perspective taking, and they are better able to engage in mutually beneficial interactions.

Until age 15 or 16, there is generally more antagonism than attraction toward the opposite gender, although teenagers begin to experience casual heterosexual contact through participation in group activities before actual dating begins (Berger & Thompson, 1991; Berndt, 1992; Dusek, 1996). Although some teenagers start dating earlier, more serious dating generally begins after age 15 or 16 (Steinberg, 1996), with relationships characterized by deep emotional involvement generally developing even later (Dusek, 1991). According to Steinberg, girls start dating earlier than boys and are more interested than boys in dating. Although Steinberg noted that not all romantic relationships are sexual, sexual experimentation generally increases during this period and teenagers are more likely to be sexually active (Cobb, 2001).

As they become less egocentric, adolescents realize there will be shortcomings in relationships and they are better able to accept this. In turn, they are more likely to stick with a friend through a disagreement and generally approach relationships in a more mature fashion.

Emotional Development

In contrast to the emotional upheaval characteristic of early adolescence, more emotional stability comes in mid-adolescence. Adolescents are better able to deal with emotionally charged issues, because they are less likely to be overwhelmed by their emotions. Because they are not as vulnerable, they are less defensive and more likely to ask for help if needed. This is an important development. Adolescents who are stuck in the concrete operational stage cannot handle overwhelming emotions and, therefore, use denial to deal with the situation. As a result, rather than relying on parents or professionals to help them cope with problems, they try to figure it out themselves, often unsuccessfully, rather than seek assistance and feel ashamed.

However, toward the end of this stage, many adolescents are lonely and ambivalent, gradually moving away from peers as their interests change. They may also experience anxiety and insecurity about the future (Vernon, 2004).

Although they are typically more emotionally stable, it is important to remember that there is great variability in how they deal with emotionally charged issues depending on their level of cognitive maturation, which accounts for the wide variation in how adolescents manage emotions. Those who are more emotionally mature have better coping skills and are less likely to behave impulsively or act out behaviorally (Vernon & Al-Mabuk, 1995). Those who are less mature may not have the coping skills they need to deal effectively with the increasing prevalence of stressors that occur during this period of development, and the demands of adolescence can result in helplessness, confusion, and pessimism.

A compounding factor in adolescents' emotional development is depression, which was not well addressed until recently because it was discounted as adolescent turmoil or masked depression, according to B. T. McWhirter and Burrow-Sanchez (2004). However, Lewinsohn, Hops, Roberts, Seeley, and Andrew (1993) reported that about 30% of adolescents experience periods of sadness and depressed feelings regularly, leading McWhirter and Burrow-Sanchez to conclude that depression in youth is a significant problem. Steinberg (1996) noted that "in its mild form, depression is probably the most common psychological disturbance among adolescents" (p. 511) and is more prevalent in girls than in boys (Kazdin, 1994). According to Evans, Van Velsor, and Schumacher (2002), "depression may be one of the most overlooked and under-treated psychological disorders of adolescence" (p. 211).

Severe depression increases the risk of suicide (Evans et al., 2002). The adolescent suicide rate has increased dramatically over the last 40 years (Steinberg, 1996). According to a report from the Centers for Disease Control and Prevention (1999), in 1999, 25% of female adolescents and 14% of male adolescents in Grades 9–12 had seriously considered attempting suicide. Gay and lesbian adolescents have high rates of attempts and completions (Faulkner & Cranston, 1998). Although Caucasian adolescent males complete suicide more than any other ethnic group (Canetto & Sakinofsky, 1998), suicide rates for African American adolescents have risen significantly (National Center for Injury Prevention and Control, as cited in E. H. McWhirter, Shepard, & Hunt-Morse, 2004), and Native American adolescents have the highest suicide rate of any ethnic group (Capuzzi & Gross, 2004). Helping adolescents develop more effective ways to deal with their problems is crucial because when they feel hopeless and pessimistic about their future, they may act impulsively to "end their pain."

Physical Development

Depending on when the early adolescent begins puberty, physical development in mid-adolescence may continue at a rather rapid rate or gradually begin to slow down. Generally by this time, girls have achieved full breast growth and have started to menstruate, pubic hair has developed completely, and their body weight has been redistributed, resulting in a more fully developed figure (Newman & Newman, 1991). Although many preadolescents and early adolescent girls are dissatisfied with their shape and weight, this dissatisfaction decreases gradually with age. Older girls in general have more realistic body images and are more comfortable with their bodies, according to Jaffe (1998).

Boys generally lag behind girls in rate of physical development by approximately 2 years (Berger & Thompson, 1991; Seifert & Hoffnung, 1997). Consequently, during early adolescence, girls are usually taller than boys. During mid-adolescence, this trend is reversed. By age 15, boys usually experience a lowering of their voice, and by age 15 or 16, facial hair appears. This is viewed as an important "coming of age" event for boys: The shaving of the face becomes a significant validation of gender role (Newman & Newman, 1991). Final pubic hair develops at about age 18. Seifert and Hoffnung noted that ethnic and individual differences affect the amount of facial and body hair as well as feelings about it. For example, in European cultures, women's underarm and leg hair is attractive, whereas in the United States, women spend considerable effort removing it.

These average ages are simply approximations. Healthy adolescents may be as much as 3 years ahead or behind these ages, and the sequence of changes also may vary somewhat. For example, girls may have some pubic hair before their breasts begin to develop, and boys may have facial hair before their voices change (Berger & Thompson, 1991). Genes, nutrition, and the tendency to experience puberty earlier in this contemporary society all affect physical maturation.

There are other considerations with regard to physical development. Girls in particular who continue to compare their body image with society's ideal image of beauty are especially susceptible to life-threatening eating disorders such as anorexia or bulimia (Lask, 2000). Culture may have an impact on how adolescents adjust to physical changes. Schlegel and Barry (1991) posited that "Western adolescents, and perhaps American adolescents in particular, are inordinately conscious of their appearance and overwhelmingly dissatisfied with it" (p. 205).

Cognitive Development

During mid-adolescence, formal operational thinking continues to develop, although many adolescents and even adults still have not reached this level of thinking. Steinberg (1996) stressed that advanced reasoning capabilities develop gradually, that these advanced skills are used by some adolescents more often than by other adolescents, and that when they apply the advanced skills may depend on the situation. As formal operational thinking develops, adolescents begin to think and behave in qualitatively different ways. For example, adolescent thinking is associated with the concept of possibilities (Moshman, 1999; Seifert & Hoffnung, 1997). As they become increasingly able to think abstractly, they can distinguish the real and concrete from the abstract and possible, and their thinking becomes more multidimensional and relativistic (K. B. Owens, 2002; Steinberg, 1996). They also can hypothesize, think about the future, be introspective, and combine thoughts (Dusek, 1996). Their thought processes are more flexible; they are less likely to think in either–or terms, which has a positive effect on how they problem solve (Vernon, 2004).

Development of formal operational thinking has implications for moral rules as well. Atwater (1996) noted that when adolescents are presented with a conflict, such as whether or not to tell authorities about a peer's misconduct, they are more aware of the negative consequences and are more likely to be honest. Their increased cognitive maturity also enables them to make more responsible decisions that otherwise could result in serious consequences, such as unwanted pregnancies or sexually transmitted diseases.

Formal operational thinking significantly affects how adolescents think and reason, which in turn relates to other areas of their lives such as decisions about education, careers, and romance (Jaffe, 1998). They are more adept at systematic problem solving as well (Seifert & Hoffnung, 1997). However, it is important to remember that although their cognitive abilities have improved considerably since early adolescence, 15- to 18-year-olds are still likely to be inconsistent in their thinking and behaving (Cobb, 2001). Furthermore, as Jaffe (1998) noted, "having an ability doesn't mean that it will be exercised correctly or at all" (p. 112).

Moral Development

Between the ages of 10 and 18 young people grow more in moral reasoning than during any other period of development (Colby et al., 1983). This progress is due to several factors: adolescents' ability to think more abstractly, their questioning of parental values because of their increased psychological maturity, their exposure to a wider array of values through peer group involvement, and personal experiences that force them to make independent decisions.

"It is not until mid to late adolescence that an understanding of the importance of the social system and shared rules for behavior becomes an emphasis in moral thinking" (Dusek, 1996, p. 109). During this phase of development, adolescents construct values that will help them function successfully as adults. They engage in extensive thinking, reasoning, and questioning as they become concerned with broader political, philosophical, and religious matters. Because their thinking is more flexible, they can consider different sides of an issue and adopt new viewpoints of right and wrong (Dusek, 1996). As they wrestle with everyday moral issues in their own lives, they are better able to identify consequences. However, this does not always translate into behavior consistent with their ability to reason. For instance, although mid-adolescents are increasingly operating at the conventional stage in Kohlberg's model of moral development, doing what is right and showing respect for authority (Dusek, 1996), it is not uncommon to find adolescents who cheat in school, drink alcohol or use drugs illegally, exceed the speed limit, or engage in unsafe sex even though morally they know better. "It is not surprising that adolescents do not *always* behave at the moral level of which they are capable; virtually no one does" (Dusek, 1996, p. 127).

Increasingly during mid-adolescence, teenagers are confronted with moral dilemmas. The peer group, parents, cultural norms, and personal pressures influence the level of moral decision making. According to

Atwater (1996), the development of moral reasoning is influenced by the interaction between individuals and their social environment and involves interpersonal as well as cognitive maturation. Gilligan (1990) stressed that girls typically respond to moral dilemmas in terms of interpersonal relationships, whereas boys are more autonomous and think in terms of rights and rules when making moral decisions. According to Atwater (1996), this makes adolescence more stressful for girls than for boys.

Parental Involvement During Mid-Adolescence

During this phase of development, adolescents are generally less volatile, resulting in more positive family interaction. Because they are less egocentric, they are more concerned with the feelings of parents and siblings and are more adultlike in their judgment and behavior (Jaffe, 1998). However, because they want more autonomy and the right to make their own decisions, there is often more family tension and disagreement. Power struggles over such things as chores, homework, and peer relationships interfere with the mid-adolescents' ability to address developmental tasks, and parents run the risk of alienating their adolescents when they attempt to exert too much control (Noller, 1994, as cited in Jaffe, 1998). On the other hand, it is not good for parents to abdicate control, which often occurs when they become frustrated in their attempts to maintain parental authority and support their teenager's desire for freedom (Jaffe, 1998; Nelsen & Lott, 2000). Despite the fact that adolescents may gain freedom when parents give up and become underinvolved, this is not what most adolescents want; then feel that their parents do not care.

Adolescents benefit from a supportive family climate (Steinberg & Levine, 1990). In healthy families, adolescents continue to maintain a sense of emotional attachment even though they spend less time with them. Parents continue to be an important source of support and role modeling (Wolman, 1998), and adolescents need parents' experience and guidance for important decisions such as career choices. Adapting parenting styles that take into account the adolescents' level of maturation helps parents and mid-adolescents achieve a more satisfactory relationship (Bluestein, 1993; Vernon & Al-Mabuk, 1995).

According to some scholars (Canetti, Bachar, Galili-Weisstub, De-Nour, & Shalev, 1997; Larson & Richards, 1994), there are differences in the way adolescents relate to their mothers versus their fathers. Jory, Rainbolt, Karns, Freeborn, and Greer (1996) reported that mothers reach out to their adolescents more frequently than fathers do, and because they are usually more involved in parenting, they also receive more of their wrath. According to Canetti et al., this is unfortunate because teenagers, and girls in particular, who remain close to their mothers generally are less depressed and better adjusted than those who completely shut them out. Likewise, healthy adolescent functioning is enhanced when fathers are actively involved with their lives.

Problem Assessment and Intervention:
Selected Case Studies

On a daily basis, helping professionals counsel a wide range of adolescents, from the basically well-adjusted teens who, with minimum intervention, successfully confront the challenges of mid-adolescence to the angry, defiant, or depressed teens whose coping skills are so inadequate that finding effective interventions can be very difficult. As previously described, the degree to which formal operational thinking is attained influences moral, social, self, and emotional development, and has a major impact on adolescents' perception of the world as they address issues pertinent to this period in their lives.

Problems experienced in mid-adolescence, ages 15–18, are described below, accompanied by assessment strategies and intervention techniques.

Case Study One: 15-Year-Old Clarissa

Problem overview. Clarissa, a 15-year-old Caucasian girl from a high socioeconomic family, initiated contact with the counselor because she and her mother had been at each other's throats for some time. According to Clarissa, her mother was "out of touch" with what kids today were doing, and, because of that, she treated Clarissa like a baby and never let her do anything. Even though she was the older of two children in the family, the only difference in the way she was treated, from Clarissa's perspective, was that she had to do more work around the house. Clarissa also was upset with her father for never listening to her side of the story—even though Clarissa thought he may not agree with her mother all the time, he always went with everything her mother decided. If Clarissa tried to talk to them about how unfair things were, they reminded her that they knew what was best for her and they had the right to make the rules because they were the parents. Clarissa said she thought about this problem all the time and hated to go home. Although this problem had been going on for several months, Clarissa had not rebelled to the point of disobedience, but she was angry and resentful, and there were frequent conflicts with her mother in particular.

Assessment considerations. Given that this teenager is only 15, it is quite probable that she has not attained formal operational thinking to the point where her thinking becomes less dichotomous, her emotions less volatile, and her relationships with her parents more harmonious. Parent–child conflict is not at all uncommon at this stage of development (Steinberg & Levine, 1990), in part because adolescents are beginning to notice discrepancies between themselves and their parents (Wolman, 1998), noting who really makes decisions in the household and feeling that parents' attempts to listen to their opinions are meaningless (Seifert & Hoffnung, 1997). In fact, Seifert and Hoffnung reported that parent–child conflict is a catalyst for further growth in social maturity, as well as a vehicle for adolescents to question rules, ideas, and values to form their own identities.

Assessment should be directed at both the adolescent and her parents so that neither party is labeled exclusively as "the problem." This is especially critical at this stage of development because adolescents have a tendency to overgeneralize and blow problems out of proportion, and failing to look at the problem systemically might result in an inaccurate diagnosis as well as inappropriate intervention (Vernon, 2002). Determining more about communication, parenting styles, rules and consequences, the nature of the parent–child relationship up until the last several months when Clarissa reported that the problems began, the nature of the arguments and how each party feels about them, and any other extenuating family circumstances or stressors would be important.

Assessment procedures. Even though the counselor wanted to assess this problem systemically, she started with Clarissa because she wanted to gain her trust by hearing her perspective first. To get a picture of the exact nature of the restrictions, the counselor asked Clarissa to make a list of all the things that her friends were allowed to do but that she was restricted from doing. Next, she asked her to rate each item with an A (*always*) or an S (*sometimes*) to help distinguish if she was always or just sometimes prohibited from these activities. She then asked Clarissa to participate in a role-play activity to determine the dynamics of the interaction with her parents when Clarissa was told that she was not allowed to do something. The counselor requested that Clarissa play herself while the counselor would play the role of the mother. She selected an item from Clarissa's list to use as an example for the role play. By doing this, the counselor learned that when Clarissa's mother refused to let her have the freedom she wanted, Clarissa argued with her in an aggressive way, which seemed to invite more conflict.

When the counselor suggested to Clarissa that she would like to interview her mother and father to learn more about the problem, she began to backpedal, stating that they would never come, that they would not be honest, and that there was no point in talking to them because they would never change. The counselor shared with her that she often worked with parents like that, and that since Clarissa was so frustrated with things the way they were, it might be worth a try. Reluctantly, Clarissa agreed that they could be contacted.

Meeting with the parents and Clarissa was enlightening. With Clarissa's permission, the counselor initiated the assessment session by indicating that their daughter was uncomfortable with the increased conflict at home and hoped things could change. She asked that each parent consider the problem from their daughter's perspective and write a short description of it. She asked Clarissa to do the same—to try and look at the situation from her parents' perspective. This is often difficult for an adolescent to do, but asking each party to step into each other's shoes can facilitate problem resolution.

After all three had read their perspectives out loud, the counselor normalized the issue by indicating that one of the most frequent conflicts during adolescence relates to wanting more privileges (Meece, 2002). She then asked them what they had learned about each other's perspective and invited them to clarify misconceptions or inaccuracies.

Next, she had them do an activity called Then and Now (Vernon, self-developed). She gave each of them a worksheet labeled across the top in one column *Then* (before age 13) and in another column *Now*. Down the side were listed these terms: family time, time with friends, arguments, chores, vacation, clothes, privileges. Each individual was asked to write down words in both columns that described their perceptions with regard to each of the categories.

The counselor also adapted a parenting styles questionnaire (Vernon & Al-Mabuk, 1995, pp. 15–16) to determine whether the parents were permissive, authoritarian, or authoritative. She also gave all three a description of 12 communication roadblocks (Gordon, 2000) and examples of effective communication skills and asked them to check the ones they used most frequently in their interactions with each other. Finally, she asked them each to keep a weekly log to determine the frequency, intensity, and nature of the conflicts.

After completing these assessments, it appeared that the parents tended to be a bit authoritarian and had not adjusted their parenting style to correspond with their firstborn's normal developmental desire to be more independent. At the same time, Clarissa was exaggerating when she said that they *never* let her do anything. Both parties admitted using some of the ineffective communication techniques, and it was clear from the Then and Now activity that things had not been very conflictual prior to early adolescence.

Interventions. Because Clarissa continued to maintain that her parents were being unreasonable, the counselor suggested that she develop a short survey about what others her age were allowed to do, indicating to Clarissa that she could then share the results with her parents. In the session, they developed the survey, which included questions that Clarissa felt were important: Do you get to do whatever you want? Do your parents let you hang out with friends on the weekends? Do you have a curfew? Do you have to do chores at home? And so forth. She was instructed to give it to a sampling of 10–12 friends who should respond with a *yes, no,* or *sometimes.* When Clarissa shared the results with the counselor, she seemed surprised that most of her friends also had some restrictions, which is what the counselor suspected. To help her be more realistic about what she requested and what her parents actually forbid her to do, the counselor asked Clarissa to keep a daily chart, on which she wrote the request, the response, and whether she thought the response was reasonable or unreasonable. These data also helped Clarissa put the situation in perspective.

Next, the counselor adapted an activity called Should They or Shouldn't They? (Vernon, 1989b, pp. 69–71), which helped this young client learn to distinguish between reasonable and unreasonable demands and to see the situation from other points of view. For example, Clarissa was given a sorting board and cards with statements such as: Parents should let their kids hang out with anyone they want; parents should never ask questions about what their kids are doing; parents should try to be fair; parents should always let their kids have their way; parents should listen to their kids; parents should provide food and shelter for their kids. After reading each card, Clarissa was to place it in the reasonable, unreasonable, or depends category on the board. She and the counselor then discussed whether her requests were reasonable or unreasonable on the basis of these examples.

Clarissa's parents were just as frustrated by the increased antagonism as she was. The counselor explained that developmentally it was normal for their daughter to want to spend more time with peers and also characteristic for Clarissa to overgeneralize about what she was not allowed to do (Vernon, 2002) and to think that nobody ever listens to her (Martin, 2003). As the parents shared their rules, it appeared they were being somewhat restrictive, which the counselor attributed to the fact that this was their first teenager and they needed some guidance in negotiating this phase of development. She recommended that they read *Positive Discipline for Teenagers* (Nelsen & Lott, 2000), which helps parents understand their teenagers, how to communicate with them effectively, and how to be kind but firm. The counselor also met with them and their daughter to facilitate discussion about privileges.

Evaluation/summary. The fact that this problem had not gotten out of hand with rebellious behavior and that the parents were willing to work on the issue made treatment much more successful. In addition, Clarissa's ability to eventually see that she tended to exaggerate the frequency with which she was never allowed to do anything also facilitated problem solving. The counselor continued to work with Clarissa and her parents to ease them through this stage of development. To emphasize family strengths, she asked them to complete a family "coat of arms" (Canfield & Wells, 1976, pp. 50–51). They were each invited to draw symbols or write words in the six spaces in response to the following: (a) something that you and your family enjoy doing together, (b) something you would miss if you were not together as a family, (c) something you and your family laugh about, (d) something you wish would change in your family, (e) something you appreciate about your family, and (f) something you think has improved in your family since coming to counseling.

After completing these various interventions, the counselor noted that Clarissa had more positive feelings about her family in general and that the parents were trying to be more understanding and effective in raising a teenager.

Case Study Two: 17-Year-Old Marcia

Problem overview. Marcia is a 17-year-old Native Indian from the Meskwaki (Fox) tribe in the Midwest. She lives in the Meskwaki settlement with her parents and two younger siblings. Both parents are employed by the tribe's casino. She has been attending this school for the last 2 years after transferring from her previous middle school at the settlement. Her teacher reported a 2-week absence period to the school principal. Several attempts to contact Marcia's family were not successful. When Marcia came back to school on her own volition, she appeared to be another person: Her outfits were completely different, and she gave the impression of being dressed like a mature woman. Also, her behavior had changed drastically, from being very vociferous, outgoing, and playful to being more serious and withdrawn. She refused to play any games with boys that required any type of physical contact. In addition, she did not want to participate in physical education class and refused to wear a swimsuit for swimming class. In fact, she quit the track-and-field team even though she was a successful long distance runner. The track coach tried to encourage Marcia to keep her long distance training to qualify for the state championship.

In the meantime, Marcia refused to talk about her sudden changes and seemed ashamed to address any related topics. After the counselor attempted to address the teacher's concerns, the parents threatened to home-school their daughter.

Assessment considerations. The onset of puberty is triggered by a series of hormonal effects that produce physical, emotional, and psychological changes. Generally speaking, the major events of puberty are over in 3 or 4 years, although some individuals may experience other changes during early adulthood (Berger, 1998). There were three factors that were instrumental in this case. First, it was obvious that at 17, Marcia was facing late puberty changes retarded by her intensive athletic training. It is not uncommon for serious female athletes to have a late puberty onset, to have infrequent menstrual periods, or to lose the menstrual periods while training, according to Berg and Worth. Second, the school staff was unaware of any rite of passage or rituals involved with female puberty changes for Native Indians (Fox tribe). Third, there was a gender issue associated with the discomfort expressed by Marcia when the coach and the counselor, both males, inquired about her current changes in behavior. Finally, psychotherapeutic modalities should be conducted within the context of Native Indian cultural values (e.g., goal oriented, proactive, and family oriented) and should take into consideration issues specific to them such as current and past collective trauma, acculturation, and life transitions.

Assessment procedures. After Marcia and the family were approached by the teacher and school principal, she was referred to the school counselor for further follow-up interviews. The parents agreed to sign an authorization form that allowed Marcia to be seen by the counselor, as long as the counselor was a woman and not a man. Also, the parents invited the other school counselor (female) to visit the settlement and have a conversation with the historian and one of the matriarchs of the tribe to get acquainted with the Fox culture. In addition, this counselor had prolonged conversations with some members of the tribe who had knowledge about traditional healing practices.

As previously indicated, understanding puberty, as well as the Fox culture, was instrumental in order to understand Marcia's changes in behavior. First, Marcia had undergone physical, emotional, and psychological changes due to the onset of puberty. The Fox tribe has a tradition in which once a girl enters puberty, her "children clothes" are burned and thrown away, representing the transition to adulthood. That rite of passage explained Marcia's sudden change in attire because she could no longer wear children's clothing. Similarly, as a woman, and according the Fox's traditions, Marcia was not allowed to have physical contact with men unless it was her father or husband-to-be. As a result of this tradition, Marcia's interactions toward boys in school had changed dramatically. Similarly, she was not allowed to expose her body to the public by wearing a swimsuit. Therefore, she refused to participate in physical education and swimming class.

Interventions. Technically, there is nothing "wrong" or developmentally inappropriate with Marcia's behavior. The counselor realized that her drastic changes in behavior came as a result of a rite of passage. In fact, other than her sudden serious behavior, Marcia's academic performance was above average except for the work she missed during her 2-week absence.

The counselor's only concern was related to Marcia's ability to cope effectively with the clash of cultural expectations and her acceptance and integration within her group of White Euro American peers. The counselor decided to approach the situation in a comprehensive way. She developed a classroom guidance unit on rite of passages in different cultures and how people's behavior change as a result of them. The main objective was to normalize Marcia's changes in behavior without focusing the discussion on her. The second strategy was to reaffirm and value Marcia's cultural heritage. The counselor met with Marcia once a week for 2 months and discussed a short book titled *Night Flying Woman: An Ojibway Narrative* (Broker, 1983). The book deals with the transitions and challenges faced by a Native Indian woman transitioning from puberty to adulthood. Although Marcia seemed confident about her cultural values, the counselor intervened in a preventive way with the idea of building more confidence and pride in case she was challenged by insensitive comments made by other students in the school.

Also, because Marcia was a very self-reflective individual and liked music and poetry, the counselor invited her to create a poem that depicted the "old" Marcia and the "new" Marcia written from an observer's perspective. Marcia readily engaged in this activity and wrote a poem beginning with the following line: "Ingenuous, candid, naïve, and trusting no more. That fragile girl is gone. There she was looking at someone new . . . " The counselor suggested that Marcia create a book of poems by keeping them in a binder, which would also be a good way for the counselor to track Marcia's psychosocial adjustment if she was willing to share what she wrote.

Evaluation/summary. Marcia's case is unique because, from a cultural and developmental standpoint, she was behaving according to the parameters established by the tribe. Although the school staff assumed that she was having significant problems, it was more an issue of perceived problems by the counselor and school staff rather than a real predicament. The counselor's interventions were more preventive and affirming in nature. The counselor respected Marcia's wish of not participating in athletic events and did not overly encourage her in that direction as a sign of respect to her cultural values. Marcia adapted well to her new identity as an adult and developed a new circle of friends who were developmentally mature and culturally sensitive to her needs.

Case Study Three: 16-Year-Old Laurie

Problem overview. Laurie, a 16-year-old Caucasian girl, sought counseling because her boyfriend, Todd, had been threatening to break up with her for the last few weeks. Laurie was devastated. They had been going together all year, but lately he had been ignoring her, saying that he wanted to date other girls. Because he lived an hour away, they only could see each other on the weekends. Although he used to call her frequently during the week, he did not do that very often now. When Laurie tried to call him, he was never home. As a result of this situation, Laurie was not sleeping well, had a hard time concentrating on her schoolwork, and felt miserable. She was not spending much time with her friends because she wanted to be home in case Todd tried to contact her.

Assessment considerations. Dating relationship problems are very common at this age and can be a major source of anxiety as the focus starts to shift from peer group acceptance to an intimate couple relationship (Martin, 2003). Although there generally is increased comfort around the opposite gender during mid-adolescence, the degree of threat resulting from relationship difficulties is often related to an adolescent's self-concept and his or her level of cognitive functioning, which affects the ability to interpret abstract concepts and problem solve.

Assessment should focus on the nature of the relationship: its longevity, when and how the problems began, and how conflict is handled. Depression is common with all types of loss (Crenshaw, 1990), so assessment should also include a depression screen, as well as a suicide screen, depending on the severity of the depression. Learning more about how Laurie has dealt with problems in the past would provide insight about her coping skills.

Assessment procedures. Laurie was very upset during the initial session and rambled a lot, so it was difficult to keep her focused to get a clear picture of the problem. To help pinpoint specific feelings and thoughts about the upsetting events regarding her boyfriend, the counselor asked her to write a response to the following questions:

1. Describe an upsetting circumstance involving your boyfriend. What happened?
2. How did you react? What did you feel?
3. What were you thinking to yourself about what happened?
4. What did he do or say?
5. Was the situation resolved, and if so, how?
6. Do you think you could have done anything differently to affect the outcome?

This structure allowed the counselor to develop a more comprehensive picture of the problem. This young client identified several upsetting events that had begun to occur recently in their relationship: being stood up, being ignored (lack of phone calls and attention), and constant arguing. Furthermore, she indicated that her boyfriend was very disrespectful to her, especially when they were with friends. Not only did she feel angry and upset, but she also felt depressed and hopeless because they argued so much. Her thoughts were: he must be seeing someone else; I'll never get over this; I do not know what I will do if we break up; he shouldn't treat me this way; there must be something wrong with me or he would want to go out with me; if he drops me, I will never find another boyfriend. It also became apparent that he used a lot of put-downs that Laurie soaked up like a sponge.

To get a sense of how depressed this teenager was, the counselor asked Laurie to keep a feeling chart, rating her moods on an hourly basis from 1 (*low*) to 10 (*high*). From this, he noticed that there were periods of the day when she functioned somewhat better, but for the most part, she was quite depressed. To further assess her depression, the counselor used the Reynolds Adolescent Depression Scale (Reynolds, 1987) that confirmed what the informal feeling chart had indicated. Although she was depressed, Laurie denied being suicidal, stated that she had no plan, and that she would never do anything like that. Despite these assurances, the counselor knew that he needed to monitor this closely.

Sensing codependency, the counselor gave Laurie a codependency checklist (Vernon, 1998c, p. 181) and asked her to check the characteristics she felt described her. The results confirmed his suspicions. Further discussion indicated that she was trying to change Todd so he would be more attentive to her, and she was allowing him to control her activities because she stayed home waiting for his phone calls and visits. In addition to her anger at him, she was also angry at herself for letting him put her down, but at the same time, she blamed herself, thinking "there must be something wrong with me or he'd like me better; there must be a good reason that he is treating me disrespectfully."

Interventions. The counselor addressed the relationship loss and subsequent depression in several ways. First, he encouraged Laurie to write a letter to Todd that expressed her hurt and pain, indicating that she may choose not to send it, but it would be a good catharsis. Second, he used the activity When You Need a Helping Hand (Vernon, 2002, p. 131), which involves identifying rational beliefs that Laurie can use to help her counteract the depressing effect of irrational beliefs, such as "I can't stand it if he breaks up with me," "I'll never get over this," and so forth. They also discussed whether medication was needed, but Laurie preferred not to take anything. Instead, the counselor encouraged her to make a depression "tool box," by filling the box with artifacts that were meaningful to her and gave her hope, such as pictures of her 1-year-old niece who made her laugh, her yearbook that reminded her of good times with friends, a flyer for the trip she was planning to take with her language class to France, and so forth.

To help her deal with self-esteem issues, the counselor drew a circle, divided it into six parts, and asked Laurie to label each part as an aspect of herself, such as girlfriend, student, friend, basketball player, musician, and babysitter. Next, Laurie drew a line beside each label and marked it on a 1 (*low*) to 5 (*high*) in relation to how she felt about herself in each aspect. As the counselor predicted, she felt quite good about herself in each area except as a girlfriend. He used this information to show Laurie that she was not a worthless person and also pointed out that she was only half of the relationship equation.

The counselor addressed the codependent relationship issues by explaining the concept in more detail and reviewing the codependent behaviors Laurie had marked on the checklist. Then the counselor asked her to write down some of the things she had asked Todd to do to get him to spend more time with her. Using strings tied to the counselor's arms and legs, he had Laurie pull on them as he read each of her statements to demonstrate to her that the harder she pulled, the more he resisted, so her attempts to control him did not work and only resulted in further argument. In addition, the counselor asked Laurie to list 10 good things about herself, and then challenged her to think about whether she really deserved to be treated disrespectfully through put-downs. He helped her identify some positive self-statements such as "I am a good person even if Todd might not think so" and "I don't deserve to be treated this way."

He also taught her about the concept of mind reading and encouraged her to ask Todd why he was withdrawing more from the relationship, rather than automatically assuming it was because she was lacking or that he was with someone else. As a final strategy, the counselor taught Laurie how to assert herself in relationships and followed this by role playing. He also recommended that she read *Teen Relationships* (Johnson, 1992), an insightful book about relationships, myths about romance, abusive relationships, and how to end relationships.

Evaluation/summary. Relationship problems do not disappear overnight, especially when there are underlying self-esteem issues and depression. Addressing these issues directly was helpful, and it also was enlightening to teach this client about codependent relationships and assertion, which helped Laurie deal with present and future problems. Despite her attempts to be less codependent and more assertive, Todd ended the relationship and Laurie struggled, but she survived a loss that is very common in adolescents. Although it took awhile for her to feel less depressed, she kept the feeling charts, which showed gradual elevation of mood. A follow-up administration of the Reynolds Adolescent Depression Scale also confirmed that this young client was less depressed.

Case Study Four: 17-Year-Old Mike

Problem overview. Mike, a 17-year-old male Caucasian, was referred by the school counselor to the local mental health clinic because several of Mike's friends told their counselor that Mike had been talking about killing himself. Although Mike denied this when the school counselor spoke with him about it, the counselor contacted Mike's father and recommended that he make an appointment for his son.

Assessment considerations. In the United States, suicide is the third leading cause of death among adolescents (Hoyert, Anos, Smith, Murphy, & Kochanek, 2001). According to Hoyert et al., approximately 1 million young people attempt suicide each year, and that number appears to be increasing. Furthermore, Caucasian adolescent males complete suicide more often than any other ethnic group (Metha, Weber, & Webb, 1998), so Mike is at increased risk. In Mike's case, assessment should address whether there has been any family history of suicide. Previous attempts, substance abuse, anxiety, hopelessness and depression, current family problems, recent suicide of a close friend, and other stressors must be ascertained, as well as poor impulse control, acting out, and reckless behaviors (E. H. McWhirter et al., 2004). Capuzzi and Gross (2004) noted that school failure and interpersonal conflict with a romantic partner are precipitants to suicide and that lack of family support can also be a factor, so all of these factors need to be assessed.

Assessment procedures. During their first meeting, Mike essentially refused to talk, so the counselor invited the father into the session and first relied on his information, asking him questions indicative of the warning signs of suicide (Capuzzi & Gross, 2004; Stefanowski-Harding, 1990): Had there been a sudden decline in school attendance and performance? Had there been a recent loss such as a move, death of a close friend or relative, divorce, or breakup with a girlfriend? Was he withdrawing more from peers, and were there changes in his social patterns? Were there any alternations in eating and sleeping patterns? Had there been previous suicide attempts to his knowledge? Was he verbally threatening suicide or alluding to how much better things would be if he were not alive? Had there been any recent suicides in Mike's school? Were there other stressors in his life of which his father was aware? Did Mike drink, smoke, or use drugs? How unusual was this recent behavior?

From the father's responses, the counselor learned that Mike's girlfriend had moved to another state and had broken up with him about 2 months ago. Because he was a single parent with three younger children and worked a lot of overtime, he had not had time to pay much attention to how Mike was reacting to this, except that he had noticed that he was spending more time alone in his room and appeared depressed. He was not aware of any substance abuse and suggested that the counselor contact the school for information about his school attendance and other school-related issues. He did share that Mike had recently gotten several failure notices and that he had "gotten on him" to study harder and bring his grades up.

The father was aware that Mike wrote a lot of poetry, so when the counselor met with Mike alone again later in the session, she asked if he would share some of his poems so she could understand how he was feeling and try to help him. Mike reluctantly agreed but said he did not need help and was not suicidal. The counselor told him she understood his reluctance to get help but indicated that he had experienced a loss and other complications in his life that might result in feelings of hopelessness. She explained that she worked with lots of teenagers who felt similarly, sharing a short tape in which a former suicidal client talked about her feelings and how eventually she worked through it and was glad to be alive. At the end of the first session, the counselor managed to get Mike to sign a contract stating that he would not hurt himself and that he would participate in at least three counseling sessions. She also suggested to Mike's father that they consider medication and hospitalization if it appeared that Mike was in eminent danger.

During the following session, Mike shared his poetry with the counselor. It was obvious from his responses that he was feeling very dejected because his girlfriend moved and had broken up with him, and he was convinced he never would have another meaningful relationship. Furthermore, he felt like a failure who would never amount to anything because he was on the verge of flunking out of school. He saw his future as hopeless. His writing seemed to indicate that he was very depressed, and despite his verbal assurance that he did not see suicide as a way to end the pain, there were references to this in his writing. After reading the poetry, the counselor shared a suicidal tendencies scale with Mike, attempting to get his perception of his behavior and thinking in relation to the 13-item scale, which assesses dimensions such as self-esteem, support system, depression, will to live, frequency of suicidal thoughts, and external behaviors. The counselor also administered the Suicidal Ideation Questionnaire (Reynolds, 1988). Results confirmed the seriousness of this situation, despite the fact that he appeared to have no plan.

Interventions. On the basis of the assessments, the counselor met with Mike and his father and recommended that they make an appointment with their family doctor immediately because she felt Mike needed to be on an antidepressant. Although Mike said he did not need medication, the counselor explained that it would help him through this rough time and that it was not unusual in cases like this for medication to be prescribed. She asked that Mike just try it for a few months, and predicted that medication, along with counseling, could help him feel less miserable. He reluctantly agreed and his father promised to make an appointment as soon as possible.

Because of Mike's reluctance to discuss the situation, the counselor used writing as the major intervention. She gave him a sheet of paper with the following unfinished sentences and asked him to write as much as he wanted about each:

1. Things in my life seem hopeless, because _____.
2. I don't think I will ever feel better because _____.
3. If I were dead, other people would feel _____.
4. Life would be worth living if _____ were different.
5. My obituary would say _____.

Mike agreed to share his responses, and the counselor challenged his belief that he would never feel better, sharing the analogy that now he had on a pair of "doom and gloom" glasses, meaning that he was looking at everything in his life from this negative perspective. When she asked him how long he had had this outlook, he indicated that it was when his girlfriend moved and he had become depressed. The counselor then pointed out that if he could work through this loss, he could then get rid of his doom and gloom glasses.

She then attempted to work with Mike to address the major loss of his girlfriend by asking him to talk about why he thought he never could have another relationship as good as this one. The counselor acknowledged his feelings but pointed out that he was only 17 and had many years ahead of him to be in relationships that might be even more meaningful. She asked him to do a time line of his relationships since he had begun dating, and he wrote down names of four girls he had dated. The counselor asked him to rate these relationships on a 1–3 scale: 1 (*very good*), 2 (*fair*), and 3 (*poor*). Mike's ratings indicated that two of the four relationships had been very good, so the counselor challenged his thinking that he would never have another good relationship, but pointed out to him that if he were dead, the possibility of another girlfriend would not be feasible. This seemed to have an impact on him, and as a homework assignment, the counselor asked him to do an "into the future" assignment, writing two different scenarios to his life: one in which he lived to be 85 years old, and one in which he ended his life soon because he did not think he could tolerate the pain.

In the following sessions, Mike shared his stories and they discussed the fact that in his story about living to age 85, he did have other relationships, and Mike conceded that this might be possible but that he still could not get over his former girlfriend. The counselor actively worked with Mike to help him see that the loss of a girlfriend is a relatively normal, albeit painful, teenage problem with which he could learn to deal. She encouraged him to continue to use his poetry as a means to express his feelings about what the relationship meant to him.

She also wanted to show Mike that there was hope—that he could overcome his depression and belief that suicide was the only way to end his pain. She shared two poems with him, written by a very depressed adolescent who had also contemplated suicide (Vernon, 2002, pp. 137–138). The first poem reflected the darkness and hopelessness this adolescent experienced, but the second one, written months later, described being able to overcome the obstacles. Although Mike did not say much after he had read them, the counselor sensed that she had planted a seed of hope.

She also helped him look at the other stressors in his life such as his failure to live up to his expectation that he could do better in school and his prediction that he never would amount to anything. She explained that depression interferes with concentration, making it difficult to focus on schoolwork. By having him make a graph of his school performance, she helped him see that it was only recently that he had begun to fail. She again used the analogy of the doom and gloom glasses, stating that since his previous performance had been very good, was it possible that his future performance would improve when he was able to take off the doom and gloom glasses? The counselor used a forced-field analysis to help Mike identify what was working for and against him in attaining better grades. Starting with small steps like forcing himself to get out of bed and go to school, they set goals for change.

Evaluation/summary. Over a period of several months, with medication and counseling, Mike began to feel better, as evidenced by his poetry, his improved school performance, and responses to the Suicide Ideation Questionnaire that the counselor asked him to complete once again toward the end of the counseling process.

In cases such as this, it is important to build resiliency. Helping this young man understand that there was life beyond the here and now was a critical component in assuring that he had some reason to stay alive.

Case Study Five: 18-Year-Old Rebeca

Problem overview. Rebeca, an 18-year-old, was born in El Salvador and moved to the United States when she was 3 years old. Her parents are growing extremely concerned about her, especially after she and other friends were arrested for shoplifting. The court ordered Rebeca to do 6 months of community service and seek counseling. A month after the shoplifting incident, a teacher caught her writing graffiti gang symbols on the school grounds. According to other students and teachers, she is not a gang member but only a "wannabe." Rebeca is in danger of not completing her senior year and graduating because of excessive absences and below-average grades. She also appears to be very angry against anyone who represents the "system." Rebeca's father works as a construction manager, her mother is a clerk at a marketing company, and she has an older brother and a younger sister. Rebeca was referred to the school-based mental health counselor to help her deal with the academic and behavioral problems.

Assessment considerations. Young people who reach adolescence with limited trust have trouble finding ideals to have faith in (Berk, 1999). Those with limited autonomy or initiative do not engage in the active exploration required to choose among alternatives. According to Erikson (1950, 1968), teenagers in complex societies experience an identity crisis—a temporary period of confusion and distress as they experiment with alternatives before settling on a set of values and goals. In addition to these developmental issues, immigrant adolescents of non-European background face cultural identity issues that increase the intensity of the issues faced by members of the majority. Finding an equitable balance between family expectations (culture of origin) and societal expectations becomes a challenging task. Also, developmental issues are complicated by institutional racism and oppression.

Assessment procedures. Rebeca seemed to be angry with anyone who tried to get close to her, with the exception of her inner circle of friends. The counselor tried in vain to establish rapport with Rebeca, but her conversations were limited to monosyllabic responses. In the counselor's opinion, Rebeca wanted to give the impression of being a tough gang member even though that was not the case, at least at this point. However, the counselor learned that Rebeca had recently made contact with members of the Pachucas (a local gang) inquiring about initiation rituals.

The counselor was searching for some way to connect with this young woman because previous attempts had been unsuccessful. In two separate sessions, the counselor shared videos: *Teenagers and Gangs: A Lethal Combination* (2000) and *Violence/Gangs* (1997), hoping that this would be a way to help Rebeca discuss her issues so that the counselor could assess the source of the anger, potential violence, and Rebeca's intentions about becoming a member of a gang. Although Rebeca seemed relatively interested in watching the videos, she had very little to say when the counselor asked for her reactions.

To assess Rebeca's level of anger, the counselor adapted questions from the Novaco Anger Inventory (Huss, Leak, & Davis, 1993). Rebeca was asked to rate the following questions on the basis of the following scale: *very little, little, moderate amount, much,* and *very much.*

1. You are constantly followed by an employee in a convenience store.
2. You are being singled out for a correction, while the actions of others go unnoticed.
3. You are talking to someone and they do not answer to you.
4. While you are struggling to carry four cups of coffee to your table at a cafeteria, someone bumps into you, spilling the coffee.
5. You have hung up your clothes, but someone knocks them to the floor and fails to pick them up.
6. You have made arrangements to go somewhere with a friend who backs out at the last minute and leaves you dangling.
7. You are being joked about or teased.

8. Someone makes a mistake and blames it on you.
9. You are trying to concentrate, but a person near you is tapping his foot.
10. You are in a discussion with someone who persists in arguing about a topic she knows very little about.
11. Someone sticks his or her nose into an argument between you and someone else.
12. You are being mocked by a small group of people as you pass them.
13. In a hurry to get somewhere, you tear a good pair of trousers/skirt on a sharp object.
14. You use your last coin to make a phone call, but you are disconnected before you finish dialing and the coin is lost.

Because the counselor only used selected items, she did not score the inventory. Instead, the counselor contextualized each of the items to Rebeca's reality. As an illustration, the counselor pointed out that Rebeca had responded "very much" on Item 12 and asked Rebeca if she could give an example of when that had happened to her. By listening to Rebeca's response and asking open questions, paraphrasing, and reflecting feelings, the counselor learned more about her client as she used the same process with other items on the inventory. It became very clear that Rebeca's anger was related to adults who impose rules and her own frustration about fitting in with the Latinos as well as the rest of the student population.

The issue of fitting in is a typical one for most adolescents, but it was more difficult for this client who was trying to find her place in two groups. This was confirmed when the counselor then presented Atkinson et al.'s (1998) minority identity development model, which consists of five stages: conformity (the ethnically diverse person accepts the dominant culture's values); dissonance (the ethnically diverse person starts questioning the negatively held stereotypes about his or her own ethnic group); resistance (the person evidences guilt, shame, and anger at the dominant group); introspection (the person begins to question his or her ethnocentric basis for judging themselves and others); and integrative awareness (the person develops a true appreciation for one's own culture and selective appreciation of the dominant White European culture). It was evident that Rebeca identified with the resistance stage in which she rejected the majority culture and engaged in antisocial behaviors "to get back to others." Rebeca reported that she was angry with anyone who wanted to exert power and control over her.

To rule out other related issues, the counselor inquired about alcohol and drug use. It is not uncommon for adolescents to either explore or cope with their feelings of inadequacy by using illegal substances and alcohol. Although Rebeca denied any involvement, the counselor used two surveys with her parents: Signs and Symptoms of Drug Abuse (Steinberg & Levine, 1990) and Signs and Symptoms of Alcohol Abuse (Parrott, 1993). From their responses, it seemed that there might be occasional experimentation, but nothing significant at this point.

Interventions. The counselor developed an intervention plan consisting of the following goals: to explore and develop appropriate coping skills to deal with anger-related issues, to strengthen Rebeca's cultural identity, and to discourage gang involvement.

Because the counselor had limited knowledge about the gang culture and adolescents, she proceeded to consult with the antigang unit of the police department. They suggested using ex-gang members as speakers and gave her the names of several whom they knew were willing to speak to groups of young people. Because the counselor was housed in the school, she consulted with the principal, who agreed that such a presentation would be good for the student body. The counselor then invited two ex-gang members, a female who had served time in prison and a male who was paralyzed from the waist down as a result of a gun shot to the spinal cord, to speak at a school assembly. These antigang unit speakers explained that they had joined a gang out of curiosity and the need for power, and they had used the gang as an outlet for their anger and frustrations. They elaborated on the legal, personal, and familial consequences of joining a gang.

In addition, the counselor used a combination of music and art therapy to help Rebeca. During various sessions, the counselor played different songs from Latino singers such as Marc Anthony, Jennifer López, Santana, and Tito Nieves. Then, she let Rebeca paint (using acrylics on cardboard instead of canvas) the images evoked by these songs. As she was painting, the counselor did not wait until Rebeca had completed the paintings to talk about them. Instead, throughout the process, the counselor asked her about the meanings, thoughts, and feelings attached to the paintings. Similarly, the counselor played songs by Beethoven, Vivaldi, Handel, Ravel, and Strauss and she let Rebeca draw or paint the images related to this music. By the use of painting and drawing, the counselor was conversing with Rebeca "through the paintings" as opposed to a more intimidating face-to-face conversation.

By this point, the relationship was better, so the counselor worked more directly on Rebeca's anger and her desire to be a more independent person without the approval of any group, including a gang. The counselor created symbolic exercises such as the following to help Rebeca address these issues:

I consider myself to be:
1. An eagle or a dove
2. A car or a truck
3. A pencil or a pen
4. A rock or sand
5. Liquid water or ice
6. A mountain cabin or a city house

The counselor explored issues of victim versus abuser, permanent versus momentary, strength versus weakness, leader versus follower, and disconnected versus gregarious. The main goal was to create awareness of the deceiving benefits provided by a gang and how the family or true friends are more reliable and safe as sources of support.

Evaluation/summary. The counselor monitored Rebeca's progress on the basis of her school attendance, her eventual disenfranchisement from gang ideology, and the absence of behavioral problems in school. The counselor also recommended a different school schedule and involvement in community-based organizations that could keep Rebeca occupied when she was not in school. Rebeca appeared to respond well to the counseling interventions and demonstrated a genuine interest about Latinos who have been successful in the United States. She expressed interest in attending the local community college and working part time in a clothing store.

Case Study Six: 18-Year-Old Scott

Problem overview. Scott, an 18-year-old male Caucasian, initially made an appointment to meet with his school counselor because he needed financial aid forms. When he returned them, he and the counselor talked about what he was planning to do after high school. He said that he was enrolled at a state university, but as the end of his senior year approached, he did not know if he wanted to go to college. He told the counselor that all of his friends seemed excited about graduation, but he had very mixed feelings, because, as he stated, "Nothing will ever be the same again." Sensing loss and transition issues, in addition to uncertainty about his future, the counselor made several appointments for him.

Assessment considerations. High school graduation represents a significant turning point for most adolescents, but one that is met with mixed emotions. There is a sense of excitement and anticipation about the future, but this transition can also result in ambivalence and loss (Vernon & Al-Mabuk, 1995). Saying goodbye to friends and family and leaving the familiar behind can be complicated and stressful (Daigneault, 1999), and confusion about career choice is often prevalent (Youngs, 1995). Often the last few months of high school result in increased parent–child conflict, as the adolescent struggles with his or her ambivalence about leaving home. In Scott's case, assessment should focus on his feelings about the transition, his coping skills, and his career goals.

Assessment procedures. Scott was not very clear about his feelings or thoughts other than the awareness that everything was going to change. To develop a clearer idea of his concerns, the counselor engaged him in a transitions assessment exercise. She gave him a sheet of paper divided into four squares, each square with one of the following labels: roles, relationships, routines, and resources (time, money, skills). The counselor asked her client to think about how his life would change after high school in relation to each of these areas and to write his thoughts in the corresponding spaces. Scott's responses helped the counselor understand how he perceived this transition. As they discussed his responses in more detail, the counselor noted in particular the loss themes in the relationships category and anxiety about money.

As part of his assessment, the counselor also reviewed Scott's ACT scores, which were very good, and his grade point, which was very high.

She suggested that he take another career inventory to help him clarify his interests.

Intervention. Based on their discussion of the transitions assessment exercise, the counselor decided to first address the loss issue, because Scott seemed very concerned about leaving his friends, some teachers, and family members. The counselor had Scott list the people he would miss the most, and because Scott liked art, she invited him to draw pictures or use photographs to make a collage of some of his happiest memories with these people. The collage, a concrete way to remember these people, was something Scott could take with him and look at when he went to college. The counselor and Scott also talked about ways to have meaningful closure with these people. Scott decided once again to use art and make cards for some of the teachers, female peers, and other adults who were significant to him. He was hesitant about doing this with his male friends, because they might think it was too sentimental, so the counselor suggested that he could make the cards but not send them. In this way, he could express how he felt and perhaps, when the time was right, he could follow through and share them. Together they identified some meaningful activities that Scott could initiate with these buddies, such as camping out or having one last backyard basketball game.

To deal with the anxiety about the future, the counselor summarized the data from the assessment exercise and listed the concerns: financial (Will I have enough money? Will I find a job?); friends (Will I make any new friends and how?); and school (Am I smart enough to make it?). She then asked Scott to describe how he had dealt with these concerns in the past and which strategies he could continue to use. The counselor had Scott examine his academic record and previous performance in difficult subjects that might indicate his chances for success in new areas, and she discussed possible sources of support such as the counseling and career placement centers at the college. She also gave Scott names of two students who were attending this school and suggested that Scott contact them and perhaps spend a day with them to get a feel for what it was like before he actually started attending.

To help Scott deal with some of his ambivalence about going to college, the counselor adapted an activity titled What's Next? (Vernon, 2002, pp. 281–282), which helped him look at options and rate them as things he would be very likely, somewhat likely, or not at all likely to do. From the results of this activity, Scott learned that he in fact did want to go to college, but that his confusion stemmed more from what he specifically wanted to major in—he thought he had to have that figured out before he went. The counselor used several worksheets from Farr and Christophersen's (1991) book, *Knowing Yourself: Learning About Your Skills, Values, and Planning Your Life*, to assist Scott with this matter, while at the same time normalizing that most high school students about to graduate did not know exactly what they wanted to do and that part of the purpose of college was to take courses to help students clarify their interests and values. She encouraged him to keep a career awareness journal to become more attuned to the various dimensions of jobs that he came in contact with, saw on television, read about, or observed, explaining that this might help him see the importance of considering multiple dimensions in selecting a career.

Evaluation/summary. Because the anxiety primarily was about the future, the counselor did what she could to help Scott examine the facts as well as his previous problem-solving abilities to give him more confidence about dealing with these upcoming issues. Although the counselor knew the concrete activities would help deal with the loss, in reality Scott may continue to grieve periodically as a natural way of working through the issues.

Other Typical Developmental Problems

As an elementary-age child, I (Ann Vernon) recall sitting on the couch with my friend watching *American Bandstand* on television. We were weak with envy, watching the teenagers dance to rock and roll, whirling about in their bobby socks, felt skirts, and rolled-up shirt sleeves. Later that night, we planned to spy on our teenage babysitter and her boyfriend who we knew would be "necking" on the porch after they thought we were asleep.

As a helping professional, I sometimes have trouble juxtaposing my memory of what I thought being a teenager was all about with the reality I see with some adolescents today. It is safe to say that life is more complex nowadays because of a variety of factors: changing family structures, poverty, increased stresses and differences among cultures, a faster pace of life, changing values with fewer clear-cut notions of what is right or wrong, and a societal crisis characterized by such things as higher unemployment, conflict, and tension (Thompson & Rudolph, 1992; Thompson et al., 2004). If we superimpose these factors on normal developmental problems that most adolescents experience to some degree, it should not be too surprising to see increases in violence among youth (Barta, 2000), alcohol and drug abuse (Gloria & Kurpius (2000), eating disorders (Berg, 1997; Wright, 2000), teen pregnancy (Annie E. Casey Foundation, 1999; Sherwood-Hawes, 2000), and teen suicide (King, Price, Telljohann, & Wahl, 2000; Thompson et al., 2004). Although many teens see these behaviors as ways to deal with problems, the behaviors become problems.

In addition to these problems that far too many adolescents experience, career development is a major concern for most young people. The high school student is actively involved in career exploration, first in the form of career fantasy about what he or she will be and, later, a reality testing as the adolescent considers such factors as ability, interest, and training requirements (Ginsberg, 1990, as cited in Atwater, 1996). Mitchell (1986) noted that many adolescents feel overwhelmed with the task of making realistic career choices, because the job picture changes so rapidly.

Youngs (1985, 1995) identified other, more typical, concerns for the high school student, which may vary depending on one's culture. These are discussed below.

Age 15

Major sources of stress at this age include the fear of being disliked or unpopular, as well as concern about peers stealing their friends or sweethearts, which results in irrational jealousy and possessiveness. They continue to have tremendous insecurity about their sexuality. Depending on whether or not they have completed puberty, adolescents still may have raging hormones that cause mood swings. Consequently, they are very sensitive to criticism and may exaggerate simple occurrences. They feel as if they are the only ones going through difficult times, which further exacerbate their stress.

Ages 16 and 17

"Facing the world" (Youngs, 1995, p. 135) is a major worry at this age: getting a car, making decisions about the future, taking college entrance exams, and having enough money. They still worry about whether they are meeting their peers' expectations and have bigger fears about adult authority: They want independence, but at the same time, they experience anxiety about it. A great deal of stress relates to sexuality: They struggle with what their parents tell them (responsibility and abstinence) and with their own physical desires.

Age 18

Making life decisions is the biggest source of stress for 18-year-olds. They fear that adults will define roles for them, worry that they have had inadequate training in high school (express confusion about career choices), and fear their lack of preparation after graduation (may appear irresponsible in actions or decisions). As they struggle to develop their own values and discard family values, there can be intense strain on the family. Another source of stress is high school graduation: losing friendships, feeling inadequate if their peers receive more scholarships or better postsecondary opportunities, and leaving a comfortable and familiar environment.

Summary

Mid-adolescence is a period of development in which many new capacities emerge and existing ones increase. Not only are cognitive skills more powerful, but new types of relationships develop, along with more differentiation of feelings and greater reflection on these feelings. Mid-adolescence serves an important function as a stepping stone to the young adult world, where there are even greater challenges and new opportunities.

It is difficult to say whether mid-adolescence is becoming more stressful for the majority of youngsters. It is clear that self-defeating methods of dealing with problems are seen as options more frequently; feelings of invulnerability and immortality can lead teenagers to act recklessly (Youngs, 1995). Conscious efforts at both intervention and prevention will help adolescents negotiate this significant stage of development.

Conclusion

＊

There is no way to push the pause button on growth and development. In some cases, what literally occurs at one moment in time never will be repeated: losing the first tooth, successfully tying a shoe for the first time, or being asked out for the first date. There are so many "firsts" during the school-age years that it is hard to account for them all. On reflection, it is apparent that these are the significant stepping stones for later development.

＊

Equally significant are experiences that occur within the context of the child's culture. Practitioners must be sensitive to ethnic and racial identity, acculturation, religious and traditional beliefs, customs, social class, health care practices, and poverty, for example, in adopting a multicultural approach to assessment and intervention (Sattler, 1998). In addition, environmental factors influence how a child functions in various circumstances. For example, if adults provide specific support, children may be able to function effectively at a higher developmental level in some situations, but without that support their ability to function might be lower.

In reality, assessment and intervention with children are complex endeavors. Developmental stages must be seen as indicators of what generally occurs; the concept must be interpreted liberally. When parents and professionals ask, "What is typical?" our response is that we have guidelines, not prescriptions, of what to expect. Although some may find this frustrating, it would be equally disconcerting to neatly sort children into categories based on whether they specifically match the criteria for a particular developmental stage. Similarly, culturally competent practice dictates that we realize that "one size does not fit all," that there is as much diversity within specific ethnic groups as there is between them. Integrating knowledge about culture and development with sensitivity will increase the effectiveness of the assessment and intervention process.

The intent of this book was to provide helping professionals with characteristics of children and adolescents across a variety of dimensions: self, social, emotional, physical, cognitive, and moral development. This information can be used in relation to assessment in two ways: as a barometer of where a child is in his or her development, and as an indicator of how to structure developmentally appropriate assessment instruments. The information is also critical in selecting and designing effective intervention strategies that correspond to the child's developmental level. A further emphasis of this work was to increase knowledge about multicultural assessment and intervention, which by necessity begins with cultural self-awareness.

Helping professionals and parents are equally challenged as they work with and support young people in their journey through life. This journey may be even more challenging for ethnically diverse children and adolescents. The intent of this book was to provide a developmental and cultural perspective to assist practitioners in their assessment and intervention efforts with young clients.

References

Adler, D. (1993). *A picture book of Frederick Douglass.* New York: Holiday House.

Aldridge, D., Gustorff, D., & Neugebauer, L. (1995). A preliminary study of creative music therapy in the treatment of children with developmental delay. *Arts in Psychotherapy, 22,* 189–205.

Allen, J., & Klein, R. (1996). *Ready, set, release.* Watertown, WI: Inner Coaching.

American Counseling Association. (1995). *Code of ethics and standards of practice.* Alexandria, VA: Author.

American Psychiatric Association. (2000). *Diagnostic and statistical manual of mental disorders* (4th ed., Text Revision). Washington, DC: Author.

Ancona, G. (1993). *Powwow.* San Diego, CA: Harcourt Brace Jovanovich.

Annie E. Casey Foundation. (1999). *Why teens have sex: Issues and trends.* Baltimore: Author.

Arnett, J. J. (1999). Adolescent storm and stress reconsidered. *American Psychologist, 54,* 317–326.

Artman, J. (1981). *Indians: An activity book.* Carthage, IL: Good Apple.

Atkinson, D. R., Morten, G., & Sue, D. W. (1998). *Counseling American minorities.* Boston: McGraw-Hill.

Atwater, E. (1996). *Adolescence* (4th ed.). Upper Saddle River, NJ: Prentice Hall.

Balgassi, H. (1996). *Peacebound trains.* Boston: Houghton Mifflin.

Barker, P. (1990). *Clinical interviews with children and adolescents.* New York: Norton.

Barona, A., & Miller, J. A. (1994). Short Acculturation Scale for Hispanic Youths (SASH-Y): A preliminary report. *Hispanic Journal of Behavioral Sciences, 16,* 155–162.

Barrish, I. J., & Barrish, H. H. (1989). *Surviving and enjoying your adolescent.* Kansas City, MO: Westport.

Barta, M. T. (2000). Death in the classroom: Violence in schools. In D. Capuzzi & D. R. Gross (Eds.), *Youth at risk: A prevention resource for counselors, teachers, and parents* (3rd ed., pp. 385–408). Alexandria, VA: American Counseling Association.

Barth, F. (1998). *Ethnic groups and boundaries.* Prospects Heights, IL: Waveland Press.

Baruth, L. G., & Manning, M. L. (2003). *Multicultural counseling and psychotherapy: A lifespan perspective* (3rd ed.). Upper Saddle River, NJ: Pearson Education.

Bayley, N. (1993). *The Bayley Scales of Infant Development–II.* New York: Psychological Corporation.

Beaty, J. J. (1998). *Observing development of the young child.* Upper Saddle River, NJ: Merrill/Prentice Hall.

Bee, H. (1992). *The developing child.* New York: HarperCollins.

Bee, H. (2000). *The developing child* (9th ed.). Needham Heights, MA: Allyn & Bacon.

Bee, H., & Henslin, J. (2003). *The developing child* (10th ed.). Needham Heights, MA: Allyn & Bacon.

Benedikt, R., Wertheim, E. H., & Lave, A. (1998). Eating attitudes and weight-loss attempts in female adolescents and their mothers. *Journal of Youth and Adolescence, 27,* 43–57.

Berg, F. M. (1997). *Afraid to eat: Children and teens in weight crisis.* Hettinger, ND: Healthy Weight Publishing Network.

Berger, K. S. (1998). *The developing person through the life span* (4th ed.). New York: Worth.

Berger, K. S. (2003). *The developing person through childhood* (3rd ed.). New York: Worth.

Berger, K., & Thompson, R. (1991). *The developing person through childhood and adolescence.* New York: Worth.

Berk, L. E. (1999). *Infants, children, and adolescents* (3rd ed.). Boston: Allyn & Bacon.

Berk, L. E. (2003). *Child development* (6th ed.). Boston: Allyn & Bacon.

Bernard, M., & Joyce, M. (1984). *Rational-emotive therapy with children and adolescents.* New York: Wiley.

Berndt, T. J. (1992). *Child development.* Orlando, FL: Harcourt Brace Jovanovich.

Berry, J. (1990). *Good answers to tough questions about physical disabilities.* New York: Children's Press.

Bierhorst, J. (1992). *Lightening inside you and other Native American riddles.* New York: William & Company.

Bireley, M., & Genshaft, J. (1991). *Understanding the gifted adolescent.* New York: Teachers College Press.

Bjorklund, D. F. (2000). *Children's thinking: Developmental function and individual differences* (3rd ed.). Belmont, CA: Wadsworth.

Bluestein, J. (1993). *Parents, teens, and boundaries: How to draw the line.* Deerfield Beach, FL: Health Communications.

Boat, B. W., & Everson, M. D. (1989). The anatomical doll project: An overview. In J. Garbarino & F. Stott (Eds.), *What children can tell us* (pp. 170–202). San Francisco: Jossey-Bass.

Borders, L., & Drury, S. (1992). Comprehensive school counseling programs: A review for policymakers and practitioners. *Journal of Counseling & Development, 70,* 487–498.

Bourne, E. J. (1995). *The anxiety and phobia workbook.* Oakland, CA: New Harbinger.

Bowman, R. P. (1987). Approaches for counseling children through music. *Elementary School Guidance and Counseling, 21,* 284–291.

Bracero, W. (1998). Confianza, gender, and hierarchy in the construction of Latino-Latina therapeutic relationship. *American Psychological Assessment, 4,* 264–277.

Bradley, L. (1988). Developmental assessment: A life-span approach. In R. Hayes & R. Aubrey (Eds.), *New directions for counseling and human development* (pp. 136–157). Denver, CO: Love Publishing.

Bradley, L. J., Gould, L. J., & Hendricks, P. B. (2004). Using innovative techniques for counseling children and adolescents. In A. Vernon (Ed.), *Counseling children and adolescents* (3rd ed., pp. 75–110). Denver, CO: Love Publishing.

Brafford, C. J. (1992). *Dancing colors: Paths of Native American women.* San Francisco: Chronicle Books.

Brazelton, T. B., & Greenspan, S. I. (2000). *The irreducible needs of children: What every child must have to grow, learn, and flourish.* Cambridge, MA: Perseus.

Brems, C. (2002). *A comprehensive guide to child psychotherapy* (2nd ed.). Boston: Allyn & Bacon.

Bridges, R. (1999). *Through my eyes.* New York: Scholastic Press.

Broker, I. (1983). *Night flying woman: An Ojibway narrative.* St. Paul: Minnesota Historical Society.

Bromfield, R. (1999). *Doing child and adolescent psychotherapy: The ways and whys.* Northvale, NJ: Jason Aronson.

Brooks-Gunn, J., & Warren, M. P. (1989). Biological and social contributions to negative affect in young adolescent girls. *Child Development, 60,* 40–55.

Bukatko, D., & Daehler, M. W. (1992). *Child development: A topical approach.* Boston: Houghton Mifflin.

Burbach, D. J., Farha, J. G., & Thorpe, J. S. (1986). Assessing depression in community samples of children using self-report inventories: Ethical considerations. *Journal of Abnormal Child Psychology, 14,* 579–589.

Button, E., Sonuga, R., Barke, J., Davies, J., & Thompson, M. (1996). A prospective study of self-esteem in the prediction of eating problems in adolescent school girls. *British Journal of Clinical Psychology, 35,* 193–203.

Campbell, D. W., & Eaton, W. O. (1999). Sex differences in the activity level of infants. *Infant and Child Development, 8,* 1–17.

Canetti, L., Bachar, E., Galili-Weisstub, E., De-Nour, A. K., & Shalev, A. Y. (1997). Parental bonding and mental health in adolescence. *Adolescence, 32,* 381–394.

Canetto, S. S., & Sakinofsky, I. (1998). The gender paradox in suicide. *Journal of Suicide and Life-Threatening Behavior, 28,* 1–23.

Canfield, J., & Wells, H. (1976). *100 ways to enhance self-concept in the classroom.* Englewood Cliffs, NJ: Prentice-Hall.

Capuzzi, D., & Gross, D. R. (2004). I don't want to live: The adolescent at risk for suicidal behavior. In D. Capuzzi & D. R. Gross (Eds.), *Youth at risk: A prevention resource for counselors, teachers, and parents* (4th ed., pp. 275–302). Alexandria, VA: American Counseling Association.

Carlson, J., & Lewis, J. (Eds.). (2002). *Counseling the adolescent: Individual, family, and school interventions* (4th ed.). Denver, CO: Love Publishing.

Carlson, L. (1999). *American eyes: New Asian American short stories for young adults.* New York: Econo-Clad.

Carlson, N. (1982). *Harriet's recital.* Bergenfield, NJ: Penguin.

Carlson, N. (1992). *What if it never stops raining?* New York: Penguin.

Cattell, R. B., Eber, H. W., & Tatsuoka, M. M. (1970). *Handbook for the 16 Personality Factor Questionnaire.* Champaign, IL: Institute for Personality and Ability Testing.

Centers for Disease Control and Prevention. (1999). *HIV/AIDS surveillance report, 11* (2). Atlanta, GA: National Center for HIV, STD, TB Prevention.

Charkow, W. (1998). Inviting children to grieve. *Professional School Counselor, 2,* 117–127.

Charlesworth, R. (2003). *Understanding child development* (6th ed.). Albany, NY: Delmar.

Chess, S., & Thomas, A. (1984). *Origins and evolution of behavior disorders: From infancy to early adult life.* New York: Brunner/Mazel.

Childswork, Childsplay. (2003). [Resource catalog]. King of Prussia, PA: Center for Applied Psychology.

Chittooran, M., & Miller, T. L. (1998). Informal assessment. In H. B. Vance (Ed.), *Psychological assessment of children* (2nd ed., pp. 13–59). New York: Wiley.

Christie, D. (2000). Cognitive-behavioural therapeutic techniques for children with eating disorders. In B. Lask & R. Bryant-Waugh (Eds.), *Anorexia nervosa and related eating disorders in childhood and adolescence* (2nd ed., pp. 205–226). East Sussex, UK: Psychology Press.

Christie, D., Watkins, B., & Lask, B. (2000). Assessment. In B. Lask & R. Bryant-Waugh (Eds.), *Anorexia nervosa and related eating disorders in childhood and adolescence* (2nd ed., pp. 105–125). East Sussex, UK: Psychology Press.

Clemente, R. (2004). Counseling culturally and ethnically diverse youth. In A. Vernon (Ed.), *Counseling children and adolescents* (3rd ed., pp. 227–256). Denver, CO: Love Publishing.

Clemente, R., & Collison, B. (2000). Interdependent perspective of functions and relations perceived by school counselors, ESL teachers, European American, and Latino students. *Professional School Counselor, 3,* 339–348.

Clemente, R., Collison, B., & Clark-Hanify, A. (2001). Bosnian refugees in the U.S.A.: Implications for the counseling profession. *Dimensions of Counseling: Research, Theory, and Practice, 29,* 11–19.

Cobain, B. (1998). *When nothing matters anymore: A survival guide for depressed teens.* Minneapolis, MN: Free Spirit.

Cobb, N. J. (2001). *The child: Infants, children, and adolescents.* Mountain View, CA: Mayfield.

Cohen, M. R. (1997). Individual and sex differences in speed of handwriting among high school students. *Perceptual and Motor Skills, 84* (3, Pt. 2), 1428–1430.

Colangelo, N., & Dettmann, D. F. (1985). Characteristics of moral problems and solutions formed by students in Grades 3–8. *Elementary School Guidance and Counseling, 19,* 260–271.

Colby, A., Kohlberg, L., Gibbs, J., & Lieberman, M. (1983). A longitudinal study of moral development. *Monographs of the Society for Research in Child Development, 48*(1–2, Serial No. 200).

Cole, M., & Cole, S. R. (1996). *The development of children* (3rd ed.). New York: Freeman.

Colten, M. E., & Gore, S. (1991). *Adolescent stress: Causes and consequences.* New York: Aldine de Gruyter.

Constantino, G., & Malgady, R. G. (1996). Cuento and hero/heroine modeling therapies for Hispanic children and adolescents. In E. Hibbs & P. S. Jensen (Eds.), *Psychological treatments for child and adolescent disorders: Empirically based strategies for clinical practice* (pp. 639–669). Washington, DC: American Psychological Association.

Constantino, G., Malgady, R. G., & Rogler, L. H. (1986). Cuento therapy: A culturally sensitive modality for Puerto Rican children. *Journal of Consulting and Clinical Psychology, 54,* 639–645.

Crenshaw, D. A. (1990). *Bereavement: Counseling the grieving throughout the life cycle.* New York: Crossword.

Crick, N. R., & Grotpeter, J. K. (1995). Relational aggression, gender, and social-psychological adjustment. *Child Development, 66,* 710–722.

Crombie, G., & Desjardins, M. J. (1993, March). *Predictors of gender: The relative importance of children's play, games, and personality characteristics.* Paper presented at the meeting of the Society for Research in Child Development, New Orleans, LA.

Cuellar, I., Arnold, B., & Maldonado, R. (1995). Acculturation Rating Scale for Mexican Americans-II: A revision of the original ARSMA scale. *Hispanic Journal of Behavioral Sciences, 17,* 275–304.

Cunningham, B., & Hare, J. (1989). Essential elements of a teacher in-service program on child bereavement. *Elementary School Guidance and Counseling, 23,* 175–182.

Curtis, C. P. (1997). *The Watsons go to Birmingham—1963.* CA: Bantam Books.

Cutler, J. (1993). *Darcy and gran don't like babies.* New York: Scholastic Press.

Daigneault, S. D. (1999). Legacies and leaving home. *Professional School Counselor, 3,* 65–73.

Davis-Kean, P. E., & Sandler, H. M. (2001). A meta-analysis of measures of self-esteem for young children: A framework for future measures. *Child Development, 72,* 887–906.

Delgado, R., & Stefancic, J. (1997). *Critical White studies: Looking behind the mirror.* Philadelphia: Temple University Press.

DiGiuseppe, R. (1999). Rational emotive behavior therapy. In H. T. Prout & D. T. Brown (Eds.), *Counseling and psychotherapy with children and adoles-*

cents: Theory and practice for school settings (pp. 306–338). New York: Wiley.

Doll, B., & Doll, D. (1997). *Bibliotherapy with young people: Librarians and mental health professionals working together.* Englewood, CO: Libraries Unlimited.

Drum, D., & Lawler, A. (1988). *Developmental interventions: Theories, principles, and practice.* Columbus, OH: Merrill.

Drummond, R. (2000). *Appraisal procedures for counselors and helping professionals* (4th ed.). New York: Merrill.

Drummond, R. J. (2004). *Appraisal procedures for counselors and helping professionals.* Upper Saddle River, NJ: Pearson Prentice Hall.

Dusek, J. B. (1991). *Adolescent development and behavior.* Englewood Cliffs, NJ: Prentice-Hall.

Dusek, J. B. (1996). *Adolescent development and behavior* (3rd ed.). Upper Saddle River, NJ: Prentice Hall.

Dustin, D., & Ehly, S. (1992). School consultation in the 1990s. *Elementary School Guidance and Counseling, 26,* 165–175.

Eaton, W. O., & Yu, A. P. (1989). Are sex differences in child motor activity level a function of sex differences in maturational status? *Child Development, 60,* 1005–1011.

Edwards, C., & Springate, K. (1995). Encouraging creativity in childhood classrooms. *Dimensions of Early Childhood, 22,* 9–12.

Eichoness, M. (1989). *Why can't anyone hear me? A guide for surviving adolescence.* Sepulveda, CA: Monroe.

Eisenberg, N., Martin, C. L., & Fabes, R. A. (1996). Gender development and gender effects. In D. C. Berliner & R. C. Calfee (Eds.), *The handbook of educational psychology* (pp. 358–396). New York: McMillan.

Elkind, D. (1974). *Children and adolescents: Interpretive essays on Jean Piaget.* New York: Oxford University Press.

Elkind, D. (1984). *All grown up and no place to go: Teenagers in crisis.* Reading, MA: Addison-Wesley.

Elkind, D. (1988). *The hurried child: Growing up too fast too soon.* Reading, MA: Addison-Wesley.

Elkind, D. (1991). Development in early childhood. *Elementary School Guidance and Counseling, 26,* 12–21.

Ellis, A., & MacLaren, C. (1998). *Rational emotive behavior therapy: A therapist's guide.* Atascadero, CA: Impact.

Ellison, R. (1982). *The invisible man.* New York: Random House.

Epanchin, B. C., & Paul, J. L. (1987). *Emotional problems of childhood and adolescence: A multidisciplinary perspective.* Columbus, OH: Merrill.

Erikson, E. H. (1950). *Childhood and society.* New York: Norton.

Erikson, E. H. (1963). *Childhood and society* (2nd ed.). New York: Norton.

Erikson, E. H. (1968). *Identity: Youth and crisis.* New York: Norton.

Erk, R. R. (2004). *Counseling treatment for children and adolescents with DSM–IV–TR diagnosis.* Upper Saddle River, NJ: Prentice Hall.

Evans, J. R., Van Velsor, P., & Schumacher, J. E. (2002). Addressing adolescent depression: A role for school counselors. *Professional School Counselor, 5,* 211–219.

Fadely, J., & Hosler, V. (1980). *Developmental psychometrics: A resource book for mental health workers and educators.* Springfield, IL: Charles C Thomas.

Farber, N. (2003). Just a girl in the world. *ASCA School Counselor, 41*(5), 12–17.

Farr, J., & Christophersen, S. (1991). *Knowing yourself: Learning about your skills, values, and planning your life.* Indianapolis, IN: JIST Works.

Faulkner, A. H., & Cranston, K. (1998). Correlates of same-sex sexual behavior in a random sample of Massachusetts high school students. *American Journal of Public Health, 88,* 262–266.

Fischetti, B. (2001). Use of play therapy for anger management in the school setting. In A. Drewes, L. Carey, & C. Schaefer (Eds.), *School-based play therapy* (pp. 238–256). New York: Wiley.

Fisher, J. L., Munsch, J., & Greene, S. M. (1996). Adolescence in intimacy. In G. R. Adams & R. Montejaror (Eds.), *Psychosocial development during adolescence* (Vol. 8, pp. 95–129). Thousand Oaks, CA: Sage.

Flanery, R. (1990). Methodological and psychometric considerations in child reports. In A. LaGreca (Ed.), *Through the eyes of the child: Obtaining self-reports from children and adolescents* (pp. 57–82). Boston: Allyn & Bacon.

Flavell, J. H. (1985). *Cognitive development* (2nd ed.). Englewood Cliffs, NJ: Prentice-Hall.

Frank, A. (1963). *The diary of a young girl.* New York: Washington Square Press.

Frankenburg, W. K., Dodds, J., Archer, P., Shapiro, H., & Bresnick, B. (1992). The Denver II: A major revision and restandardization of the Denver Developmental Screening Test. *Pediatrics, 89,* 91–97.

Frisch, R. E. (1991). Puberty and body fat. In R. M. Lerner, A. C. Petersen, & J. Brooks-Gunn (Eds.), *Encyclopedia of adolescence* (pp. 355–392). New York: Garland.

Galassi, J. P., & Perot, A. R. (1992). What you should know about behavioral assessment. *Journal of Counseling & Development, 70,* 624–631.

Garbarino, J., & Kostelny, K. (1992). Child maltreatment as a community problem. *Child Abuse and Neglect, 16,* 144–164.

Garbarino, J., & Stott, F. M. (1992). *What children can tell us: Eliciting and interpreting critical information from children.* San Francisco: Jossey-Bass.

Garber, J., Kelley, M. K., & Martin, N. C. (2002). Developmental trajectories of adolescents' depressive symptoms: Predictors of change. *Journal of Consulting and Clinical Psychology, 70,* 79–95.

Gardner, R. (1971). *Therapeutic communication with children: The mutual story-telling technique in child psychotherapy.* New York: Aronson.

Gardner, R. (1986). *The psychotherapeutic technique of Richard A. Gardner.* Northvale, NJ: Jason Aronson.

Gardner, R. A. (1979). Mutual storytelling technique. In C. E. Schaefer (Ed.), *The therapeutic use of child's play* (pp. 313–321). New York: Jason Aronson.

Gauvain, M. (2001). *The social context of cognitive development*. New York: Guilford Press.

Ge, X., Conger, R. D., & Elder, G. H. (1996). Coming of age too early: Pubertal influences on girls' vulnerability to psychological distress. *Child Development, 67*, 3386–4000.

Gibson, R. L., & Mitchell, M. H. (1990). *Introduction to counseling and guidance*. New York: Macmillan.

Gilligan, C. (1982). *In a different voice*. Cambridge, MA: Harvard University Press.

Gilligan, C. (1990). Teaching Shakespeare's sister: Notes from the underground of female adolescence. In C. Gilligan, N. Lyons, & T. Hanmer (Eds.), *Making connections: The relational worlds of adolescent girls at Emma Willard School* (pp. 6–29). Cambridge, MA: Harvard University Press.

Ginter, E. J., & Glauser, A. (2001). Effective use of the *DSM* from a developmental/wellness perspective. In E. R. Welfel & R. E. Ingersoll (Eds.), *The mental desk reference* (pp. 69–77). New York: Wiley.

Ginter, E. J., & Glauser, A. S. (2004). Assessment and diagnosis: The developmental perspective and its implications. In R. R. Erk (Ed.), *Counseling treatment for children and adolescents with DSM–IV–TR disorders* (pp. 2–36). Upper Saddle River, NJ: Prentice Hall.

Gladding, S. T. (1987). Poetic expressions: A counseling art in elementary schools. *Elementary School Guidance and Counseling, 21*, 307–311.

Gladding, S. T. (1995). Creativity in counseling. *Counseling and Human Development, 28*, 1–12.

Gladding, S. T. (1998). *Counseling as an art: The creative arts in counseling* (2nd ed.). Alexandria, VA: American Counseling Association.

Gladding, S. T. (2005). *Counseling as an art: The creative arts in counseling* (3rd ed.). Alexandria, VA: American Counseling Association.

Gladding, S. T., & Gladding, C. T. (1991). The ABC's of bibliotherapy. *The School Counselor, 39*, 7–13.

Glass, J. C. (1991). Death, loss, and grief among middle school children: Implications for the school counselor. *Elementary School Guidance and Counseling, 26*, 139–148.

Gloria, A. M., & Kurpius, S. E. (2000). I can't live without it: Adolescent substance abuse from a cultural and contextual framework. In D. Capuzzi & D. R. Gross (Eds.), *Youth at risk: A prevention resource for counselors, teachers, and parents* (3rd ed., pp. 409–439). Alexandria, VA: American Counseling Association.

Goldman, L. (1990). Qualitative assessment. *The Counseling Psychologist, 18*, 205–213.

Goode, J. (2001). Against cultural essentialism. In I. Susser & T. C. Patterson (Eds.), *Cultural diversity in the United States*. Malden, MA: Blackwell.

Gordon, T. (2000). *Parent effectiveness training: The proven program for raising responsible children*. New York: Three Rivers Press.

Graham, S., & Weintraub, N. (1996). A review of handwriting research: Progress and prospects from 1980–1994. *Educational Psychology Review, 8,* 7–87.

Gray, E., & Cosgrove, D. (1985). Ethnogentric perception of childrearing practices in protective services. *Child Abuse and Neglect, 9,* 389–396.

Green, J. (1999). *Cultural awareness in the human services.* Englewood Cliffs, NJ: Prentice Hall.

Greenspan, S. I. (1981). *Psychopathology and adaptation in infancy and early childhood: Principles of clinical diagnoses and preventive intervention.* New York: International Universities Press.

Greenspan, S. I., & Lieberman, A. F. (1980). Infants, mothers, and their interaction: A quantitative clinical approach to developmental assessment. In S. I. Greenspan & G. H. Pollock (Eds.), *The course of life: Psychoanalytic contributions toward understanding personality development* [Special issue] (Vol. 1). Washington, DC: U.S. Government Printing Office.

Greenspan, S. I., & Porges, S. W. (1984). Psychopathology in infancy and early childhood: Clinical perspectives on the organization of sensory and affective thematic experience. *Child Development, 55,* 49–70.

Guidubaldi, J., DeZolt, D., & Myers, M. A. (1991). Assessment and diagnostic services for prekindergarten children. *Elementary School Guidance and Counseling, 26,* 45–56.

Gysbers, N. C., & Henderson, P. (2000). *Developing and managing your school guidance program* (3rd ed.). Alexandria, VA: American Counseling Association.

Hall, M. (1971). *Go Indians! Stories of the great Indian athletes of the Carlisle school.* Los Angeles: Ward Richie Press.

Harris, J. R. (1998). *The nurture assumption: Why children turn out the way they are.* New York: Free Press.

Hart, D. H. (1972). *The Hart sentence completion test for children* [Unpublished manuscript]. Salt Lake City, UT: Educational Support Systems.

Harter, S. (1983). Developmental perspectives on the self-system. In P. H. Mussen (Series Ed.) & E. M. Heatherington (Vol. Ed.), *Handbook of child psychology: Vol. 4. Socialization, personality, and social development* (4th ed., pp. 275–385). New York: Wiley.

Harter, S. (1999). *The cognitive and social construction of the developing self.* New York: Guilford Press.

Harter, S. (2001). *The construction of the self: A developmental perspective* (2nd ed.). New York: Guilford Press.

Hartup, W. W. (1984). The peer context in middle childhood. In W. A. Collins (Ed.), *Development during middle childhood: The years from six to twelve* (pp. 240–282). Washington, DC: National Academy Press.

Hartup, W. W., & Stevens, N. (1999). Friendships and adaptation across the lifespan. *Current Directions in Psychological Science, 8,* 76–79.

Head, J. (1997). *Working with adolescents: Constructing identity.* Washington, DC: Falmer Press.

Helms, J. (1989). Considering some methodological issues in racial identity counseling research. *The Counseling Psychologist, 17,* 227–252.

Helms, J. (1995). An update of Helm's White and people of color racial identity models. In J. G. Ponterotto, J. M. Casas, L. A. Suzuki, & C. M. Alexander (Eds.), *Handbook of multicultural counseling* (pp. 181–198). Thousand Oaks, CA: Sage.

Helms, J. E., & Cook, D. A. (1999). *Using race and culture in counseling and psychotherapy.* Boston: Allyn & Bacon.

Hills and Valleys: Teen Depression. (1998). [Video]. (Available from Discovery Channel School, P.O. Box 6027, Florence, KY 41022–6027; www.discoveryschool.com)

Hodges, E. E., Boivin, M., Vitaro, F., & Bukowski, W. M. (1999). The power of friendship: Protection against an escalating cycle of peer victimization. *Developmental Psychology, 35,* 94–101.

Hoffman, T., Dana, R., & Bolton, B. (1985). Measured acculturation and MMPI–168 performance of Native American adults. *Journal of Cross-Cultural Psychology, 16,* 243–256.

Hogan-García, M. (2003). *The four skills of cultural diversity competence: A process for understanding and practice* (2nd ed.). Pacific Grove, CA: Brooks/Cole.

Hohenshil, T. H., & Brown, M. B. (1991). Public school counseling services for prekindergarten children. *Elementary School Guidance and Counseling, 26,* 4–11.

Hood, A., & Johnson, R. (2002). *Assessment in counseling: A guide to the use of psychological assessment procedures* (3rd ed.). Alexandria, VA: American Counseling Association.

Howe, J. (1990). *There's a monster under my bed.* New York: MacMillan.

Hoyert, D. L., Anos, E., Smith, B. L. Murphy, S. L., & Kochanek, K. D. (2001). Deaths: Final data for 1999 (DHHS Publication No. PH 2001–1120). *National Vital Statistics Reports 49*(8). Hyattsville, MD: National Center for Health Statistics.

Hughes, J. N., & Baker, D. B. (1990). *The clinical child interview.* New York: Guilford Press.

Huss, M. T., Leak, G. K., & Davis, S. F. (1993). A validation study of the Novaco Anger Inventory. *Bulletin of the Psychonomic Society, 31,* 279–281.

Inclan, J., & Hernandez, M. (1992). Cross-cultural perspectives and co-dependence: The case of poor Hispanics. *American Journal of Orthopsychiatry, 62,* 245–255.

Irwin, C. E., & Millstein, S. G. (1992). Biopsychosocial correlates of risk-taking behaviors during adolescence: Can the physician intervene? *Journal of Adolescent Health Care, 7,* 825–965.

Ivey, A. (2000). *Developmental therapy: Theory into practice.* North Amherst, MA: Microtraining Associates.

Izard, C. E., & Ackerman, B. P. (2000). Motivation, organization, and regulatory functions of discrete emotions. In M. Lewis & J. M. Haviland-

Jones (Eds.), *Handbook of emotions* (pp. 253–264). New York: Guilford Press.

Jaffe, M. L. (1998). *Adolescence.* New York: Wiley.

James, R. K., & Myer, R. (1987). Puppets: The elementary school counselor's right or left arm. *Elementary School Guidance and Counseling, 21,* 292–299.

Jenkins, R. L., & Beckh, E. (1993). Finger puppets and mask making. In C. E. Schaefer & D. M. Cangelosi (Eds.), *Play therapy techniques* (pp. 83–90). Northvale, NJ: Aronson.

Jensen, K. L. (2001). The effects of selected classical music on self-disclosure. *Journal of Music Therapy, 38,* 2–27.

Johnson, J. (1992). *Teen relationships.* Minneapolis, MN: Lerner.

Johnson, W., & Kottman, T. (1992). Developmental needs of middle school students: Implications for counselors. *Elementary School Guidance and Counseling, 27,* 3–14.

Jory, B., Rainbolt, E., Karns, J. T., Freeborn, A., & Greer, C. V. (1996). Communication patterns and alliances between parents and adolescents during a structured problem-solving task. *Journal of Adolescence, 19,* 339–346.

Kamphaus, R. W., & Frick, P. J. (1996). *Clinical assessment of child and adolescent personality and behavior.* Needham Heights, MA: Allyn & Bacon.

Kaplan, P. S. (2000). *A child's odyssey: Child and adolescent development* (3rd ed.). Belmont, CA: Wadsworth.

Kazdin, A. E. (1994). Psychotherapy for children and adolescents. In A. E. Bergin & S. L. Garfield (Eds.), *Handbook of psychotherapy and behavior change* (4th ed., pp. 543–594). New York: Wiley.

Keat, D. L. (1979). *Multimodal therapy with children.* New York: Pergamon.

Keat, D. L. (1990). *Child multimodal therapy.* New York: Greenwood.

Kim, B. S. K., & Abreu, J. M. (2001). Acculturation measurement: Theory, current instruments, and future directions. In J. G. Ponterotto, J. M. Casas, L. A. Suzuki, & C. M. Alexander (Eds.), *Handbook of multicultural counseling* (pp. 394–424). Thousand Oaks, CA: Sage.

Kim, B. S. K., Atkinson, D. R., & Yang, P. H. (1999). The Asian Values Scale: Development, factor analysis, validation, and reliability. *Journal of Counseling Psychology, 46,* 342–352.

Kincade, E., & Evans, K. (1996). Counseling theories, process and intervention in a multicultural context. In J. L. DeLucia-Waack (Ed.), *Multicultural counseling competencies: Implications for training and practice* (pp. 89–112). Alexandria, VA: Association for Counselor Education and Supervision.

King, K. A., Price, J. H., Telljohann, S. K., & Wahl, J. (2000). Preventing adolescent suicide: Do high school counselors know the risk factors? *Professional School Counseling, 3,* 255–263.

Klimek, D., & Anderson, M. (1989). *Inner world, outer world: Understanding the struggles of adolescence.* Ann Arbor, MI: ERIC/CAPS.

Knaus, W. (1974). *Rational-emotive education: A manual for elementary school teachers*. New York: Institute for Rational Living.

Knell, S. (2000). Cognitive-behavioral play therapy for childhood fears and phobias. In H. Kaduson & C. Schaefer (Eds.), *Short-term play therapy for children* (pp. 3–27). New York: Guilford Press.

Knell, S., & Moore, D. (1990). Cognitive-behavioral play therapy in the treatment of encopresis. *Journal of Clinical Child Psychology, 19,* 55–60.

Kohlberg, L. (1980). *The meaning and measurement of moral development.* Worcester, MA: Clark University Press.

Kohlberg, L. (1981). *The philosophy of moral development.* New York: Harper & Row.

Kohlberg, L. (1984). *The psychology of moral development.* San Francisco: Harper & Row.

Kolbisen, I. M. (1989). *Wiggle-butts and up-faces.* Half Moon Bay, CA: I Think I Can.

Koppitz, E. M. (1982). *Personality assessment in the schools.* In C. R. Reynolds & T. B. Gurkin (Eds.), *Handbook of school psychology* (pp. 273–295). New York: Wiley.

Kottman, T. (2001). *Play therapy: Basics and beyond.* Alexandria, VA: American Counseling Association.

Kottman, T. (2003). *Partners in play: An Adlerian approach to play therapy* (2nd ed.). Alexandria, VA: American Counseling Association.

Kottman, T. (2004). Play therapy. In A. Vernon (Ed.), *Counseling children and adolescents* (3rd ed., pp. 111–136). Denver, CO: Love Publishing.

Kottman, T., & Ashby, J. (2000). Perfectionistic children and adolescents: Implications for school counselors. *Professional School Counseling, 3,* 182–188.

Kottman, T., & Johnson, V. (1993). Adlerian play therapy: A tool for school counselors. *Elementary School Guidance and Counseling, 28,* 42–51.

Kottman, T., & Stiles, K. (1990). The mutual storytelling technique: An Adlerian application in child therapy. *Individual Psychology, 46,* 148–156.

Kramer, E. (1998). *Childhood and art therapy* (2nd ed.). Chicago: Magnolia Street.

Krickeberg, S. K. (1991). Away from Walton Mountain: Bibliographies for today's troubled youth. *The School Counselor, 39,* 52–56.

Kroen, W. C. (1996). *Helping children cope with the death of a loved one: A guide for grownups.* Minneapolis, MN: Free Spirit.

Kurcinka, M. S. (2000). Kids, parents, and power struggles: Winning for a lifetime. New York: Harper Collins.

Kwanzaa: An African American Celebration. (1995). [Videotape]. (Available from National Geographic, School Publishing, 1145 17th Street N.W., Washington, DC 20036–4688)

Kwiatkowska, H. (2001). Family art therapy: Experiments with new techniques. *American Journal of Art Therapy, 40,* 27–39.

LaGreca, A. (1990). *Through the eyes of the child: Obtaining self-reports from children and adolescents.* Boston: Allyn & Bacon.

Laible, D. J., & Thompson, R. A. (1998). Attachment and emotional understanding in preschool children. *Developmental Psychology, 34,* 1038–1045.

Lamb, M. E., & Fauchier, A. (2001). The effects of question type on self-contradictions by children in the course of forensic interviews. *Applied Cognitive Psychology, 15,* 483–491.

Landreth, G. L. (1991). *Play therapy: The art of the relationship.* Muncie, IN: Accelerated Development.

Landreth, G. L. (2002). *Play therapy: The art of the relationship* (2nd ed.). New York: Brunner-Routledge.

Landrine, H., & Klonoff, E. A. (1994). The African American Acculturation Scale: Development, reliability, and validity. *Journal of Black Psychology, 20,* 104–127.

Lapsley, D. K. (1993). Toward an integrated theory of adolescent ego development: The "new look" at adolescent egocentrism. *American Journal of Orthopsychiatry, 63,* 562–571.

Larsen, R., & Asmussen, L. (1991). Anger, worry, and hurt in early adolescence: An enlarging world of negative emotions. In M. E. Colten & S. Gore (Eds.), *Adolescent stress: Causes and consequences* (pp. 21–41). New York: Aldine de Gruyter.

Larson, R., & Richards, M. H. (1994). *Divergent realities: The emotional lives of mothers, fathers, and adolescents.* New York: Basic Books.

Lask, B. (2000). Aetiology. In B. Lask & R. Bryant-Waugh (Eds.), *Anorexia nervosa and related eating disorders in childhood and adolescence* (2nd ed., pp. 63–79). East Sussex, UK: Psychology Press.

Laursen, B., Coy, K. C., & Collins, W. A. (1998). Reconsidering changes in parent–child conflict across adolescence: A meta analysis. *Child Development, 69,* 817–832.

Lazar, A., & Torney-Purta, J. (1991). The development of the subconcepts of death in young children: A short-term longitudinal study. *Child Development, 62,* 1321–1333.

Lazarus, A. A. (1976). *Multimodal behavior therapy.* New York: Springer.

Lee, L. (1996). *The Japanese Americans.* New York: Scholastic Press.

LeFrancois, G. R. (1992). *Of children: An introduction to child development.* Belmont, CA: Wadsworth.

Lewinsohn, P. M., Hops, H., Roberts, R., Seeley, J. R., & Andrew, J. (1993). Adolescent psychopathology: Prevalence and incidence of depression and other *DSM–III–R* disorders in high school students. *Journal of Abnormal Psychology, 102,* 183–204.

Lewis, J. A. (2002). Working with adolescents: The cultural context. In J. Carlson & J. Lewis (Eds.), *Counseling the adolescent: Individual, family, and school interventions* (4th ed., pp. 3–16). Denver, CO: Love Publishing.

Loden, M. (1996). *Implementing diversity.* Chicago: Irwin.

Loevinger, J. (1976). *Ego development.* San Francisco: Jossey-Bass.

Loevinger, J., Wessler, R., & Redmore, C. (1978). *Measuring ego development* (Vols. 1 & 2). San Francisco: Jossey-Bass.

Lynch, E. W. (1992). From culture shock to cultural learning. In E. W. Lynch & M. J. Hanson (Eds.), *Developing cross-cultural competence* (pp. 19–34). Baltimore: Paul H. Brookes.

Malina, R. M. (1991). Growth spurt, adolescent. In R. M. Lerner, A. C. Petersen, & J. Brooks-Gunn (Eds.), *Encyclopedia of adolescence* (pp. 244–289). New York: Garland.

Marcia, J. (1980). Identity in adolescence. In J. Adelson (Ed.), *Handbook of adolescent psychology* (pp. 145–185). New York: Wiley.

Marín, G., & Gamba, R. J. (1996). A new measurement of acculturation for Hispanics: The Bidimensional Acculturation Scale for Hispanics (BAS). *Hispanic Journal of Behavioral Sciences, 18,* 297–316.

Martin, D. G. (2003). *Clinical practice with adolescents.* Pacific Grove, CA: Brooks/Cole.

Martínez, R., Norman, R. D., & Delaney, H. D. (1984). A children's Hispanic background scale. *Hispanic Journal of Behavioral Sciences, 6,* 103–112.

Maslow, A. (1998). *Toward a psychology of being* (3rd ed.). New York: Wiley.

Mathias, C. E. (1992). Touching the lives of children: Consultative interventions that work. *Elementary School Guidance and Counseling, 26,* 190–201.

Mayers, K. (1995). Songwriting with traumatized children. *Arts in Psychotherapy, 22,* 495–498.

McCarthy, D. (1972). *McCarthy scales of children's abilities.* New York: Psychological Corporation.

McDevitt, T. M., & Ormrod, J. E. (2002). *Child development and education.* Upper Saddle River, NJ: Pearson Education.

McFarland, W. P., & Dupuis, M. (2001). The legal duty to protect gay and lesbian students from violence in school. *Professional School Counselor, 4,* 171–179.

McGlauflin, H. (1998). Helping children grieve at school. *Professional School Counseling, 1*(5), 46–49.

McPhee, L. (2000). *Dying to be thin.* Boston: WGBH Educational Foundation.

McWhirter, B. T., & Burrow-Sanchez, J. J. (2004). Preventing and treating depression and bipolar disorders in children and adolescents. In D. Capuzzi & D. R. Gross (Eds.), *Youth at risk: A prevention resource for counselors, teachers, and parents* (4th ed., pp. 117–142). Alexandria, VA: American Counseling Association.

McWhirter, B. T., McWhirter, J. J., Hart, R., & Gat, I. (2000). Preventing and treating depression in children and adolescents. In D. Capuzzi & D. Gross (Eds.), Youth at risk: A prevention resource for counselors, teachers, and parents (3rd ed., pp. 141–169). Alexandria, VA: American Counseling Association.

McWhirter, E. H., Shepard, R. E., & Hunt-Morse, M. P. (2004). Counseling at-risk children and adolescents. In A. Vernon (Ed.), *Counseling children and adolescents* (3rd ed., pp. 311–353). Denver, CO: Love Publishing.

Meece, J. L. (2002). *Child and adolescent development for educators* (2nd ed.). New York: McGraw Hill.

Meeus, W., Iedema, J., Helsen , M., & Vollebergh, W. (1999). Patterns of adolescent identity development: Review of literature and longitudinal analysis. *Development Review, 19,* 571–621.

Merritt, J. E. (1991). Reducing a child's nighttime fears. *Elementary School Guidance and Counseling, 25,* 291–295.

Merry, S. (2001). Racialized identities and the law. In I. Susser & T. C. Patterson (Eds.), *Cultural diversity in the United States.* Malden, MA: Blackwell.

Metha, N., Weber, B., & Webb, L. D. (1998). Youth suicide prevention: A survey and analysis of policies and efforts in the 50 states. *Journal of Suicide and Life-Threatening Behavior, 28,* 150–164.

Miller, L. J. (1982). *Miller assessment for preschoolers.* San Antonio, TX: Psychological Corporation.

Milliones, J. (1980). Construction of a Black consciousness measure: Psychotherapeutic implications. *Psychotherapy: Theory, Research, and Practice, 17,* 175–182.

Mintz, L., O'Halloran, M., Mulholland, A., & Schneider, P. (1997). Questionnaire for eating disorder diagnoses: Reliability and validity of operationalizing *DSM–IV* criteria into a self-report form. *Journal of Counseling Psychology, 44,* 63–71.

Mitchell, J. (1986). *The nature of adolescence.* Calgary, Alberta, Canada: Detselig.

Moran, H. (2001). Who do you think you are? Drawing the ideal self: A technique to explore a child's sense of self. *Clinical Child Psychology and Psychiatry, 6,* 599–604.

Morrison, A. (1992). *The new leaders, guidelines on leadership diversity in America.* San Francisco: Jossey-Bass.

Moshman, D. (1999). *Adolescent psychological development: Rationality, morality, and identity.* Mahwah, NJ: Erlbaum.

Murphy, B. C., Eisenberg, N., Fabes, R. A., Shepard, S., & Guthrie, I. K. (1999). Consistency and change in children's emotionality and regulation: A longitudinal study. *Merrill-Palmer Quarterly, 45,* 413–444.

Myrick, R. D. (1987). *Developmental guidance and counseling: A practical approach.* Minneapolis, MN: Educational Media.

Myrick, R. D. (1997). *Developmental guidance and counseling: A practical approach* (3rd ed.). Minneapolis, MN: Educational Media.

Nelsen, J., & Lott, L. (2000). *Positive discipline for teenagers: Empowering your teen and yourself through kind and firm parenting.* Roseville, CA: Prima.

Nelson, R. C. (1987). Graphics in counseling. *Elementary School Guidance and Counseling, 22,* 17–29.

Newcomb, N. S. (1994). Music: A powerful resource for the elementary school counselor. *Elementary School Guidance and Counseling, 28,* 150–155.

Newman, B. M., & Newman, P. R. (1991). *Development through life: A psychosocial approach.* Pacific Grove, CA: Brooks/Cole.

Newton, M. (1995). *Adolescence: Guiding youth through the perilous ordeal*. New York: Norton.

Nicolopoulou, A. (1993). Play, cognitive development, and the social world: Piaget, Vygotsky, and beyond. *Human Development, 63*, 227–241.

Nolen-Hoeksema, S. (2001). Gender differences in depression. *Current Directions in Psychological Science, 10*, 173–176.

O'Connor, K. J. (1991). *The play therapy primer: An integration of theories and techniques*. New York: Wiley.

O'Connor, K. J. (2000). *The play therapy primer* (2nd ed.). New York: Wiley.

O'Connor, K. J., & Schaefer, C. E. (1993). *Handbook of play therapy: Advances and innovations*. New York: Wiley.

Orton, G. L. (1997). *Strategies for counseling with children and their parents*. Pacific Grove, CA: Brooks/Cole.

Oster, G. D., & Gould, P. (1987). *Using drawings in assessment and therapy: A guide for mental health professionals*. New York: Bruner/Mazel.

Owens, K. B. (2002). *Child and adolescent development: An integrated approach*. Belmont, CA: Wadsworth.

Owens, R. E., Jr. (1996). *Language development* (4th ed.). Boston: Allyn & Bacon.

Palmer, P. (1977). *The mouse, the monster, and me*. San Luis Obispo, CA: Impact.

Paniagua, F. A. (1998). *Assessing and treating culturally diverse clients: A practical guide*. Thousands Oaks, CA: Sage.

Pardeck, J. A. (1995). Bibliotherapy: An innovative approach for helping children. *Early Childhood Development and Care, 110*, 83–88.

Pardeck, J. T., & Pardeck, J. A. (Eds.). (1993). *Bibliotherapy: A clinical approach for helping children*. Yverdon, Switzerland: Gordon & Breach Science.

Parker, J. G., & Asher, S. R. (1993). Friendship and friendship quality in middle childhood: Links with peer group acceptance and feelings of loneliness and social dissatisfaction. *Developmental Psychology, 29*, 611–621.

Parrott, L. (1993). *Helping the struggling adolescent*. Grand Rapids, MI: Zonderwan.

Pedersen, P. (2000). *A handbook for developing multicultural awareness* (3rd ed.). Alexandria, VA: American Counseling Association.

Pedersen, P. B., Draguns, J. G., Lonner, W. J., & Trimble, J. E. (Eds.). (2002). *Counseling across cultures* (5th ed.). Thousand Oaks, CA: Sage.

Pennells, M., & Smith, S. C. (1995). *The forgotten mourners: Guidelines for working with bereaved children*. London: Jessica Kingsley.

Petersen, A. (1987). The nature of biological and psychosocial interactions: The sample case of early adolescence. In R. M. Lerner & T. T. Foch (Eds.), *Biological and psychosocial interactions in early adolescence: A life-span perspective* (pp. 35–61). Hillsdale, NJ: Erlbaum.

Petersen, A., Kennedy, R., & Sullivan, P. (1991). Coping with adolescence. In M. E. Colten & S. Gore (Eds.), *Adolescent stress: Causes and consequences* (pp. 93–110). New York: Aldine de Gruyter.

Phinney, J. (1990). Ethnic identity in adolescents and adults: Review of research. *Psychological Bulletin, 108,* 499–514.

Phinney, J., Ong, A., & Madden, T. (2000). Cultural values and intergenerational value discrepancies in immigrant and non-immigrant families. *Child Development, 71,* 528–539.

Piaget, J. (1967). *Six psychological studies.* New York: Random House.

Pincus, D. (1990). *Feeling good about yourself: Strategies to guide young people toward more positive, personal feelings.* Carthage, IL: Good Apple.

Ponterotto, J. G., Baluch, S., & Carielli, D. (1998). The Suinn–Lew Asian Self-Identity Acculturation Scale (SL-ASIA): Critique and research recommendation. *Measurement and Evaluation in Counseling and Development, 31,* 109–124.

Porter, L. (2003). *Young children's behavior: Practical approaches for caregivers and teachers* (2nd ed.). Baltimore: Paul H. Brookes.

Potter-Efron, R. (1993). *How to control your anger before it controls you.* Minneapolis, MN: Johnson Institute.

Prout, H. T. (1999). Counseling and psychotherapy with children and adolescents: An overview. In H. T. Prout & D. T. Brown (Eds.), *Counseling and psychotherapy with children and adolescents: Theory and practice for school and clinical settings* (3rd ed., pp. 1–25). New York: Wiley.

Pruitt, D. B. (Ed.). (1998). *Your child: what every parent needs to know about childhood development from birth to preadolescence.* New York: Harper Collins.

Pumphrey, J., & Pumphrey, J. (2003). *Creepy things are scaring me.* Scranton, PA: Harper Collins.

Quintana, S. (1999). Role of perspective taking abilities and ethnic socialization in development of adolescent ethnic identity. *Journal of Research on Adolescence, 9,* 161–184.

Rathus, S. A. (2004). *Voyages in childhood.* Belmont, CA: Wadsworth.

Reddy, L., Spencer, P., Hall, T., & Rubel, E. (2001). Use of developmentally appropriate games in a child group training program for young children with attention-deficit/hyperactivity disorder. In A. Drewes, L. Carey, & C. Schaefer (Eds.), *School based play therapy* (pp. 256–276). New York: Wiley.

Reynolds, W. M. (1987). *Reynolds Adolescent Depression Scale.* Odessa, FL: Psychological Assessment Resources.

Reynolds, W. M. (1988). *Suicidal Ideation Questionnaire.* Odessa, FL: Psychological Assessment Resources.

Reynolds, S. (1993). Interventions for typical developmental problems. In A. Vernon (Ed.), *Counseling children and adolescents: A practitioner's guide* (pp. 55–84). Denver, CO: Love Publishing.

Rezentes, III, W. C. (1993). Na Mea Hawai'I: A Hawaiian acculturation scale. *Psychological Reports, 73,* 383–393.

Ridley, C. R., Espelage, D. L., & Rubinstein, K. J. (1997). Course development in multicultural counseling. In D. B. Pope-Davis & H. L. K. Coleman (Eds.), *Multicultural counseling competencies: Assessment, education and training, and supervision* (pp. 131–158). Thousand Oaks, CA: Sage.

Robinson, E. H., Rotter, J. C., Fey, M. A., & Robinson, S. L. (1991). Children's fears: Toward a preventive model. *The School Counselor, 38,* 187–192.

Rogoff, B. (1990). *Apprenticeship in thinking: Cognitive development in social context.* New York: Oxford University Press.

Rotter, J. B., & Rafferty, J. E. (1950). *Manual for the Rotter Incomplete Sentence Blank.* New York: Psychological Corporation.

Roysircar-Sodowsky, G., & Frey, L. L. (2003). Children of immigrants: Their worldviews value conflicts. In P. B. Pedersen & J. C. Carey (Eds.)., *Multicultural counseling in high schools: A practical handbook* (pp. 61–83). Boston: Allyn & Bacon.

Rubin, K. H., Bukowski, W., & Parker, J. G. (1998). Peer interactions, relationships, and groups. In W. Damon (Series Ed.) & N. Eisenberg (Vol. Ed.), *Handbook of child psychology: Vol. 3. Social, emotional, and personality development* (5th ed., pp. 619–700). New York: Wiley.

Ruffman, T. (1999). Children's understanding of logical inconsistency. *Child Development, 70,* 872–886.

Saarni, C., Mumme, D. L., & Campos, J. J. (1998). Emotional development: Action, communication, and understanding. In W. Damon (Series Ed.) & N. Eisenberg (Vol. Ed.), *Handbook of child psychology: Vol. 3. Social, emotional, and personality development* (5th ed., pp. 237–309). New York: Wiley.

Sadker, M. P., & Sadker, D. (1994). *Failing at fairness: How our schools cheat girls.* New York: Touchstone.

Santrock, J. (2000). *Child development* (9th ed.). New York: McGraw-Hill.

Santrock, J., & Yussen, S. (1992). *Child development: An introduction.* Dubuque, IA: William C. Brown.

Sattler, J. M. (1993). *Assessment of children* (3rd ed., Rev. reprint). San Diego, CA: Jerome M. Sattler.

Sattler, J. M. (1998). *Clinical and forensic interviewing of children and families: Guidelines for the mental health, education, pediatric, and child maltreatment fields.* San Diego, CA: Jerome M. Sattler.

Savin, M. (1995). *The moon bridge.* New York: Scholastic Press.

Scarano-Osika, G., & Maloney, K. (2004). Adolescents and eating disorders. In R. R. Erk (Ed.), *Counseling treatment for children and adolescents with DSM–IV–TR disorders* (pp. 305–341). Upper Saddle River, NJ: Merrill Prentice Hall.

Schaefer, C. E., & Reid, S. E. (2000). *Game play: Therapeutic use of childhood games.* New York: Wiley.

Schave, D., & Schave, B. (1989). *Early adolescence and the search for self: A developmental perspective.* New York: Praeger.

Schickedanz, J. A., Schickedanz, D. L., Forsyth, P. D., & Forsyth, G. A. (1998). *Understanding children and adolescents* (3rd ed.). Needham Heights, MA: Allyn & Bacon.

Schlegel, A., & Barry, H., III. (1991). *Adolescence: An anthropological inquiry.* New York: Free Press.

Schmidt, J. J. (1996). *Counseling in schools: Essential services and comprehensive programs* (2nd ed.). Boston: Allyn & Bacon.

Seifert, K. L., & Hoffnung, R. J. (1997). *Child and adolescent development* (4th ed.). Boston: Houghton Mifflin.

Self-Esteem Shop. (2003). *Playtime* [Resource catalog]. Royal Oak, MI: Author.

Selman, R. (1980). *The growth of interpersonal understanding: Developmental and clinical analyses.* New York: Academic Press.

Selman, R. (1981). The child as a friendship philosopher. In S. R. Asher & J. M. Gottman (Eds.), *The development of children's friendships* (pp. 242–272). New York: Cambridge University Press.

Selman, R., & Schultz, L. H. (1998). *Making a friend in youth: Developmental theory and pair therapy.* New York: Walter de Gruyter.

Semrud-Clikeman, M. (1995). *Child and adolescent therapy.* Boston: Allyn & Bacon.

Shamir, H., DuRocher Schudlich, T., & Cummings, E. M. (2001). Marital conflict, parenting styles, and children's representations of family relationships. *Parenting: Science & Practice, 1,* 123–151.

Shapiro, L. E. (1996). *Short-term therapy with children: Make-a-game instructions.* King of Prussia, PA: Center for Applied Psychology.

Sherwood-Hawes, A. (2000). Children having children: Teenage pregnancy and parenthood. In D. Capuzzi & D. R. Gross (Eds.), *Youth at risk: A prevention resource for counselors, teachers, and parents* (3rd ed., pp. 243–280). Alexandria, VA: American Counseling Association.

Shostron, E. (1974). *Personal orientation inventory.* San Diego, CA: Educational and Industrial Testing Service.

Siegler, R., DeLoache, J., & Eisenberg, N. (2003). *How children develop.* New York: Worth.

Silver, R. (1988). *Draw a story.* New York: Ablin Press.

Silver, R. (1993). *Draw a story* (Rev. ed.). New York: Ablin Press.

Silverstein, A., & Silverstein, V. (1991). *So you think you're fat?* New York: HarperCollins.

Simon, N. (1986). *The saddest time.* Morton Grove, IL: Whitman.

Sippola, L., Bukowski, W. M., & Noll, R. B. (1997). Age differences in children's and early adolescents' liking for same-sex and other-sex peers. *Merrill-Palmer Quarterly, 43,* 547–561.

Sleeter, C., & McLaren, P. (1995). *Multicultural education, critical pedagogy, and the politics of difference.* New York: State University of New York Press.

Sloan, G. (2003). *Give them poetry!* New York: Teachers College Press.

Smolak, L., Levine, M., & Gralen, S. (1993). The impact of puberty and dating on eating problems among middle school girls. *Journal of Youth and Adolescence, 22,* 355–368.

Snowden, L. R., & Hines, A. M. (1999). A scale to assess African American acculturation. *Journal of Black Psychology, 25,* 36–47.

Stefanowski-Harding, S. (1990). Child suicide: A review of the literature and implications for school counselors. *The School Counselor, 37,* 328–336.

Steinberg, L. (1996). *Adolescence* (4th ed.). New York: McGraw Hill.

Steinberg, L., & Levine, A. (1990). *You and your adolescent: A parent's guide for ages 10–20.* New York: Harper Collins.

Stone, W., & Lemanek, K. (1990). Developmental issues in children's self-reports. In A. LaGreca (Ed.), *Through the eyes of the child: Obtaining self-reports from children and adolescents* (pp. 18–56). Boston: Allyn & Bacon.

Strub, R. (1990/1991). Concerns I have. In A. Vernon & R. Strub (Eds.), *Developmental guidance program implementation* (pp. 97–98). Cedar Falls: University of Northern Iowa Press.

Sue, D. W., Arredondo, P., & McDavis, R. J. (1992). Multicultural counseling competencies and standards: A call to the profession. *Journal of Counseling & Development, 70,* 644–688.

Sue, D. W., Carter, R. T., Casas, J. M., Fouad, N. A., Ivey, A. E., Jensen, M., et al. (1998). *Multicultural counseling competencies: Individual and organizational development.* Thousand Oaks, CA: Sage.

Sue, D. W., & Sue, D. (2002). *Counseling the culturally diverse: Theory and practice* (4th ed.). New York: Wiley.

Sycamore, J. E., Corey, A. L., & Coker, D. H. (1990). Reducing test anxiety. *Elementary School Guidance and Counseling, 24,* 231–233.

Tarver-Behring, S., & Spagna, M. E. (2004). Counseling with exceptional children. In A. Vernon (Ed.), *Counseling children and adolescents* (4th ed., pp. 189–225). Denver, CO: Love Publishing.

Tatum, B. D. (1993). Talking about race, learning about racism: The application of racial identity development theory in the classroom. *Harvard Educational Review, 62*(1), 1–24.

Taylor, M. (1981). *Let the circle be unbroken.* New York: Dial Press.

Teenagers and gangs: A lethal combination. (2000). [Videotape]. (Available from Discovery Channel School, P.O. Box 6027, Florence, KY 41022–6027; www.discoveryschool.com)

Thomas, P. (2000). *I miss you: A first look at death.* New York: Barrons.

Thompson, C. L., & Rudolph, L. B. (1992). *Counseling children.* Pacific Grove, CA: Brooks/Cole.

Thompson, C. L., & Rudolph, L. B. (2000). *Counseling children* (5th ed.). Pacific Grove, CA: Brooks/Cole.

Thompson, C. L., Rudolph, L. B., & Henderson, D. (2004). *Counseling children* (6th ed.). Pacific Grove, CA: Brooks/Cole.

Tollerud, T., & Nejedlo, R. (2004). Designing a developmental counseling curriculum. In A. Vernon (Ed.)., *Counseling children and adolescents* (3rd ed., pp. 391–423). Denver, CO: Love Publishing.

Triandis, H. C. (1995). *Individualism and collectivism.* Boulder, CO: Westview Press.

Turiel, E. (1983). *The development of social knowledge.* Cambridge, England: Cambridge University Press.

Turiel, E. (1998). The development of morality. In N. Eisenberg (Ed.), *Handbook of child psychology* (Vol. 3, pp. 863–932). New York: Wiley.

Vance, H. B. (1998). (Ed.). *Psychological assessment of children: Best practices for school and clinical settings* (2nd ed.). New York: Wiley.

Vernon, A. (1989a). *Thinking, feeling, behaving: An emotional education curriculum for adolescents.* Champaign, IL: Research Press.

Vernon, A. (1989b). *Thinking, feeling, behaving: An emotional education curriculum for children.* Champaign, IL: Research Press.

Vernon, A. (1998a). *The passport program: A journey through emotional, social, cognitive, and self-development (Grades 1–5).* Champaign, IL: Research Press.

Vernon, A. (1998b). *The passport program: A journey through emotional, social, cognitive, and self-development (Grades 6–8).* Champaign, IL: Research Press.

Vernon, A. (1998c). *The passport program: A journey through emotional, social, cognitive, and self-development (Grades 9–12).* Champaign, IL: Research Press.

Vernon, A. (1999). Counseling children and adolescents: Developmental considerations. In A. Vernon (Ed.), *Counseling children and adolescents* (2nd ed., pp. 2–29). Denver, CO: Love Publishing.

Vernon, A. (2001). Creative approaches to counseling. In D. Capuzzi & D. R. Gross, Eds., *Introduction to the counseling profession* (3rd ed., pp. 224–248). Needham Heights, MA: Allyn & Bacon.

Vernon, A. (2002). *What works when with children and adolescents: A handbook of individual counseling techniques.* Champaign, IL: Research Press.

Vernon, A. (2004). Counseling children and adolescents: Developmental considerations. In A. Vernon (Ed.), *Counseling children and adolescents* (3rd ed., pp. 1–34). Denver, CO: Love Publishing.

Vernon, A., & Al-Mabuk, R. H. (1995). *What growing up is all about: A parent's guide to child and adolescent development.* Champaign, IL: Research Press.

Violence/Gangs. (1997). [Videotape]. (Available from Discovery Channel School, P.O. Box 6027, Florence, KY 41022–6027; www.discoveryschool.com)

Wagner, W. G. (2003). *Counseling, psychology, and children: A multidimensional approach to intervention.* Upper Saddle River, NJ: Merrill Prentice Hall.

Walker, L. J., & Taylor, H. H. (1991). Family interaction and the development of moral reasoning. *Child Development, 62,* 264–283.

Waterman, A. S. (1999). Identity as an aspect of optimal psychological functioning. In G. R. Adams, T. P. Gullotta, & R. Montemayor (Eds.), *Adolescent identity formation* (pp. 50–72). Newbury Park, CA: Sage.

Weinshenker, N. (2002). Adolescence and body image. *School Nurse News, 19*(3), 13–16.

Weinstein, G., & Alschuler, A. (1985). Education and counseling for self-knowledge development. *Journal of Counseling & Development, 64,* 19–25.

Weisfeld, G. (1999). *Evolutionary principles of human adolescence.* New York: Basic Books.

Whiston, S. C. (2000). *Principles and applications of assessment in counseling.* Belmont, CA: Wadsworth.

Wilde, J. (2000). *Hot stuff to help kids chill out: The anger and stress management book.* Richmond, IN: LGR Publishing.

Winkelman, M. (1999). *Ethnic sensitivity in social work.* Dubuque, IA: Eddie Bowers.

Wolman, B. B. (1998). *Adolescence: Biological and psychosocial perspectives.* Westport, CT: Greenwood Press.

Worden, J. W. (1996). *Children and grief.* New York: Guilford Press.

Wrenn, C. G. (1962). The culturally encapsulated counselor. *Harvard Educational Review, 32,* 444–449.

Wright, K. (2000). The secret and all-consuming obsessions: Eating disorders. In D. Capuzzi & D. R. Gross (Eds.), *Youth at risk: A prevention resource for counselors, teachers, and parents* (3rd ed., pp. 193–242). Alexandria, VA: American Counseling Association.

Yep, L. (2000). *Cockroach cooties.* New York: Harper Collins.

Yoder, A. E. (2000). Barriers to ego identity status formation: A contextual qualification of Marcia's identity status paradigm. *Journal of Adolescence, 23,* 95–106.

Youngs, B. B. (1985). *Stress in children.* New York: Arbor House.

Youngs, B. B. (1990). *Friendship is forever, isn't it?* Berkeley Springs, WV: Learning Tools.

Youngs, B. B. (1995). *Stress and your child: Helping kids cope with the strains and pressures of life.* New York: Ballantine Books.

Yule, W. (1993). Developmental considerations in child assessment. In T. H. Ollendick & M. Hersen (Eds.), *Handbook of child and adolescent assessment* (pp. 15–25). Boston: Allyn & Bacon.

Zimbabwe: The Lost City of Africa. (2000). [Videotape]. (Available from National Geographic, School Publishing, 1145 17th Street N.W., Washington, DC 20036–4688)

Zuniga, M. E. (1992). Using metaphors in therapy: Dichos and Latino clients. *National Association of Social Workers, 37*(1), 55–60.

Index

A

Abstract thought
  in early adolescence, 165, 167
  in mid-adolescence, 200
  stage of development and design
    of interventions, 74–75
Academically gifted children and
  writing activities, 37
Accommodation, 10
Activity-based interventions, 94–96. *See
  also specific activities (e.g., art, writing,
  etc.)*
Activity sheets, use of, 87–88
ADHD. *See* Attention-Deficit/
  Hyperactivity Disorder
Adios Anger (game), 90–91
Adolescence
  art activities, use of, 40
  assessment and intervention
    early adolescence, 159–192. *See
      also* Early adolescence
    mid-adolescence, 193–222. *See
      also* Mid-adolescence
  counselor's relationship in, 25, 75
  design of interventions for, 76
  emotional understanding in, 16
  music activities, use of, 44
  person perception, 17
  psychosocial development
    assessment instruments for, 46
  self, concept of, 16
  16 Personality Factors for
    Adolescents, 49
  writing activities, use of, 37
Advice column writing, use of, 87
African Americans. *See* Cultural
  differences

Age-appropriate behavior, 3, 18
  design of interventions for, 76
Aggression in middle childhood, 138
Alternative solutions, 5
American Counseling Association code
  of ethics, 57
Animism, 113
Anorexia. *See* Eating disorders
Anxiety
  case study of early childhood,
    116–118, 123–126
  case study of middle childhood,
    147–149
    test-taking anxiety, 149–151
  in early adolescence, 167, 190–191
  in mid-adolescence, 198, 222
Art activities, use of, 40, 96–98
Art artifacts, use of, 97–98
Artificialism, 113
Aspects of Culture or Ethnicity, 66
Assertiveness and cultural differences,
  61–62
Assessment. *See also* Developmental
  assessment
  childhood problems, 17–19
  defined, 4–5
  drawbacks of testing, 7
  early adolescence, 159–192
    case studies, 171–192
  early childhood, 107–133
    case studies, 116–133
  effective child assessment, 21–30
  of emotional understanding, 15–16
  informal, 34
  mid-adolescence, 193–222
    case studies, 203–222
  middle childhood, 135–158
    case studies, 142–156

Assessment (*continued*)
    multicultural, 57–72. *See also*
      Multicultural assessment
    process with children, 14–17, 20
    relationship with counselor, 22–27
    significant others, involvement of,
      29–30
Assimilation, 10
Associative play in early childhood, 109
Atkinson, D.R., 217
Attention-Deficit/Hyperactivity
    Disorder (ADHD), 18, 20
Attention span and design of
    interventions, 75
Atwater, E., 159, 160, 200, 202
Autobiography writing, use of, 86–87
Autonomy, 12
    in early adolescence, 164, 170
    in mid-adolescence, 202
      case study, 203–206
    shame and doubt vs., 11

B

Barker, P., 50
BASIC ID, 52
Bayley Scales of Infant Development—
    Second Edition, 44
Bee, H., 137
Behavior graphs, use of, 42
Behavior Toss (game), 91
Bender Visual-Motor Gestalt Test, 47–48
Berg, F.M., 178, 207
Berger, K. & Thompson, R., 112, 135, 181
Berger, K.S., 111
Berk, L.E., 9, 15–16, 110, 111, 113, 114,
    139, 160
Bibliotherapy, use of, 40–41, 71, 93–94
Body outlines, use of, 96–97
Borders, L. & Drury, S., xiv
Bowman, R.P., 98
Bradley, L., 5, 88
Brain activity in early childhood, 110
Brazelton, T.B. & Greenspan, S.I., 135
Brems, C., 96, 103
Bulimia. *See* Eating disorders

Bullying, 138
Burbach, D.J., Farha, J.G. & Thorpe, J.S.,
    31

C

Campbell, D.W. & Eaton, W.O., 111
Canetti, L., 202
Cartoons, use of, 97
Case studies of problem assessment
    and intervention
      early adolescence, 159–192
      early childhood, 116–133
      mid-adolescence, 203–222
      middle childhood, 142–156
Cattell, R.B., Eber, H.W. & Tatsuoka,
    M.M., 49
Centers for Disease Control and
    Prevention report on adolescent
    suicide, 199
Centration, 111–112
Charkow, W., 142
Checklists or rating scales of
    developmental characteristics, 35–36
Chess, S. & Thomas, A., 115
Child development. *See also four specific*
    stages: Early childhood, Middle
    childhood, Early adolescence, Mid-
    adolescence
    balancing with culture and
      psychopathy, 19–21
    heightened interest in field of, xiii
Children's Personality Questionnaire, 49
Chittooran, M. & Miller, T.L., 34
Classroom guidance, xiv
Client involvement and qualitative
    method, 6
Cobb, N.J., 108, 113, 135, 136, 163, 166,
    167, 195
Cognitive-behavioral play therapy, 102
Cognitive development, 9–10
    assessment instruments for, 45–46
    in early adolescence, 167–169
    in early childhood, 111–113
    interviewing techniques for
      assessment, 51

in mid-adolescence, 200–201
in middle childhood, 139–140
Coining, 145–147
Colangelo, N. & Dettmann, D.F., 38, 141
Communication style and cultural
    norms, 28
Concept Assessment Kit, 46
Concrete operational thought stage of
    development, 10
    designing interventions for, 74–75
    interviewing techniques for
        assessment, 51
    in middle childhood, 139
    shift to formal operational thinking
        in adolescence, 167, 198
Confidentiality, 31
Conformist stage, 12
    cultural awareness and, 62
    in early adolescence, 163
Conscientious stage, 12
Constructivist approach to cognitive
    development, 9
Conventional moral reasoning, 12, 169
Coopersmith Self-Esteem Inventory, 7
Core identity, 61
Counseling. *See also* Assessment
    child's resistance, reluctance, or
        discomfort toward, 22, 30
    relationship with counselor, 22–27
        designing developmentally and
            culturally responsive
            interventions, 75–79
        games, use of, 39–40
    school counseling programs, xiv
Counselor's Self-Assessment of
    Cultural Awareness Scale, 58–61
Crenshaw, D.A., 142, 143
Crick, N.R. & Grotpeter, J.K., 138
Crisis Intervention Game, The, 92
Cuentes (short stories), 68, 71
Cultural differences
    art activities, use of, 40
    assertiveness and, 61–62
    assessment taking into account,
        57–72. *See also* Multicultural
        assessment

awareness of, 28, 58–61
balancing with child development
    and psychopathy, 19–21
case study of early adolescence,
    184–187
case study of early childhood,
    119–121, 126–129, 145–147
case study of middle childhood,
    152–154
designing responsive interventions
    to, 73–104
early adolescence and, 160, 165, 170
Erikson developmental theory
    and, 11
formal operational thinking and,
    169
importance of, xiv, 223
interventions taking into account,
    73–104. *See also* Developmentally
    and culturally responsive
    interventions
in mid-adolescence, 195
    case studies, 206–207, 215–219
moral decision making and, 169
music activities, use of, 43
self-assessment of counselor's
    cultural awareness, 58–61
self-monitoring techniques, use of,
    41
storytelling, use of, 40–41, 71
suicide and, 199
unfinished sentences and, 37
Cultural Formulation Concepts, 66

D

D Is for Decision (activity sheet), 87–88
Dating in mid-adolescence, 198
    case study, 209
Death of relative, middle childhood
    case study, 142–145
Decision making, 5
    dilemmas and, 38–39
Defining Issues Test, 46
Denver Developmental Screening Test
    II, 49–50

Depression
in early adolescence, 165, 167
case study, 182–184
in mid-adolescence, 199
case study, 209
middle childhood case study,
154–156
Design process for developmentally
and culturally responsive
interventions, 73–81
age-appropriate, 76
evaluation stage, 80–81
flexibility and perseverance, 77
guidelines for, 74–79
language choice and, 77–78
learning style, suited to, 76–77
overstructuring, 78
reason for choice of, 78
relationship with counselor, 75–79
timing of, 77
Developmental assessment. *See also*
Assessment
art activities, use of, 40
awareness of issues of, 27–28
bibliotherapy and storytelling, use
of, 40–41, 71, 93–94
checklists or rating scales, 35–36
comprehensive model for, 52–54
decision-making dilemmas, use of,
38–39
defined, 5–9
designing instruments for, 34–44
games, use of, 39–40
importance of, 33
instruments for, 44–50. *See also*
Instruments for developmental
assessment
methods of, 33–55
music activities, use of, 43–44
play therapy, 42–43
role-playing activities, use of, 42
self-monitoring techniques, use of,
41–42
self-rating scales, use of, 43
unfinished sentences, use of, 36–37
writing activities, use of, 37–38

Developmental psychology, 8
Developmental reference point errors, 27
Developmental theories, 9–14
cognitive development, 9–10
defined, 9
ego development, 11–12
interpersonal development, 13–14
moral development, 12–13
Developmental vectors, 18
Developmentally and culturally
responsive interventions, 73–104
activity-based interventions, 94–96
activity sheets, use of, 87–88
art activities, use of, 96–98
design process for, 73–81
drama, use of, 100–101
four-stage design process (case
study), 81–83
implementation stage, 79–80
literature, use of, 93–94
music, use of, 98–101
planning stage for, 73–74
play, use of, 101–103
puppets, use of, 103–104
therapeutic games, use of, 88–92
types of interventions, 83–104
writing exercises, use of, 84–87
*Diagnostic and Statistical Manual of
Mental Disorders—Fourth Edition—
Text Revision (DSM–IV–TR)*, 4
balancing with culture and child
development, 19–21
using for diagnosis of childhood
problems, 17–19
Dichos (popular sayings), 68, 71
Differentiation of assessment levels, 8
Disability, child with, middle childhood
case study, 154–156
Diversity competence, 57. *See also*
Cultural differences
continual reassessment of, 79
cultural awareness and, 63–64
Doll, B. & Doll, D., 147
Drama as intervention, 100–101
Draw-a-Person Test, 48
Drum, D. & Lawler, A., xiv, 8

Drummond, R.J., 7, 33, 34, 44, 45, 46, 48
DSM–IV–TR. *See Diagnostic and
Statistical Manual of Mental Disorders—
Fourth Edition—Text Revision*
Dusek, J.B., 160, 194, 197, 201

✳
E

Early adolescence
assessment and intervention,
159–192
case studies, 171–192
characteristics of, 161–169
cognitive development in, 167–169
emotional development in,
164–165, 191
moral development in, 169
other typical concerns in, 190–192
parental involvement in, 169–170
physical development in, 165–167
self-development in, 161–162, 191
social development in, 162–164, 191
Early childhood
assessment and intervention,
107–133
case studies, 116–133
characteristics of, 107–114
cognitive development in, 111–113
counselor's relationship with
preschool children, 24
developmental tests or screening
for, 44
emotional development in, 109–110
games, use of, 39–40
language development in, 112
moral development in, 113–114
motor skills in, 110–111
other typical developmental
problems, 133–134
parental involvement, 114–116
physical development in, 110–111
play therapy, use of, 42–43
self-development in, 108
social development in, 109
Early School Personality Questionnaire,
49

Eating disorders
in early adolescence, 166
case study, 178–181
in mid-adolescence, 200
Ego development, 11–12
in middle childhood, 137
Egocentric perspective taking, 14
in early adolescence, 161–162, 164
Elkind, D., 112, 133, 140, 162, 194–195
Emotional development
assessment of, 15–16
in early adolescence, 164–165, 191
in early childhood, 109–110
language skills and, 17
in mid-adolescence, 198–199
in middle childhood, 138–139
person perception and, 16–17
testing of, 45
Enuresis, case study of preschooler,
123–126
Epanchin, B.C. & Paul, J.L., 7
Erikson, Erik, 8, 10–11, 119, 196, 216
Erk, R.R., 18
Ethical considerations, 30–31
multicultural assessment and, 57
Ethical Reasoning Inventory, 46
Ethnic differences. *See* Cultural
differences; Multicultural assessment
Evaluation stage of developmentally
and culturally responsive
interventions, 80–81
Evans, J.R., Van Velsor, P. &
Schumacher, J.E., 199
Exercise charts, use of, 42
Experiments with clients, 80
Exploration, 196
Extended Cultural Evaluation Form,
66–67
Eye contact and cultural norms, 28

✳
F

Fact or Belief? (game), 89
Fadely, J. & Hosler, J., 7, 46, 49
Fairy tale writing, use of, 87
Family drawings, use of, 48, 97

Family Happenings (game), 92
Farber, N., 161
Fear of dark, case study of preschooler, 121–123
Feeling charts, use of, 41
FID (Frequency Intensity Duration) Scale, 21–22
Find Someone Who . . . (activity-based intervention), 95–96
Fish for Feelings (game), 90
Flanery, R., 3
Flip for Feelings (game), 92
Food charts, use of, 42
Formal operations stage of development, 10
    interviewing techniques for assessment, 51
    transition to in adolescence, 167, 168, 200–201
Frankenburg, W.K., 49–50
Frequency Intensity Duration (FID) Scale, 21–22
Friendships
    in early adolescence, 163–164
    in mid-adolescence, 197
    in middle childhood, 137–138

G

Gain With Goals (activity sheet), 88
Galassi, J.P. & Perot, A.R., 22
Games, use of, 39–40
    commercially produced games, 92
    as intervention, 88–92
Garbarino, J. & Kostelny, K., 176
Garbarino, J. & Stott, F.M., 44, 45, 50, 112
Garber, J., 165
Gardner, R.A., 41
Gender differences
    in early adolescence, 160, 161, 163, 165, 166
    in early childhood, 109
    Erikson studies, 11
    Kohlberg's model, 13
    in mid-adolescence, 197–198, 199–200, 202
    in middle childhood, 137–138, 139
Gibson, R.L. & Mitchell, M.H., 86
Gilligan, C., 11, 12–13, 202
Ginter, E.J. & Glauser, A., 4, 18–19, 33
Gladding, S.T., 84, 98, 100
Gladding, S.T. & Gladding, C.T., 93
Good Behavior Game, The, 92
Graphics, use of, 97
Greenspan, S.I., 45
Greenspan, S.I. & Lieberman, A., 45
Greenspan, S.I. & Porges, S.W., 45
Grieving children, middle childhood case study, 142–145

H

Hall, G.S., 160
Hart Sentence Completion Test for Children, 47
Harter, S., 40, 137
Head, J., 160
HELPING model, 52
    example of use of, 53–54
    middle childhood case study and, 150
Hierarchical stages of development, xiv, 8, 9
Hierarchy of needs, 48
High school graduation, transition from, 222
    case study, 219–221
High School Personality Questionnaire, 49
Hodges, E.E., 138
Homework assignments, 80
Homosexuality and suicide, 199
Hood, A. & Johnson, R., 4, 22
Hostile children. *See also* Rebelliousness
    counselor's relationship with, 25
    games, use of, 39–40
House-Tree-Person Test, 48
Houston Test for Language Development, 45
Hoyert, D.L., 212
Hughes, J.N. & Baker, D.B., 50

I

Identity achievement, 197
Identity-change model, 62
Identity diffusion, 196
Identity foreclosure, 196
Identity issues
  case study of early adolescent, 184–187
  case study of preschooler, 119–121
  in mid-adolescence, 195
  role confusion vs., 11
Identity moratorium, 196
"Imaginary audience" concept, 162
Implementation stage of developmentally and culturally responsive interventions, 79–80
Impulsive stage, 11
Inclan, J. & Hernandez, M., 170
Independence. *See also* Autonomy
  in early adolescence, 164, 170
  Erikson developmental theory and, 11
  in mid-adolescence, 202, 222
  case study, 203–206
Individualistic stage, 12
Individualized interventions, 84
  games as, 89
Industry vs. inferiority, 11
Infants and developmental tests or screening, 44, 49–50
Informal assessments, 34
Information obtained from child, 3, 52
Initiative vs. guilt, 11
Instruments for developmental assessment, 34–50. *See also specific instrument by name*
  acculturation scales, 68, 69
  cognitive stages, 45–46
  designing of, 34–44
  interviewing techniques, 50–51
  language development, 45
  moral development, 46
  psychosocial development, 46
Integrated stage, 12
Interpersonal development, 13–14

Interventions
  developmentally and culturally responsive, 73–104. *See also* Developmentally and culturally responsive interventions
  early adolescence, 159–192
    case studies, 171–192
  early childhood, 107–133
    case studies, 116–133
  mid-adolescence, 193–222
    case studies, 203–222
  middle childhood, 135–158
    case studies, 142–156
Interviews
  as interventions, 94–95
  techniques for, 50–51
Invincibility fable, 162
Irwin, C.E. & Millstein, S.G., 167
Ivey, A., xiv, 8, 51, 54

J

Jaffe, M.L., 159, 163, 194, 197, 199, 201
James, R.K. & Myer, R., 103
Jealousy of new baby, case study of preschooler, 130–133
Jellies in a jar, use of, 42
Jenkins, R.L. & Beckh, E., 104
Jory, B., 202
Journaling. *See* Writing activities, use of

K

Kamphaus, R. W. & Frick, P.J., 7
Kaplan, P.S., 9, 12, 13, 167
Keat, D.L., 52, 53
Kincade, E. & Evans, K., 84
Kinetic Family Drawing Test, 48
Klimek, D. & Anderson, M., 160
Kohlberg, L., 12–13, 39, 46, 113, 114, 140, 169, 201
Koppitz, E.M., 47, 48
Kottman, T., 88, 101–102, 124
Kottman, T. & Johnson, V., 103
Kwiatkowska, H., 40

L

LaGreca, A., 29
Landreth, G.L., 102
Language development, 17
  in early childhood, 112
  testing of, 45
Larsen, R. & Asmussen, L., 187
Lask, B., 178
Latinos. *See* Cultural differences
Lazar, A. & Torney-Purta, J., 143
Lazarus, A.A., 52, 53
Learning style, interventions suited to,
  76–77
Letter writing, use of, 86
Lewinsohn, P.M., 199
Limerick writing, use of, 86
Literalness of preschoolers, 133
Literature, use of. *See* Bibliotherapy,
  use of
"Locker room phobia" of early
  adolescents, 166
Loevinger, J., 11
Loevinger, J., Wessler, R. & Redmore,
  C., 47

M

Mad music, use of, 100
Make-believe play, 113
Marcia, J., 196
Martin, D.G., 160
Masks, use of, 96
Maslow, A., 48
McCarthy Scales of Children's Abilities,
  44
McDevitt, T.M. & Ormrod, J.E., 14, 162,
  169
McWhirter, B.T., 182
McWhirter, B.T. & Burrow-Sanchez, J.J.,
  199
Measures of Psychosocial Development
  (MPD), 46
Media, use of, 95
Meece, J.L., 159, 161, 165, 166, 167, 170,
  195, 196

Meeus, W., 196
Menstruation, onset of, 166, 191
Mid-adolescence
  assessment and intervention,
    193–222
  case studies, 203–222
  characteristics of, 193–202
  cognitive development in, 200–201
  emotional development in, 198–199
  moral development in, 200,
    201–202
  other typical problems, 221–222
  parental involvement in, 202
  physical development in, 199–200
  self-development in, 195–197
  social development in, 197–198
  stages of, 194
Middle childhood
  assessment and intervention,
    135–158
  case studies, 142–156
  Bender Visual-Motor Gestalt Test,
    47–48
  characteristics of, 136–141
  cognitive development in, 139–140
  counselor's relationship with
    children, 24
  emotional development in, 138–139
  gender differences in, 137–138
  moral development in, 140–141
  motor skills in, 139
  other typical developmental
    problems, 156–157
  parental involvement, 141
  physical development in, 139
  play therapy, use of, 42–43
  self-development in, 136–137
  self-monitoring techniques, use of,
    41
  social development in, 137–138
Miller Assessment for Preschoolers,
  44
Mitchell, J., 221
Mood swings
  in early adolescence, 164, 191
  in mid-adolescence, 222

Moral development, 12–13
  assessment instruments for, 46
  decision-making dilemmas and, 38–39
  in early adolescence, 169
  in early childhood, 113–114
  in mid-adolescence, 200, 201–202
  in middle childhood, 140–141
Moral imperative, 113–114
Moral Judgment Interview, 46
Moral Judgment Inventory, 46
Motor skills
  in early childhood, 110–111
  in middle childhood, 139
Move It! (game), 90
Multicultural assessment, 57–72
  acculturation scales, 68, 69
  culturally sensitive assessments, 68–71
  ethical issues and, 57
  example of, 64–65
  guidelines for, 67–68
  integrating culture into assessment process, 65–68
  list of culturally appropriate books to use in, 68, 70
  personal culture and cultural awareness, 61–65
  personal exploration of cultural sensitivity and competency, 58–61
  stages in, 62–64
Multicultural Counseling Competencies and Standards, 57
Multimodal Child Interview Schedule (MCIS), 52
Music as intervention, 98–101
Music/mood collages, use of, 99
Myrick, R.D., 34, 76

N

New identity stage and cultural awareness, 63
Newman, B.M. & Newman, P.R., 113, 140, 168
Newton, M., 187

Nicolopoulou, A., 113
Nighttime fears, case study of preschooler, 121–123
Nolen-Hoeksema, S., 165
Nonverbal children
  interviewing techniques for assessment, 51
  music activities, use of, 44
Novaco Anger Inventory, 216

O

O'Connor, K.J., 102
Options (game), 89–90
Orton, G.L., 86, 93, 96, 103–104, 135
Oster, G.D. & Gould, P., 40

P

Paniagua, F.A., 66
Paper dolls, use of, 97
Pardeck, J.T. & Pardeck, J.A., 93
Parental involvement
  in assessment, 29–30
  in early adolescence, 169–170
  in early childhood, 114–116
  in mid-adolescence, 202
  in middle childhood, 141
  in play therapy, 102
  Social Recognition Skills Checklist for, 49
Parental support groups, 141
Peer relations
  in early adolescence, 163–164
  case study, 187
  in mid-adolescence, 197, 222
Perfectionistic behavior, case study of preschooler, 130–133
Person perception, 16–17
Personal culture and cultural awareness, 61–65
Personal Orientation Inventory, 48–49
Personality vs. personal culture, 61
Physical development
  in early adolescence, 165–167
  in early childhood, 110–111

Physical development (*continued*)
in mid-adolescence, 199–200
in middle childhood, 139
Piaget, Jean, 8, 9, 45, 111, 139
Planning stage for developmentally
and culturally responsive
interventions, 73–74
Play
in early childhood, 109
use in therapy, 42–43, 101–103
Poetry writing, use of, 85
Political correctness, 58
Postconventional moral reasoning, 13
Preconventional moral reasoning, 12, 169
Preoperational thought stage of
development, 10
in early childhood, 111
interviewing techniques for
assessment, 51
Preschool children. *See* Early childhood
Presocial stage, 11
Prevention, xiv
Problem identification, 5, 21–22
Prout, H.T., 3, 21
Psychological System Survey, 46
Psychosocial development, 10–11
assessment instruments for, 46
Puberty. *See* Early adolescence
Puppets, use of, 103–104

✳
Q

Qualitative vs. quantitative methods, 6

✳
R

Racial differences. *See* Cultural
differences; Multicultural assessment
Rapport building with clients, 22–27
Rathus, S.A., 139
Rating scales of developmental
characteristics, 35–36
Rebelliousness
in early adolescence, 165
case study, 187–190
in mid-adolescence, case study,
215–219

Redefinition stage and cultural
awareness, 63
Reinforcement and design of
interventions, 75
Resistance stage and cultural
awareness, 62–63
Reynell Developmental Language
Scale, 45
Reynolds, W.M., 73
Road to Achievement, The (game), 91
Rogoff, B., 169
Role playing, 42, 101
Rubin, K.H., Bukowski, W. & Parker,
J.G., 138

✳
S

Sattler, J.M., 22
Schave, D. & Schave, B., 160, 161, 167
Schlegel, A. & Barry, H., III, 200
School avoidance, case study in early
adolescence, 171–175
School counseling programs, xiv
School Form of the Coopersmith Self-
Esteem Inventory, 7
Second-person reciprocal perspective
taking, 14
Seifert, K.L. & Hoffnung, R.J., 200,
203
Self-assessment of cultural awareness
of counselor, 58–61
Self-aware stage, 12
Self-composed music, use of, 99
Self-concept, 16
case study of preschooler,
126–129
in early childhood, 108
in middle childhood, 137
Self-conscious behavior in early
adolescence, 162, 166–167, 191
case studies, 171–178
Self-development
in early adolescence, 161–162,
191
in early childhood, 108
in mid-adolescence, 195–197
in middle childhood, 136–137

Self-esteem, 7
    case study in mid-adolescence,
        209–212
    in early adolescence, 161
    in early childhood, 108
    in middle childhood, 137
Self-identity chart, 185–186
Self-monitoring techniques, use of,
    41–42
Self-protective stage, 12
Self-rating scales, 43
Selman, R., 13–14, 36, 42, 109
Selman, R. & Schultz, L.H., 13–14, 42, 138
Semrud-Clikeman, M., 31
Sensorimotor stage of development,
    9–10
Separation anxiety of preschoolers,
    133–134
Sexual identity
    of mid-adolescents, 195–196
    of preschoolers, 108
Sexuality
    early adolescent awareness of, 191
    in mid-adolescence, 194, 222
Shapiro, L.E., 89
Shostron, E., 48–49
Shy children's relationship with
    counselor, 25
Sibling rivalry, case study of
    preschooler, 130–133
Silly songs, use of, 99
16 Personality Factors for Adolescents,
    49
Social contract, 13
Social conventions, 113–114
Social development
    in early adolescence, 162–164, 191
    in early childhood, 109
    in mid-adolescence, 197–198
    in middle childhood, 137–138
Social Recognition Skills Checklist, 49
Song lyrics (line savers), use of, 99
Starr, J. & Raykovitz, J., 52
Steinberg, L., 159, 160, 164, 165, 168,
    171, 193, 197, 198, 199, 200
Stone, W. & Lemanek, K., 14, 16

Stop, Relax, and Think (game), 92
Storytelling, use of, 40–41
Story-writing activities. *See* Writing
    activities, use of
Subjective perspective taking, 14
Sue, D.W. & Sue, D., 28
Suicide in mid-adolescence, 199
    case study, 212–215

T

Tape-recorded activities, 95
Tardiness as cultural norm, 28
Team play in middle childhood, 137
Temper graphs, use of, 42
Test-taking anxiety, middle childhood
    case study, 149–151
Testing. *See* Assessment
Therapeutic fairy tale writing, use of, 87
Thinking. *See* Cognitive development
Third-person mutual perspective
    taking, 14
This Is My Bag (art activity), 98
Thompson, C.L., 101
Thompson, C.L. & Rudolph, L.B., 50,
    101
"Time warp" concept, 161
Timing of interventions, 77
Toys. *See* Play
Triandis, H.C., 169
Trotter Incomplete Sentence Blank, 47
Trust vs. mistrust, 11
Turiel, E., 114

U

Unfinished sentences, use of, 36–37
    Washington University Sentence
        Completion Test, 47
Universal ethical principles, 13

V

Vance, H.B., 34, 36
Verification, 5
Vernon, A., 3, 29
Video drama, use of, 100

W

Wach Analysis of Cognitive Structures, 46

Wagner, W.G., 3, 29, 103, 104

Walker, L.J. & Taylor, H.H., 141

Washington University Sentence Completion Test, 47

Waterman, A.S., 196

Weinstein, G. & Alschuler, A., 51

Whiston, S.C., 4, 28, 31, 50

White identity development model, 62

Wolman, B.B., 164

Worry boxes, use of, 42

Wrenn, C.G., 65

Writing activities, use of, 37–38, 84–87

Y

Yoder, A.E., 195

Youngs, B.B., 126, 130, 134, 157, 221

Yule, W., 3, 33, 35, 44